Best Wishes

Gary Schuster

11/23/94

Successful Life Insurance Selling

How To Prosper in the Year 2000 and Beyond

Gary Schulte

Dearborn
Financial Publishing, Inc.

While a great deal of care has been taken to provide accurate and current information, the ideas, suggestions, general principles and conclusions presented in this text are subject to local, state and federal laws and regulations, court cases and any revisions of same. The reader is thus urged to consult legal counsel regarding any points of law—this publication should not be used as a substitute for competent legal advice.

Publisher: Anita A. Constant
Senior Associate Editor: Karen A. Christensen
Managing Editor: Jack L. Kiburz
Editorial Assistant: Stephanie Schmidt
Interior Design: Lucy Jenkins
Cover Design: Design Alliance, Inc.

Printed in the United States of America

95 96 97 10 9 8 7 6 5 4 3 2 1

Library of Congress Cataloging-in-Publication Data

Schulte, Gary. 1946–
    Successful life insurance selling : how to prosper in the year
2000 and beyond / Gary Shulte.
        p.   cm.
    Includes index.
    ISBN 0-7931-1041-6 : $24.95
    1. Selling—Life insurance—United States.   2. Insurance, Life—
United States—Marketing.   3. Life insurance agents—United States.
I. Title.
HG8876.S28   1994
368.3′2′00688—dc20   94-26906
                                                                  CIP

Dedication

To Roger G. Molski, CLU
   A Shepherd of Leaders
   A Role Model for Students
   An Example to All

Acknowledgements

Much of this book is a collection of information, philosophies and practices I have learned from the industry greats I have been privileged to work with: Jack and Garry Kinder, Guy Baker, Barry Kaye, Tom Wolff and many others. Some of my observations rely heavily on my readings from the works of specialists in human behavior, such as Dr. Stephen Covey, Dr. Tom Stanley and Dr. Warren Bennis.

The remainder of the book was drawn from the long learning curve provided by the hundreds of agents who over two decades taught me how to manage, while I attempted to teach them how to sell. To all of them I extend my gratitude.

I also wish to thank my wife Marcia for her patient support and unwavering faith in me, my friend Larry Patterson who typed, formatted and reviewed every page, and my friend Johnny Mazzola for bringing Dearborn Financial Publishing and me together.

Contents

Preface

This book was written to provide life insurance agents with a new perspective for today, the turn of the century and beyond. I have long believed that most life insurance agents build their professional careers on the tips of icebergs with titles like "motivation," "positive mental attitude," "goal setting" and "selling skills." This book contains an ample portion of these basic ingredients for success and, I believe, adds meaningful fresh perspectives that will make a difference in the lives of those who apply what they learn. By the year 2000 and beyond, however, life insurance agents wishing to succeed will need to understand (1) that portion of the iceberg that historically has been less apparent; (2) carrier financial analysis, product integrity, point-of-sales liability and other forces that are at work driving the life insurance industry into the next century; and (3) that economics, politics, regulation and our new global economy will all play crucial roles by the year 2000. It is for these reasons I felt compelled to write this book.

I had the good fortune to launch my life insurance career as an agent in the legendary Jack and Garry Kinder Agency. With their guidance over the years, I learned much about coaching agents through the incipient stages of their careers and into the established sales force. To these teachings I have added my own experience as an agency manager and marketing officer, to create the contemporary portions of this blueprint to successful life insurance selling.

However, it was the journey that I took after leaving the traditional role of agency manager that gave me the knowledge to create a more complete work on successful life insurance selling for the year 2000 and beyond. My experiences in senior management allowed me to view the industry from places seldom exposed to the sales and marketing force.

Recent times have taken the life insurance industry from a sleeping giant to a key player in the financial services industry. As chief marketing officer of Executive Life during the last half of the 1980s and as an independent consultant, author and lecturer on life insurance marketing, I spent more than a decade on the very cusp of the financial services revolution. It was an incredible ride that, despite great personal loss and hardship, provided me with an education in the marketing of life insurance, present and future.

During 1985 to 1991 I oversaw what, at the time, was the industry's largest independent distribution system (PPGA–Brokerage). I also worked in a senior capacity with the industry's first producer group and with the first agent-owned reinsurance company. After writing my first book about these experiences, *The Fall of First Executive* (1991), I was invited to consult with many of the industry's more innovative companies to plan new product and distribution concepts. These experiences taught me that there is more going on beneath the "selling" surface than ever before. These changes will profoundly affect today's agent.

Yes, knowledge, attitude, habits and skills still deliver high performance, but other factors are at work that, if not understood, can be roadblocks to success. Overcoming these roadblocks will require a firm grasp of the dynamics at work in the financial services spectrum. Through a set of unique circumstances over the past 25 years—some fortunate, some disastrous and a few golden—I feel prepared for these challenging times and want to help you, the reader, prepare for the journey as well.

1

Market Specialization

"If it is to be, it's up to me."
—Jack and Garry Kinder

The business you are in is no business at all, except for the business you create. You create your life insurance practice by carving out a population of individuals and businesses who come to know you as their insurance planning professional.

Before you can build a successful practice with an eye toward the year 2000 and beyond, however, you must have a clear backdrop against which to structure it. This becomes your frame of reference— or your guiding principle, if you will.

First, you must understand that ours is a proactive business, meaning that good things happen only because you *make* them happen. Prospects are found only if you find them. They will buy only if you help them solve a problem. They will refer you to others only if they trust and respect you. Everything is in the hands of the agent. On a good day, that means being in charge of your own destiny, but on a bad day, it can simply be a heavy burden!

Building *your* practice involves a lot of responsibility. This, of course, is why *you* came into the business in the first place; you wanted to chart your own course—to be the architect of your own future. We must never forget this double-edged sword of total control of our actions and total responsibility for our results. We must be convinced that we wouldn't have it any other way if we are to succeed.

Once you understand this basic tenet of our business—not just intellectually but emotionally, too—you can begin your task of successful life insurance selling. For if you can create trusted relationships with people who can and will buy life insurance, the business will do the rest. It will give you all you deserve—no less, no more. In the scheme of things today, that is indeed a remarkable outcome.

This book is intended to help you create a blueprint for the construction of your life insurance practice. Our focus will be on sound business principles and practices and how, by thoughtful understanding, you can make the right choices and create the result that best fits your ambitions and talents.

We are going to plow some new ground in areas such as carrier and product analysis as well as revisit the most time-tested habits and skills of success. We are going to go through a process that starts with basic choices and finishes with the payoff of someday selling your practice. Let's get to work!

EXAMINING YOUR OPTIONS

When you went off to college, you were given a year or so to get the lay of the land and a feel for your choices regarding a career path. Then, during your sophomore year, your student adviser or your parents probably began to urge you to declare a major.

Your life insurance career is similar. After a few years of doing whatever it takes to move forward, you should begin to think about an area of specialization. It's no secret that a high level of expertise in an important field is one way to ensure economic security in most professions. That doesn't mean that a general practitioner can't enjoy a successful career in life insurance. On the contrary, as we shall soon see, it may be the best market of all. However, if that is your choice, make certain it is just that: a choice, not a decision by default. Most successful agents focus on a particular market that appeals to them and in which they have a comfort level. Rather than drifting into one market or another, it may make more sense to go through an intelligent, logical selection process.

Let's begin drawing a blueprint for building a successful life insurance career with an exercise that I believe every agent should engage in at least once in his or her career. If you have already chosen your area of specialization, this exercise still has value. In fact, many agents, upon revisiting their feelings on specialization, discover that changes in their careers or newly discovered talents could cause them to shift or modify their area of specialization. As we shall see later, many agents build and sell more than one practice over their careers, each of which is focused around a specific market or specialty.

First, a word about market choices. When we talk about choosing a specialty, we include a mixture of people, products and markets. For our purposes here, we include professionals such as teachers or physicians; products such as disability income or mortgage redemption; concepts such as qualified pension and needs programming; and markets such as qualified plans or business insurance. In other words, our definition of markets may not conform with those of a good business school, but they will make sense to life insurance agents.

Thus, we don't want to get too scientific. If an agent wants to work mostly with schoolteachers selling a variety of needs-related products ranging from insuring their mortgages to planning for their children's educations, that's one market. If another agent wants to focus on writing qualified plans for everyone from corporations to street vendors, that's another market. We define a market specialty as the area of focus in your practice in which *you* have developed some expertise. If *you* know who your prospects are and what you like to sell them, you have a market specialty. Beyond that, you can become more sophisticated in your definitions as time goes on. But for starters, knowing what and to whom you sell is the first big step.

Who Am I?

One of the great benefits of our business is that we get to do business with people we like and we can avoid those people and situations we don't care for. So the first step involves taking advantage of this opportunity by profiling the type of clientele we want to focus on.

With What Type of People Do I Work Well? Look at personality styles: analytical, amiable, driving or expressive. In what type of professions do you find people that you work well with? For example, engineers, salespeople, lawyers, nurses and teachers all tend to possess personality traits that drew them to their profession.

It's usually preferable to work with people who share in our belief system. The life insurance industry affords us the opportunity to do just that. We can gravitate toward prospects who share similar values and life experiences. If you want to work with people from your previous profession, members of your church or temple, or those of your own political persuasion, you can; in fact, you probably should. After all, ours is a people business, and our best chance of building the necessary rapport that precedes most sales is to have as much in common as possible with the prospect.

What Expertise Do I Bring from My Previous Experience?
Another great thing about our business is that everything you did before coming into it helped you to prepare for it. Everything it takes to succeed in life—discipline, goal orientation, empathy, conviction, determination, integrity, sincerity and, above all, the love of people—is essential to success in life insurance selling. All of those qualities we were encouraged to foster by our teachers, parents and clergy are important to a successful career in life insurance sales. Our profession tends to attract the well-developed, socially desirable personality. Then, by choosing prospects carefully, we can create a clientele that fits our personality like a glove! This, in my view, is the best definition of vocational fulfillment: a job that lets you use all of your strengths and permits you to work around your weaknesses.

Add to this the experiences of your previous job. Whatever it was, there were things about it you liked that, if developed, could help you be more successful as an agent. For example, if you were a teacher, you enjoyed conveying concepts, counseling and sharing. These qualities can be transferred to your new career and should be considered when selecting your area of specialization. A teacher might do very well in the young family market, where a lot of education and guidance are sought by first-time buyers. On the other hand, complicated markets like ESOPs (Employee Stock Ownership Plans) require presentations to groups, such as company management, and a lot of explanation. Again, this could be very attractive to many teachers.

Thus, a thoughtfully constructed clientele, built by targeting prospects you are comfortable working with, is a primary key to your job satisfaction.

What Would I Most Enjoy Selling? It's worth thinking carefully about your comfort level with regard to the type of sale you prefer. For example, if you focus on the family market, you will probably tend to write a lot of cases, because the premiums are typically smaller while the needs are many. (The average family buys between five and seven life insurance policies over a lifetime.)

In the corporate market, the sales are usually much larger but often fewer and further between because much more development time is involved.

Initially, newer agents feel more comfortable in the family market but often aspire to the "big-ticket" business or estate-planning case. However, we must remember why we entered the business in the first place. Many of us wanted to be in control of our own careers. When we rely upon the "yea" or "nay" of one big prospect to make our month or even our year, we relinquish that control. On the other hand, when we are making 10 or 15 smaller sales each month, no one prospect can meaningfully affect our performance. In my view, a high case rate (over 100 paid cases per year) is the best way to be sure that you are in complete control of your practice. If you enjoy a single, one-shot sales call, you will want to focus on a single-needs sale, such as mortgage insurance or disability coverage.

If you enjoy multiple-call selling where the stakes are high, you may focus on business insurance, such as COLI (Corporate Owned Life Insurance). Just remember, *it's fun to hunt elephants, but it's only rewarding if you bag one with regularity!*

If service to clients is not your long suit, avoid markets that are easy to sell but difficult to service, such as group insurance or casualty insurance.

Where Do I Think My Biggest Potential Lies? In our business there are many ways to be successful, but you are only likely to truly excel if you spend your time mastering those key tasks that are vital to building a successful practice.

You will be a star if you master certain things for which you have aptitudes that are also solid paths to sales performance.

For example, if you have a natural aptitude for the technical and complex, you may do well in the tax-oriented sale, such as estate planning. These markets involve a lot of research and verification of the authority by which you make your recommendations. You will need explanations and sound answers to complicated questions from financial advisers, such as CPAs and attorneys. Preparation is central to success in this market.

If you are not technically oriented but like the upscale market, there are many big single-needs sales to be made to the high net worth individual. Deferred compensation, key person insurance and pension maximization are just a few examples.

A final thought on this suitability issue: The biggest factor in call reluctance and low levels of productivity is lack of conviction. If you believe you have a product, concept or idea that, once acted upon by your prospects, will accrue to their benefit, you will go to the marketplace with a mission. If you truly believe that the people you call on need what you sell more than you need to sell it, you will succeed. Take the time to think about the best forum in which to tell your story and the best people to tell it to. If you're convinced you have something of real value to offer, you will have no trouble finding people to offer it to.

What Are the Markets of the Third Millennium?

While some markets will always be good, many big premium dollars of the future will come from new and emerging markets. In actuality, a "new market" is most often merely a new approach to an existing market. It has been said that there are no new ideas in the life insurance business, just new approaches to presenting the old ideas. This is an accurate generalization, but don't think it means the opportunity to be creative isn't better than ever.

As long as our business has been around, there have really been only two markets for our product. In the broadest sense, all life insurance is sold to solve one of two problems. Years ago we called these two problems "dying too soon" or "living too long." Today, as we try to appeal to a more educated consumer, we have restated these two problems as wealth accumulation and wealth conservation. From these two basic challenges that every American faces—accumulating money with assurances and hanging on to it once you have it—all life insurance sales are made.

A while back, a wealthy friend of mine told me that by his reckoning, the definition of a millionaire changed with the excesses of the 1980s. "A millionaire," he explained, "is no longer someone with a net worth of $1 million. That's nothing special. A millionaire is someone with a net income of $1 million per year!"

Arrogant as it sounds, my friend has a point. A million dollars isn't anything close to what it was when the term *millionaire* and the image it brings to mind was coined. So for purposes of compiling my list of Million-Dollar Markets for the year 2000, I took my friend's new definition into account. We will only discuss markets in which I personally know and work with at least one agent who earns $1 million or more annually in first-year commissions. Granted, that's not net income after expenses, but it's good enough to warrant our attention all the same. Using this criteria, my list comes to ten markets for the year 2000.

Let's take a "catalog look" at various ways that today's life insurance superstars address these two age-old problems of wealth accumulation and wealth conservation. Our aim here is not to teach you the markets, but to point out the characteristics of each market so you can match them against your talents.

Qualified Plans   Pension and profit-sharing or qualified plans (so called because, upon IRS approval, these plans *qualify* for favorable tax treatment, such as tax-deductible annual deposits or tax-free accumulation) have long been a lucrative market for sophisticated agents who are good at administration. I believe this market has an extraordinarily strong future and poses opportunity beyond any of its previous heights. In the 1960s and 1970s, qualified pension plans were regarded as a growth market and, to be sure, they still represent a major share of life insurance company revenues. However, legislation enacted by Congress in the 1980s limited the attractiveness of qualified pension plans for many smaller corporations and businesses, especially professional corporations, such as medical practices. The increasing administration expenses needed to accommodate the new laws cut deeply into the returns available for smaller businesses. In addition, a series of limitations levied upon the key person or business owner made qualified plans much less beneficial to those who had to pay for them. These limitations present themselves in three primary areas.

First, the dominant buying motive for most qualified plans in the small-business market was that the business owner could set aside a major share of the contribution for himself or herself. Various pieces of legislation enacted in the 1980s substantially restricted the amount of contributions and benefits that could accrue to the principal owners. Plans that discriminate even moderately in favor of those who pay for them will not qualify with the Internal Revenue Service (IRS) for tax deductibility.

Second, the IRS reporting and administrative requirements for small qualified plans became cumbersome and expensive. If a doctor is putting $30,000 per year into a qualified plan and the reporting and administrative expenses run about $1,500 per year, then the first 5 percent of yields on the plan are eaten up by administration expenses. This obviously diminishes the attractiveness of such a plan.

Finally, the maximum individual tax bracket on marginal income declined from a high of about 90 percent in the late 1960s to a low of about 33 percent in the late 1980s. Thus, the government subsidies of such plans declined dramatically. The tax benefits to a high-income business owner created enough leverage for the owners to include employees in the plan and still come out ahead of most regular nonqualified savings plans. Lower taxes, ironically, did away with this selling point.

It has been our experience that the congressional pendulum always swings. When Congress tries to restrict the fruit borne of a particular tax advantage by chopping down the tree, its members usually regret it. With the growing public concern about the retirement needs of older Americans, legislation has been and will continue to be proposed to liberalize the restrictions on qualified plans.

Simultaneously, individual income tax rates are increasing, and that trend is not likely to reverse anytime soon. Higher taxes are never good news, but they do increase the attractiveness of the term "tax-free benefit."

Most advanced underwriting experts seem to agree that the qualified plan market is poised to explode as we approach the turn of the century. The potential for up-and-coming agents to catch this wave is truly exciting.

A word of caution: The qualified plan market requires a lot of knowledge and resources—knowledge because, in addition to understanding tax law and complex product design, you must usually work hand-in-hand with the client's other advisers, namely the CPA and the attorney; resources because a qualified plan is a complicated sale that requires a lot of bench strength from your company. You should be sure your company wants qualified plan business before you enact a plan for giving it to them. If a company is not geared up to support the agent and service the client for this kind of business, success is unlikely.

The qualified plan market is back, and it will emerge over the next few years as the platform for the launching of some of the industry's greatest success stories.

Surprisingly, at the moment there are few agents focused on this opportunity. My bet is that those agents who major in qualified plans over the next few years will experience meteoric success.

The Life Insured Retirement Plan   One thing about life insurance agents we can count on is that every time Congress tries to fill what it perceives to be a hole in the tax code, agents go to the place where a fresh hole has been dug and fill it with new sales concepts. Clamping down on tax shelters in the 1980s made traditional split-dollar plans look much more attractive. The inside buildup of cash within a life insurance policy is one of the few untaxed capital growth items left today. The industry quickly addressed the problem and is now selling the concept as a life insurance purchase. Depending on whether a split-dollar approach is used, these plans vary between a traditional life insurance sale and variations on split dollar.

The nonqualified deferred compensation plan, using split-dollar life insurance, is one of the hottest markets in our industry. Section 162 and split-dollar plans, which vary from company to company in format, were sometimes known as Private Pension Plans. This term was deemed to be misleading, however, in that it was not always clear as to what was being sold. By and large, companies have adopted new language to ensure clarification of the concept used for this sale.

The nonqualified deferred compensation plan is a simple life insurance sale that provides an excellent vehicle for the safe accumulation of cash values for retirement along with the added security of a death benefit. It needs no window dressing and, in my view, will sell very well when presented as exactly what it is—a life insurance policy. There are two approaches: one for businesses and one for individuals.

For businesses, typically the company pays for a life insurance policy on the owner(s) of the business by giving them a bonus in the form of a premium to the life insurance carrier for a policy on the life of the owner(s) or key executives. Because the policy is actually owned by the insured, he or she is responsible for the income tax on the dollar amount of the premium. The company may choose to offset this additional tax cost to the insured by paying an additional amount to the insured to cover the tax (single bonus) or by paying a bonus to cover all additional tax costs (gross up).

Because Life Insured Retirement Plans do not require IRS prototypes or approval, they are much more flexible than qualified plans. Usually, they allow clients to discriminate at will in favor of key employees, including themselves. The Life Insured Retirement Plan is a package sale in sophisticated wrapping. Once mastered, it can be fun, profitable and relatively easy to sell. The prospects for this market include virtually all small businesses and closely held corporations (especially C corporations, which retain some earnings after the owners are paid). The key element is the presence of at least one highly compensated individual (usually the owner) who wants to put aside funds for retirement in the most cost-effective, tax-favored way. Doctors and dentists, for example, often fit this profile.

The Life Insured Retirement Plan actually can complement an existing qualified retirement plan as an extra layer of benefits for the business owner and any other key employees. It also can be a perfect entrée to other business insurance sales, such as buy/sell and key person insurance. Because it is a novel and attractive-sounding concept, the Life Insured Retirement Plan approach in direct mail and cold calling can generate more appointments than other more commonplace approaches. As we all know, the challenge is to have a reason to contact a qualified prospect. At this time, the Life Insured Retirement Plan seems to look very much like a door opener.

Essential to this package sale is a sound understanding of split-dollar life insurance and Section 162 plans. Despite the amount of ink devoted to split-dollar over its past 25 or so years of popularity, few agents really have a complete understanding of how it works. We won't attempt to explain it here, but I can tell you it's not all that complicated. Split-dollar is a concept sale. It offers an IRS-approved method of moving dollars out of a business on a tax-favored basis. This is accomplished through various methods of joint ownership of a life insurance policy by the business and the employee. A wealth of articles and books on the subject are available through industry trade journals and publishers. My suggestion is to read as much as you can stand on the subject, then take a split-dollar expert with you on a few joint calls. Nothing brings education into focus like a fat commission check!

The second form of Life Insured Retirement Plans is for individuals and is much simpler. This approach emphasizes the use of high-cash-value life insurance policies as savings vehicles for retirement planning. Most companies have various products that allow clients to maximize annual premiums with the emphasis on cash accumulation.

As a supplement to other retirement planning, life insurance is a wonderful vehicle. It goes a long way toward providing peace of mind both in the safety of the cash values and in the assurances it provides should premature death, disability or emergencies occur along the way. This is a use of life insurance you can proudly sell for exactly what it is: a safe, sound value to the consumer.

A word of caution: In recent years, life insurance policies as retirement planning vehicles have drawn sharp criticism when compared with alternative investments. This is not because life insurance doesn't compare favorably to other investments, because it surely does. The problem has been that the nature of some presentations obscured the customer's view of what was being sold. Never allow this to happen. Follow your company's rules to the letter and make sure everyone knows that you are selling life insurance.

Corporate Owned Life Insurance and Deferred Compensation
COLI and the related deferred compensation market both involve a variety of sales built around providing an additional layer of compensation (usually at retirement) for key executives. The COLI market is most often associated with larger companies wanting to do something special for top management or, occasionally, their board of directors. However, in recent years this market has virtually exploded due to the introduction of the concept of using cash-value life insur-

ance to fund certain additional balance sheet obligations for large companies. For example, if a corporation has promised postretirement benefits to its employees, such as Medicare supplement coverage or additional retirement income outside its pension plan, these benefits must be carried on its books as a liability. Under current accounting rules, it has become a requirement that most companies establish a sinking fund or other plan to assure that retired employees will have these funds when needed. Life insurance, with its tax-deferred accumulation of cash values and track record for safety and security, has proven—in many cases—to be a perfect funding vehicle for these obligations.

Similarly, when a large company wishes to add an extra retirement benefit on top of its pension plan for top management, life insurance has proven to be an excellent choice. These deferred compensation plans often involve large life insurance policies on key executives that provide cash at retirement as well as liquidity for estate tax purposes.

The premiums generated by COLI and deferred compensation sales can often run into the hundreds of thousands and even millions of dollars. However, clients often require that the insurance company design special low-load policies that generally pay the agent commissions that are only a fraction of those paid on traditional policies. The good news is that even a lower commission rate on premiums the size of the typical COLI case result in substantial compensation to the agent. The fact is that the top COLI producers are probably the highest paid salespeople in America.

Agents wishing to specialize in this market should realize that they will be "majoring in the majors." This market is the purview of the industry's most sophisticated Top of the Table producers. The rewards are big, but the learning curve is steep. This is not so much because of the complexity of the product as it is due to the often arduous sales process. The COLI or "big-ticket" deferred compensation sale typically involves presentation for approval to management compensation committees, human resource departments and boards of directors. The approval process usually also involves review from outside compensation consultants, accountants and lawyers. It is not uncommon for a sale to take a year or longer to complete.

COLI is a market that agents usually *evolve* into rather than break into. It requires substantial knowledge of compensation and benefit analysis at the senior executive level. Companies don't install COLI plans for their executives until their boards are convinced that the decision is supported by adequate research and analysis of their entire compensation packages. Especially today, bonus and deferred compensation plans must be fully explained and defendable to shareholders, security analysts and even company customers. This market is the ultimate elephant hunt. The work is challenging in every way—but the rewards are usually well worth it!

Employee Stock Ownership Plans Perhaps the most esoteric of the so-called advanced underwriting markets, ESOPs and ESOTs (Employee Stock Ownership Trusts) have been popular for about 25 years.

The sale is built around a classic problem of most family-owned, closely held, medium-size corporations. A non–publicly traded company, built around the personality and skills of its founder, is seldom very liquid upon the founder's death. Because the company often represents the bulk of the deceased's estate, there can be real problems when the estate taxes need to be paid. Many people with large estates tied up in an ongoing business don't realize that estate taxes can take over 50 percent of their wealth in a single bite—usually due no more than nine months after the death of the business owner. People are further mistaken if they think the bite taken by taxes is an even, across-the-board bite. It is not.

When the tax bill comes due, the liquid assets are sacrificed first, usually at 100 cents on the dollar. Then, if liquid assets are inadequate, the semiliquid assets—such as homes, personal property and "underwater" investments (e.g., stocks or bonds selling below the purchase price)—are sold at market value. Finally, if money is still owed, the business itself may be sold, almost always at significantly less value than it would have had if the owner was living and was a willing seller negotiating with a willing buyer. The results can be assets sacrificed at a deep discount to pay a tax based on market value at the owner's death, causing the effective tax rate to far exceed 50 percent. This whipsaw can be devastating.

ESOPs are plans that enable an owner or family to create a market for its business prior to the founder's death by selling it to the employees. This way, everyone wins. The founder capitalizes his or her corporation to conserve the value for family members; the employees perpetuate the enterprise through their ownership and thus secure both their jobs and their economic futures. All of this has been made possible by special legislation that facilitates such a transaction, so long as it is made available to most of the employees. The legislation allows owners to sell a minimum of 30 percent of their stock to the ESOP for no taxable gain, provided certain conditions are met.

Like estate planning, life insurance is not an integral part of the plan itself but rather the logical vehicle for a complicated transaction. In estate planning, we arrange property in a way that minimizes estate taxes. Then we calculate the tax that cannot be avoided through planning and demonstrate how life insurance is the best way to pay the bill.

When we enact an ESOP plan, we create a program whereby employees purchase stock in the company from the owners over time, usually in installments. The plans are fairly complicated. They involve not only CPAs and attorneys but also banks or other financial institutions, which lend the employees the money to purchase the company. The insurance sale can materialize in several ways, but the most common is the need to pay off the bank and other loans in the event the owner dies prematurely, or in the event an employee who bought stock dies before it is paid for. The ESOP is the vehicle; life insurance is the fuel.

Like the COLI market, ESOPs and ESOTs are also elephant hunts. The stakes are high but the competitors are surprisingly few. This is not just because they are complicated sales, but also because the agent must create banking relationships that understand and are receptive to the concepts. Virtually all sales in this market involve group presentations to sophisticated advisers and also presentations to key employees to be sure they "buy in to the buyout." For those with the energy and patience to take it on, this can be among the most rewarding of the advanced markets. Once the learning curve for the ESOP/ESOT market is behind you, the view is pretty spectacular!

125 Cafeteria/401(k) Section 125 of the Internal Revenue Code enables certain employees to pay for health insurance and related welfare benefits with before-tax dollars. Enacting a 125 Plan frees up both employee and employer dollars for the purchase of additional benefits.

Typically, by moving the dollars used to pay for things like health insurance, eye care and day care for employees' children to a before-tax status, the employees' disposable income may increase by $25 to $50 per month. The agent installing a 125 Plan then shows the employees how to divert this little windfall into a life insurance policy, annuity or mutual fund that can be purchased on a payroll deduction basis. It is an ideal way to help the average working person find those scarce premium dollars needed for additional insurance coverage or savings.

The 401(k) market (which allows tax-deferred contributions to personalized retirement plans) is a part of this significant segment of the payroll deduction market.

Under Section 401(k) of the Internal Revenue Code, employees can vote to institute a tax-favored savings plan that permits them to put up to about 8 percent of their gross income aside on a nontaxable basis. Employers can enrich the plan with matching contributions up to 50 percent, which are also not currently taxed to the employee. Employer contributions usually vest over a period of time, about five years, while employee contributions are immediately vested and portable.

I see this as a package sale market that allows agents the opportunity to enter the business insurance field on a turnkey basis. For the agent who wants to grow into the corporate market in a profitable and focused way, there is no better opportunity than the Section 125 and 401(k).

The keys to breaking the entry barriers to this market are systems and sales tracks. No special gift is required for success. Rather, it is picking the right track to run on and perfecting your skills with repetition and experience. The larger sales in this market involve the recruitment of enrollers and often require travel to multiple locations to reach the company's work force. Such cases require specialized training and expertise. For most readers, we suggest focusing on the 10- to 100-employee market at a single location. At least initially, this is the best way to learn the payroll deduction/401(k) business. Also, these types of cases will tend to develop more easily into business insurance sales if the company owners are local.

Key to any decision to enter this market is the assurance that your company has the resources and commitment needed for long-term success. The payroll deduction/401(k) market is very administrative-intensive. It involves many smaller policies that require specialized underwriting, servicing and premium accounting.

For a long while, many industry experts believed that payroll deduction was the most cost-effective way for the average working person to buy small amounts of competitively priced life insurance. With the help of audiovisual enrollment services, computerized underwriting and policy issue improvements, along with other innovations, this is rapidly becoming the case. Payroll deduction/(401(k) plans are another big wave waiting to be caught by forward-thinking agents.

The International Market We have all heard about the new global economy and the level playing field being created by reduced trade barriers between the countries of the world. The North American Free Trade Agreement (NAFTA) is only the beginning. This is such an enormous issue that it is almost difficult to comprehend. The opportunity is becoming bigger than many ever expected. For the life insurance industry, the international market is truly the dawn of a new epoch.

The life insurance and related products that we sell have long been regarded by the rest of the world as among the best anywhere. Despite its ups and downs in recent years, the U.S. dollar is still regarded as one of the best places to put wealth and savings over the long term.

Buying American, when it comes to life insurance, is a powerful lure to the upper class and new emerging middle class in exploding Third-World economies. But the availability of traditional American life insurance products is only part of the story. The last great American technology that has never been exported or duplicated is advanced life underwriting and business insurance. With a couple of exceptions such as Great Britain and Germany, business insurance as we know it is virtually unheard of throughout the rest of the world.

Today, the industrial complex in South America and the manufacturing resources in the Pacific Rim countries are becoming the economic centers of gravity for our new global economy. The owners of these businesses, large and small, have the same business insurance needs as their American counterparts: buy/sell, key person and executive benefit planning, to mention just a few. Yet to date no meaningful delivery system exists to address this market with the intelligent solutions offered by the U.S. life insurance industry.

In an exciting response to this opportunity, many North American companies are beginning to look at accepting business from foreign nationals (non-U.S. citizens or residents). This is not just a market for agents living in coastal or border states, such as Florida, Texas or California. Almost every American city has immigrant communities filled with first-generation professionals and businesspeople. To begin with, these people are often excellent prospects themselves in a market that can become a great nest. This can be especially important because in the development of the offshore business, it can take a long time from prospect to paycheck.

An ideal example is the physician or other highly trained professional from Asia, the Pacific Rim or South America. Such persons usually got to the United States because families back home had the means to send them to the best schools and finance their immigration to the United States. These people are often prominent, influential and affluent in their own countries. They are eager to build new relationships in the United States and want to find ways to anchor their economic security with a plan that assures them they can live the American dream. So use the techniques outlined in this book to target this market, establish a relationship, build a strong image and win their respect. If that's all that happens, you'll still come out a winner.

However, if you can reach prospects among professional members of the immigrant community in your city, you may find the gateway to the biggest individual market of the next 20 years!

Once you have clients here whose roots, lineage and family wealth lie offshore, the key is to find the right conditions for an entrée. For this to happen, certain circumstances must be present:

- You must be certain there is wealth available for the purchase of a U.S. dollar–denominated life insurance contract. Most affluent foreigners have offshore wealth built over a period of time that is available for foreign investments. Be certain that the family has a way to buy your product directly or through a third party without getting you involved in any foreign currency transactions.

- Try to focus on wealthy relatives who visit the client here in the United States from time to time. Travel is expensive, and many companies require applications and exams to be completed here in the United States.

- Be sure you're dealing with legitimate prospects. This is why it is important to make a client out of your local center of influence first. Unfortunately, there have been some incidents of fraudulent death claims in Third-World markets that have caused some companies to balk at offshore business. Your company will likely frown on any claim that turns out to be "rocks in a box."

- Understand any cultural or foreign law differences before you make recommendations that could backfire. For example, some countries have no estate tax; others prohibit the purchase of life insurance from a nondomestic carrier. In Asia, to buy life insurance is considered bad luck. However, policies with emphasis on cash accumulation and lower death benefits are well received.

Despite the obstacles, the energetic, creative agent willing to "cross the border" will find that the new international market truly has no boundaries. The barriers that exist will soon fall, just as they have in many other areas of international trade.

The international market is not for everyone. It will take a lot of time and effort to establish yourself and make clients of the U.S. residents who can lead you to this market. Yet the potential rewards are almost unlimited. The wealthy and successful citizens of most of the world have all of the insurance planning problems of their U.S. counterparts but none of the solutions! Remember, the expertise, technology and sales skills for advanced markets reside almost entirely in the United States. In my opinion, for the agent with vision, ambition and patience, there is no greater opportunity in our business today.

Over Age 50   There is a bulge of so-called "baby boomers" in our population. Most of them will have reached their 50th birthday by the year 2000. The primary event going on with this huge segment of our population is change. With regard to their economic future, most are at one of three crossroads: wealth conservation concern, wealth preservation fear or wealth accumulation crisis.

Wealth conservation concern refers to the need for proper estate planning. Those baby boomers who have succeeded in attaining some wealth have a need for estate planning, but often lack a sense of urgency to do something about it. Only the substantially wealthy are usually more than mildly concerned about liquidity for estate taxes.

A much larger segment of the baby boomer population has become moderately successful financially. These individuals genuinely fear losing their wealth due to a long-term illness or disability. Most of the baby boomers are now experiencing the declining health or death of their parents. What they have learned is that they face the prospect of "freighting"! Most of us no longer grow old, get sick and die. Most of us grow old and go into a slow glide of medically supported declining health. This can go on for a protracted period of time, burning through the entire net worth of the typically financially comfortable senior citizen. It's not a problem for the rich, nor is it a problem for the poor. It is a problem for the middle-class citizen who has done everything he or she was supposed to do to plan for retirement. Yet they have seen their life's savings wiped out by long-term stays in extended-care facilities.

People in their 50s and 60s who have lived through this sad drama with elderly loved ones have a valid fear. The fact is, most of us will finish our lives in an extended-care facility. That's bad enough—and so is the dissipation of a lifetime of savings. But what about the spouse we leave behind, who may have to get by for several years, then face the same end? Only this time, the spouse has to depend on government programs.

Sadly, baby boomers have even more to fear than their parents did. Funding for social programs for the elderly will, no doubt, feel the pinch of funding national health care. For example, there is a movement in Congress to pay Social Security on a qualifications basis, which means that if you can't prove you need it, you may not get it. That's going to be a tough pill to swallow for many baby boomers who paid the maximum Social Security tax all their lives, only to be denied the benefit because they were disciplined enough to plan for their retirement.

It's a tough problem and one that, in my view, can be solved only by the products and services offered by the life insurance industry.

The third segment of the baby boomers are those who have failed to plan for their retirement. Remember, this was originally the "now generation"—the "me firsters." I know; I've been part of this group my whole life, and of one thing I am certain: They have been the biggest spenders and the poorest savers of any developed country in the post–World War II era. Now there is genuine alarm among many of them about their economic security. They are ready to listen to you!

It isn't just that many baby boomers have overspent and undersaved, either. The rules they were playing by have changed, too. The inflation that made an expensive home a safe harbor has been gone for over a decade—yet the mortgages remain.

The cost of raising and educating children has continued to escalate while the income to fund it has increased at a much slower rate. The parents they thought were financially secure until death are outliving their savings and being sustained by a health-care system that is out of control with costs.

The consolidation of much of American industry has eliminated millions of middle-management and skilled labor jobs and, with it, retirement benefits that were previously taken for granted.

What all of this means to you is opportunity—not just to earn a good living, but also to make a genuine contribution to the resolution of a serious social problem. The baby boomer market is a marketer's dream: an enormous need that has yet to be converted to outright consumer demand. Those responsible for pulling this switch will be part of one of the biggest windfalls in financial services history. They will also help to solve one of society's looming problems—the care and economic security of our elderly.

Estate Planning   Although estate planning will eventually involve many members of the baby boomer market, it is currently most prevalent among a separate and distinct segment. Today, the estate planning market consists largely of the fastest-growing segment of our population, those over age 65. An outgrowth of the affluence of our society, this market has exploded and will continue to expand. The following statement says it all:

Experts predict that by the year 2010, over $14 trillion will pass from one generation to the next in America!

The need for proper estate planning, once the problem of the elite, has become a middle-class epidemic. With Congress contemplating reductions of the exemption equivalent, anyone owning a home probably has an eventual estate tax problem—a problem that even industry outsiders agree can best be solved with the purchase of a life insurance policy.

However, operating in the estate planning market involves a lot more than the sale of a life insurance policy. Life insurance is to an estate plan what fuel is to an automobile: It makes the whole thing go. But first someone must build the car—or, in this case, the plan.

To succeed in estate planning the agent must learn tax law; must understand trusts, wills and probate; and must be able to win the total confidence of the prospect to gather the necessary information to prepare a proper plan.

Above all, the estate planning agent must subscribe to the team approach to financial planning. This means working in a credible, supportive and cooperative capacity with the client's other advisers. Specifically, the attorney and accountant should be included in most sales presentations or kept "in the loop" throughout the sales process.

If the accountant or lawyer doesn't understand what you are trying to do in an estate planning case, he or she will fight you. And, if they fight you, they will usually win! To be an estate planner, you will need to be good at working with and supporting those other professionals upon whom your client relies for advice. Frankly, if you cannot win the support of other credible advisers, given the litigious world we live in, you should back off. You simply cannot afford the legal exposure of persuading clients to go against the wishes of their noninsurance professional advisers.

In recent years, concerns about attitudes of CPAs and attorneys have been somewhat relieved by the emergence of support among attorneys for life insurance as a key part of estate planning. One attorney organization, the National Network for Estate Planning Attorneys, has become a showcase for the team approach to the rest of the financial services industry. Founded by Bob Esperti and Renno Peterson, two of America's leading estate planning attorneys, the network has been built through cooperation with the life insurance industry. In fact, Esperti and Peterson built a 50-lawyer law practice back in the 1970s that did only estate planning. Amazingly, every client in their practice was brought to them through life insurance agents that they taught and worked with in seminars and study groups. Now this network of team approach believers has expanded across the entire nation. (For more information about the National Network of Estate Planning Attorneys, see Appendix A. A second important organization is the American Academy of Estate Planning Attorneys, 9171 Towne Centre Drive, Suite 500, San Diego, CA 92122, 800-846-1555.)

It's true that, even with the help of good attorneys, most estate planning cases are complex, require much ancillary planning not directly related to the sale of insurance and, above all, require a team approach. As one might imagine, this means that this type of sale involves a lot of specialized education and often takes months or even years to consummate. Then again, $14 trillion worth of estates offers a lot of potentially big sales! My enthusiasm for this market is shared by the many agents I have worked with in recent years who have doubled and tripled their income by developing the estate planning market as a specialty.

The Family Market This term refers to basic life insurance and financial planning for middle-class American families and individuals. It is still the backbone of the life insurance business and a most worthwhile choice for an agent to focus upon. In fact, there is a strong argument for the family market being the overall best choice, not only for entry-level and intermediate-level agents, but for veterans as well.

There are three very important reasons why today's agent should consider the traditional family market.

First, it is *grossly underserviced while the need increases.* Due to the high cost of bringing new agents into the business, fewer companies have the resources to do a thorough job of training agents to work in the family market. As a result, the penetration of this market by life insurance agents is at an all-time low. This spells big opportunity. According to LIMRA (Life Insurance Management Research Association), the average American family was called on about life insurance twice as often in the 1980s as it is in the 1990s! Yet today, more than ever before, the establishment of an insurance/financial plan is vitally important to families. Besides the fact that people change jobs more frequently and lose benefits, we are dealing with a more volatile economy and ever-increasing pressure of the cost of providing for our old age.

As mentioned previously, Congress is talking about qualification requirements for Social Security recipients based upon current income. This would mean that those above a certain income level might lose their Social Security benefits. Initially, this would affect only those who had achieved very significant financial success. However, we know only too well what happens once the camel pokes his nose under the tent. With the ever-increasing problems of providing health care for our elderly, as well as meeting their retirement needs, the average American may be ill-advised to continue to rely upon the social programs and employer benefits that once diminished the need for personal retirement planning.

Second, and closely related to the increasing need for retirement planning, is the emergence of variable life as the product of the future. In my opinion, variable life will be a wave much bigger than that of the universal/interest-sensitive revolution a decade earlier. With this product, we will have the opportunity to offer clients in the family market genuine financial planning. By covering protection needs, saving needs and even investment needs, the life insurance industry can now claim its rightful share of the American family's savings dollar—a dollar that, by all recent accounts, is growing each year, thus adding even more to our opportunity.

Third, the family market is the most time-tested, reliable path to long-term success in life insurance selling. More knowledge, sales information and good ideas are available to the student of this market than in all of the others combined!

When it comes to seeking the formulas for success, nothing can hold a candle to the family market. As we will discuss later in greater detail, the agent even has access to two foolproof systems that literally guarantee success: the One-Card System for prospecting and Financial Need Analysis for a point-of-sale track. In the individual market, if an agent follows the proven practices and formulas, predictable and consistent results must and will follow. In a world where little is certain, we can offer a simple blueprint to big results in this more-fertile-than-ever market.

Besides the average American family (which is making a comeback), other family situations have emerged in recent years that historically have been ignored. Single-parent households, single professionals and mature couples with elderly parents are a few examples.

You came into this business to be in charge of your career, to be independent and to be compensated in direct proportion to your effort and ability. No market can assure the realization of these goals better than the individual family market.

The formulas for the family market are etched in stone. All you need to do is apply yourself and predictable, consistent results will follow:

> 10 approaches (appointments scheduled under favorable conditions)
> = 6 fact-finding interviews (an agreed-to need and money commitment)
> = 2 applications

How you get those appointments and close those sales has clearly changed over the years. Telephone answering machines and voice mail have increased the number of "dials" we must make to get a live suspect on the line, and point-of-sale computer software has complicated the buying process. Still, conduct six successful fact-finding interviews every week and you'll pay for 100 sales per year. Do this for five years and you will be on your way to a dream career that is almost unmatchable.

The tenth area of specialization, marketing to the affluent, is a pervasive issue that touches all of the areas we have discussed. With this in mind, we will look at it in the next chapter, which addresses market strategies.

So far, we have discussed nine areas of specialization from which any motivated agent can choose to major in and succeed. In fact, I firmly believe that if all of the able-bodied agents and home office marketing departments in our industry chose to focus on any one of these nine areas of specialization, they still would not achieve full market penetration of their targeted specialty. It's that wide open today.

2

Marketing Strategies

"I always believed the toughest accomplishment of my career would be to reach my goal of qualifying for the Top of the Table. Once I made it, I realized the toughest accomplishment of my career would be staying focused on what got me there."

—Agent Greg Acosta

Once you decide on your specific area of specialization, it makes good sense to further delineate your activities by focusing on certain segments of your prospect pool. Specifically, focus upon those prospects who can and will buy—the affluent! This group contains many individuals and businesses whose needs encompass every area of specialization we have covered. In fact, we feel quite strongly that this particular group offers the biggest opportunity in the life insurance industry to the end of the decade and beyond.

The old definition of a prospect is as true today as it ever was: "Does he have the need? Can I motivate him? Does he have the ability to pay?" The profitability of your practice will be greatly affected by the amount of marginal income your prospects have for the purchase of life insurance. All the need and motivation in the world is of little value if the prospect can't write the check to consummate the sale. Therefore, one important way to assure profitability in life insurance selling is to focus on those prospects whose business tends to be profitable.

Agents who are intimidated by the idea of dealing with the affluent would be well advised to remember the words of Ernest Hemingway when his friend F. Scott Fitzgerald reportedly said to him, "You know, Ernest, the rich are different from you and me." Hemingway's quip: "Yes, you're right, Scott, they are. They have more money!" All other factors being equal, working with the affluent is not only more profitable, it's more fun, because you rarely have to worry about finding premium dollars. It's finding need and motivation that is the challenge. Of course, as is usually the case with results that are extremely rewarding, getting there will take some doing.

WHO ARE THE AFFLUENT?

I define the affluent as those individuals with a net worth in excess of $1 million and/or an annual income from the primary breadwinner of at least $100,000. (In many households today, both spouses are working professionals; still, to meet my definition of affluent, one spouse must be earning at least $100,000 per year.)

The most important fact about this market is that it is growing, and growing fast. In fact, it is the fastest-growing major market segment in the industry. Let's look at the characteristics of the affluent that make this market attractive.

- They have the same needs, problems and desires as other segments of the market, but their numbers are bigger.

- Research indicates that a surprising number have done little, if any, financial planning. In other words, most of this enormous market is not being called on!

- Because they have money and are usually well educated, they have the resources to make a quick decision when shown an attractive solution to a perceived problem.

- Once they become clients, they can provide a wealth of ancillary selling opportunities through their friends, their businesses, their children, and their civic and charitable associations.

- The affluent have the ability to make substantial purchases during downtimes in the economy.

- They associate with people like themselves, which makes for the best-feathered nest an agent can have.

- It has long been believed that agents tend to earn at the level of those with whom they do business.

Reaching the affluent market is simply a matter of knowing where to go. Surprisingly, it is often not the places we would assume, such as country clubs and posh resorts. The affluent are typically very hard working, usually business owners, and they seldom flaunt their wealth or waste their time.

So, if you wish to locate the affluent, you won't do it by going to places of ostentatious leisure. Rather, you will find them by getting in step with their very busy, productive lifestyles.

Business Owners The old adage that you can't judge a book by its cover was never more true than it is about the businesses you should call on to tap the affluent market.

Just like in your insurance practice, in most businesses, it isn't how much you earn that counts, it's how much you *keep* of what you earn. The most successful small businesses are often in the most understated locations or unpretentious neighborhoods.

Rather than calling on a stylish boutique in the local Galleria, you might do better with a convenience store in the less attractive part of town. The owner of a local chain of auto body shops is likely to be more affluent than the owner of a high-profile new-car dealership. The farmer who looks "dirt poor" is often "filthy rich!" The most successful contractor in your area isn't on the local links on Saturday morning; instead, he's more likely to be found at some local doughnut shop at 6 a.m.

Today, the small businesses that are successful often operate in niches serving larger industries—for example, the computer software companies serving banks and insurance companies, or vendors of computer programming, collection bureaus and quick printing/copying services. The small-business segment of our economy is booming. Take the time to ask business clients who calls on them or supplies them with a valuable product or service.

Professionals Doctors, dentists and lawyers are still wonderful segments of the affluent market, but you must be selective. First of all, a professional designation is not an automatic ticket to wealth today. It takes superior performance over a long period of time to attain affluence as a physician, dentist or lawyer. You will need to segment this market to target the affluent among it.

These prospects have been targeted for the purchase of life insurance since graduate school. They usually understand just enough about the work you do to give a fairly formidable objection to talking with you. Rarely are they actually "all set," as they like to say. More often than not, they have a piecemeal insurance program consisting of two or three purchases from various agents. The opportunity in the professional market is to offer a complete program through careful analysis, using a team approach that includes their other advisers.

Finding those professionals who fit into the affluent category can be more of a challenge than most agents think. The income is usually there, but the net worth part of the equation often is missing. Doctors, for example, spend so much time and money on their education that they are often in their 40s before they have substantial disposable income. At that point, they too often try to play "catch-up" with the creation of a lifestyle that supports their lofty image. This, of course, is a good reason for them to team up with a quality life insurance agent to help them plan properly once the money finally does start coming in. So, if this is the market you choose, you may have to grow with them to affluence rather than join them when they are already there.

In addition, this is an area of specialization that requires a lot of specific knowledge about the vagaries of the profession and the characteristics of those who practice it.

Entertainers and Athletes In recent years, there has been enormous growth among the affluent members of these two groups. This has increased the number of professional business managers who handle the wealth of these often less than financially sophisticated individuals. Life insurance planning is one of the first things the nouveau riche stars of sport and entertainment should consider. As the old question goes: "If you had a goose that laid golden eggs, which would you insure, the eggs or the goose?"

The best way to break into this market is through the business manager. Typically, celebrity management firms promote themselves as providing a full array of services to their clients, usually including life insurance and estate planning. Surprisingly, the agents we know in this market found many of the business managers receptive when they approached them about providing insurance services to their clients.

This is a narrow but very deep market, well worth pursuing if you live in an area that provides access to the financial advisers of the stars in your community.

Idle Rich   The one group of the affluent that is often easily accessible are the scions of the wealthy. However, the number of so-called idle rich is smaller than you might think, and because of the way they acquired their wealth, they are not usually the best prospects among the affluent.

A better prospect is the working offspring who has assumed the responsibility of running a family business. These individuals are often familiar with the problems of perpetuity in small businesses from firsthand experience. Because they have the responsibility for carrying on the family business (often having been chosen over siblings), they usually welcome sound advice from a third party of their own choosing. They want to make good, and if you convince them that you can be of help, you can win a role as trusted adviser.

Senior Corporate Executives   The leaders of the Fortune 500 corporations include a large segment of the affluent population. Many of these individuals have acquired substantial wealth through stock option and equity programs.

Although good prospects as individuals, they are often best accessed through their corporations. Large companies tend to reward their executives with deferred compensation and equity participation plans that work well when funded with insurance products. To access this market takes a great deal of expertise, credibility and patience. The agents who have succeeded in this market are few, but they themselves have achieved substantial affluence through their efforts.

GAINING ACCESS TO THE AFFLUENT

If you are convinced that you want to maximize your profits by building a successful practice targeted at the affluent, you will have to know how you are going to get there. It isn't easy, or that's where every agent would be selling. Yet the penetration in this market is not even remotely close to the potential it offers. I believe the main reason is twofold—one perceived, one real.

The perceived reason is the notion among many agents that they cannot succeed in this market. They feel that they lack the knowledge and skill; therefore, they lack the courage to tackle this market. Obviously, to call on successful people, we must think of ourselves as successful and worthy of their business. If an agent can learn enough about prospects in the affluent market to open up cases, that may be all that is necessary initially. Joint work will be touted throughout this book as a key building block to a successful practice. Nowhere is the value of joint work more evident than in the affluent market. In addition to knowledge and skill, the affluent market requires a lot of backup and support not normally directly accessible to newer agents. By seeking out a seasoned veteran in their agency or community, agents secure the help they need to develop and close the cases they open up on their own. In the process, they will gain the confidence and knowledge that only experience in the field can provide.

The second reason agents hesitate to go after the affluent is that affluent people tend to do business with "their own"—people they can relate to. You don't have to be rich to call on the rich (although it doesn't hurt). Most of those in the market we have identified as affluent are professional, bright, often well educated and usually good judges of the abilities of others. So, *if you're going to play in the big leagues, you do have to be good.* You need to know your product and your market. You must be a skilled salesperson. You must have the courage of your convictions to call on the affluent. To be perfectly honest, the second reason some agents are reluctant to call on the affluent may be valid. You want to have enough of the "right stuff" in your mind. The only difference between you and the affluent prospect who is at the top of his or her profession should be timing.

They have arrived, you are on the journey. If you can believe this, you not only will succeed in calling on the affluent, you will also succeed in becoming one of them.

You should be aware of several other considerations if you hope to gain access to the affluent. Dedicated activities in these four areas will be of paramount importance.

1. **Prepare to service the affluent.**

   You will need the same state-of-the-art support in your business as the affluent client typically has in his or hers:

   - Superior staff
   - Computer support
   - Product specialist support
   - Financial planning software
   - Estate planning software
   - Due care research
   - Access to a good attorney
   - Advanced underwriting backup

   Initially you will rely on your agency, your manager and joint work with senior agents for these resources. Eventually, however, they will be your responsibility.

2. **Build your public-relations effort around the affluent.**

   - Make sure your brochure contains endorsements from people they will identify with.
   - Advertise in their trade and professional journals.
   - Indicate your specialty on your business card.
   - Belong to appropriate organizations (e.g., the Estate Planning Council).
   - Get an article published on working with high net worth individuals.

3. **Go where the affluent congregate and support their organizations.**

   - *Trade shows*—This is an often overlooked opportunity by agents.

   - *Professional conferences and annual meetings*—Become known to them in their world.

   - *Symposiums and lectures*—Learn about their business or profession.

   - *Continuing education programs*—Those in other professions usually have the same requirements as those of us in the insurance business.

4. **Once the ball is rolling:**

   - Develop centers of influence. The affluent like to know they are in good company.

   - Find a wealthy mentor to guide you. Pick a client whose success you want to emulate.

   - Insist on referrals. This is your key to anchoring yourself in this market.

   - Observe their friends and colleagues. Every moment in the habitat of the affluent offers great opportunity to prospect by personal observation.

SELLING TO THE AFFLUENT

If you have mastered the skills outlined in *Successful Life Insurance Selling for the Year 2000,* you have a start. The process of selling to the affluent, however, requires some modification. The big-ticket sale requires that every base be covered. As is always the case, each step of the process must be handled with thoroughness and professionalism. In addition to the affluent prospect, who is typically adroit, this sale usually is subject to the scrutiny of other professionals who advise him or her, such as attorneys and CPAs. If you're going to be in this market, you'll want to be a master salesperson, able to handle every step of the sales process with professional poise. The process starts out like any other, but differs as you move toward the close.

The Approach

This step is the same as it is with any prospect. Get the appointment under favorable conditions. This is one phase of the process that never changes.

Fact-Finding Interview

I recommend a fact-finding sheet customized to the high net worth individual. A good example is included in Appendix C.

The affluent typically have more complicated balance sheets and income sources. However, the focus of the initial interview is still the same: need, money and motivation.

You will want to work at developing prepared responses to the roadblocks the affluent prospect puts in your path. The objections may be more powerful than those you are used to, but it's only a matter of learning how to deal with them.

Case Preparation

The key word here is preparation. In this market, casework can be extensive. For example, you will need all of the information about the prospect's assets and how they are held (e.g., in joint tenancy, in trust, etc.), along with information about investments and other relevant documents.

Case assembly will usually require some brainstorming with your manager, other agents or a qualified third party, especially in the beginning. When working with the affluent, you cannot be over-prepared.

You may need to meet with the prospect's CPA or attorney to procure the proper information. Chapter 8 of this book is a good guide to the types of processes you will want in place.

Case Presentation

Now is the time to remember the truism, "Make every occasion a great occasion." With what's at stake, you must anticipate every development for every selling interview.

The biggest difference is that these types of cases usually require the presence of multiple parties: the client and spouse, accountant, lawyer, business associates or key personnel. You will want to be sure that all parties necessary to a buying decision are always present.

Because of the audience, your presentation format may differ. You may wish to use visual aids, slides or overheads. Otherwise, you will want to distribute ring binders containing the proposal materials. I recommend both.

The affluent differ from the nonaffluent in one important way: They know that their wealth entitles them to special privileges in the marketplace. In addition, the affluent are well aware of the complexities of managing money, of opportunities available to the prudent and of the pitfalls that await the unwary. According to a recent study from LIMRA, the majority of affluent prospects fall into three categories, and you'll want to be prepared to deal with all three.

First are those who *need to be educated* in finances. Their affluence may come from mastery of a discipline, such as brain surgery, or a gift, such as singing. They will want you to explain what each product does and to make some sense out of the information overload. These clients tend to build trusted relationships over time, but initially they will want a comfort level with regard to your competence.

The second type are those who are *goal-oriented.* They are typically younger, more aggressive, often businesspeople with an entrepreneurial bent. These clients need you to help them reach their specific objectives. I like to say that the goal-oriented affluent prospect wants the agent on his or her "board of directors"—not literally, but figuratively. They are rising stars and if you win their respect, you can develop a long-term relationship as a trusted adviser. These are the most exciting prospects among the affluent.

The third type of affluent prospects are those who have *financial problems,* such as estate liquidity or complicated family or business situations. These individuals need to be educated about their problems or options and then need to become motivated to act. Typically, these cases quickly evolve into estate planning cases. They take a while to close and usually involve advisers and outside counsel. Estate planning is, by definition, marketing to the affluent, but the sale is a wealth conservation sale, while the other two categories tend to deal with prospects in the wealth accumulation stage.

No matter what type of prospects are involved, your job is the same. Help them recognize a problem and motivate them to solve it through your services. This is the part that never changes.

Remember that the affluent are different from the nonaffluent: They have bigger needs and bigger resources to solve their problems. They also have bigger expectations of those who would ask them to part with their hard-earned money.

MARKET PENETRATION

Until now, we've had the pleasure of going through a scientific exercise to help us get ready. Unfortunately, for too many agents, the exercise of getting ready becomes an end unto itself. They spend too much time thinking and not enough time acting. The problem is as old as the business itself. Don't get trapped into the deadly cycle of "getting ready to get ready." Now that you've picked a market, let the real work begin. You must first assemble a game plan for entering that marketplace and establishing yourself as a factor.

You want to become a known and respected practitioner in your chosen field: known by your community, your friends, your prospects and clients, your industry and your competition—not just for your knowledge and expertise, but for your results as well. For if I haven't said it yet, I will say it now and often: Results are our final judge.

Overcoming Entry Barriers

If you're new to the business or new to the market you've chosen, you are going to have to overcome some obstacles. Entry barriers exist primarily in three areas: credentials, resources and access.

Credentials Just as you inspect the credentials of the professionals you depend upon for medical, accounting and legal advice, so your prospects will inspect your credentials.

However, unlike other professions, we have a unique advantage: We can practice our profession while completing our education. We must be careful with this unique privilege, however. As we move into markets we are not yet fully qualified for, we should rely on joint work and help from our management, just as an intern at a hospital relies on the senior medical staff. Meanwhile, we must acquire our own credentials.

Credentials fall into three broad categories: learned, earned and paid for.

Learned credentials in this context mean educational credentials. Ironically, the most important learned credentials ultimately come from experience. Experience, track record and reputation obviously form the ultimate credential, which, by definition, is possessed by those who have already built a successful practice.

Today there are three important learned credentials: fully licensed life and health insurance agent, which today should also include being a licensed stockbroker; Chartered Life Underwriter; and Chartered Financial Consultant or Certified Financial Planner.

Set a date and a schedule in your business plan (as described in Chapter 5) for achieving these three educational milestones. Meanwhile, make it clear to prospects and clients that you are actively pursuing these goals.

Earned credentials include Million Dollar Round Table, Court of the Table, Top of the Table and various company club levels, such as Leader's Club or President's Club.

These credentials may be more important to your own definition of success than to that of the prospect. However, never underestimate the fact that successful people like to deal with successful people. You will never regret sharing your production achievements with your clients. They will applaud you and be much more receptive to referring you to others.

Finally, earned credentials are the gateway to industry and company recognition that will lead to joint work opportunities.

Paid-for credentials are membership opportunities, such as the Estate Planning Council or the American Society of Pension Actuaries (ASPA), that allow you to participate in their meetings and learn while you earn.

Your membership in professional organizations such as the National Association of Life Underwriters (NALU) is also important. During your early years, involvement in professional organizations can serve as a credential indicating your involvement in your industry and your commitment to your profession.

Resources   The second entry barrier to be overcome is resources, in terms of people, support and money. Resources are critical to market penetration. You must have the ability to invest in the equipment needed to practice your craft. This might be estate planning software and a compendium of books and documents on estate planning that provide reference materials for your activities. It might also include computers and casework specialists to aid in putting your sales presentations together.

The most important resources are human. Do you have access to a respected expert through joint work, or a home office advanced underwriting staff? Until you are established, this access is critical to market entry. Until you are an expert, you must *borrow* one! We talk throughout this book about the value of joint work. It simply cannot be overemphasized. In every profession, the high achievers serve an internship at the feet of the masters who preceded them. Ours is no different.

Access   Finally, to enter the market you must decide how you are going to access a steady flow of qualified prospects. Remember this above all: *In the final analysis, it will be the people who teach you the business.* It is the prospects you work with who will put you through the paces until you learn your profession.

Unlike students of medicine or law, we get to practice on real live customers until we learn our profession! We hope that, like doctors and lawyers, we can intern under the supervision of skilled practitioners (joint work); still, we are permitted to wean ourselves from our teachers as our confidence grows.

How we access those on whom we practice our profession is an important matter. This is not a book about prospecting, so suffice it to say that you should develop a system that puts you in front of enough of the right kind of prospects. And during this period, until you become an expert, bring one with you!

Financial resources, capital or just plain money: However you choose to reference it, it's the scarcest resource for most new businesses. According to the U.S. Department of Commerce, most new businesses that fail do so during the first three years, and the biggest reason they fail is that they are undercapitalized. The same is true of life insurance agents; the failure rate during the first three years is extremely high. After they turn the proverbial corner, however (usually during the fifth year), you can't get them out of the business with a crowbar!

Why do agents fail? A lot of industry ink has been spent on that subject. We do know that, as new businesses go, the financial barriers to a life insurance career are among the lowest, while the financial rewards are among the highest. After all, in most cases the companies pick up most of the agent's start-up expenses, which is truly unique in so entrepreneurial a business. No one does anything of the kind for doctors, dentists or lawyers. Yet many agents fail to realize that a secretary, a computer, direct mail or other item they pay for themselves may be that extra something that puts them over the top.

Initial Investment Requirements

To enter a new market, you must do several things to package yourself, announce your presence and prepare to do business when cases begin to develop.

First, you must invest in yourself. Literally. I believe you cannot overinvest in your personal appearance; you should look as professional and successful as you can. Today it has become popular to play down personal appearance as the measure of a person. To be sure, we only have what God gave us to work with, and that is enough in virtually every case. One need only look at the industry legends of the past 30 or so years to know that we are not talking about becoming one of the "Beautiful People." You should take care of yourself physically, pay attention to your grooming and carry yourself in a way that inspires confidence. Remember, all you sell are configurations of numbers on a piece of paper, in exchange for which you are asking people to give you their money.

That's a tall order, and my point is that most agents cannot afford to lose a single sale simply because they failed to appear as credible and professional as they might have. This is not a matter of conformity or subordination to the system; it's a matter of good business. To sell right, you have to look right.

Second, you *must* (and if ever there was a place to use the word *must,* this is it) invest in an executive assistant. Initially, this person might be a part-time high school student or your spouse—someone to initiate the position of KOP (key office person). This is the person who does everything (except those things that only you can do): Manage your One-Card System, handle correspondence, schedule appointments, generate illustration, oversee the new business process from application to paycheck and do everything necessary to keep you in the field.

Your third investment is in systems and support. Here I am talking about a computer and client management software (my favorite client management software is CMS Client Management Systems, 200 South 13th Street, Ste. 214, Grover Beach, CA 93433, 800-643-4488), the purchase of lists and the maintenance of a database, and, above all, the critical due care and point-of-sales aids that help you to maintain state-of-the-art presentations materials, such as Financial Need Analysis[SM] (FNA) and Business and Estate Analysis and Review (BEAR[TM], produced by Vernon Publishing, Hartford, Conn., 213-643-7799) or the systems provided by your company.

Finally, you will want to develop a database from a highly specialized mailing list, targeted at the prospects in your community for your area of specialization. Such lists are available for almost any prospect profile through specialty mail houses. Invest in the best list you can and begin a regular direct-mail program. Every study on penetration of new markets tells us that success begins with a quality list and is developed through repetition. Repetition breeds familiarity, and familiarity is the manifestation of established presence in the marketplace.

Start with an introductory letter that includes your image brochure. Then, follow up with a regular quarterly newsletter. Consider advertising in the trade journals of your chosen market. The more often your name comes up, the more frequently those considering your services will be receptive to you.

As previously stated, your biggest investment will always be in personnel. The choice of an executive assistant or KOP may be the most important decision you make in building a successful practice. Pick someone who wants to learn your area of specialization almost as much as you do. Give him or her a career path that includes a chance to share in the profits from the enterprise. If possible, get someone with experience at working with agents in your market. Reach beyond your present capacity to pay and find someone willing to go the extra mile for back-end rewards. Then reward performance generously, and your assistant will become the foundation of your enterprise.

Financing your initial investment should come from a staunch commitment to continuing the strategy that got you this far. Before abandoning the old, be sure you're well on your way to greener pastures.

Don't be afraid to go to a bank or other lender. Compared to almost any other business, ours has among the lowest capital requirements. On the other hand, don't try to solve a fundamental problem, like prospecting, by throwing money at it. The fact is (as we will discuss later), you must be a good prospector by way of skill development. It is not something you can buy.

Establishing a Beachhead

Now that you are rolling, doing some cases and finding your footing, you will want to stake out your turf.

The first step is image building, which we will cover in detail in Chapter 6. This fits in well with the access issues we have just discussed.

Next is the development of customer profiles through market segmentation. For example, if your specialization is the Qualified Retirement Plan, the prospects for your services include professional corporations, closely held corporations, Subchapter S corporations, partnerships and sole proprietorships. Among these, you may wish to target professional corporations, with the primary focus on doctors. This is fine, but be sure you are prepared to do what it takes to make such a target market effort work for you.

First, it is important to define your *primary prospect,* because this will drive your other activities. Once you know who it is you want to offer your services to, you can build your personal marketing program around their needs.

If, for example, you are a Qualified Plan specialist, focusing on doctors, your plan to establish your presence in the marketplace would include the following activities:

1. A general mailing introducing you as a specialist in Qualified Retirement Plans.

2. A seminar for (or individual presentations to) local CPAs focused on what you can do for their doctor clients (Consider qualifying such a meeting for continuing education credits.)

3. The cultivation of a prominent doctor who will serve as a center of influence for you in this market (You need to land a center of influence as a client to make things begin to happen.)

4. A carefully prepared group presentation on Qualified Retirement Plans, complete with slides and handouts to be presented at local Rotary, Lions, church, accountants', lawyers' or other group meetings in need of speakers

5. A plan to give this presentation at local industry meetings to establish your expertise and promote joint work

Individually, each of these activities will probably yield few specific sales initially. Eventually, however, you will see that you have mounted a campaign that will yield a tidal wave of new clients over time.

Market Share

Whatever your area of specialization, if you make a good choice there will likely be substantial competition and significant pressure on profit margins. Welcome to American business and the new global economy! The day of safe harbors or profitable niches are largely gone. If you can't compete head to head with no regard for offering something different, then your days are numbered. On the other hand, there is a lot you can do to assure a solid, profitable share of your market in the specialty of your choice. A good starting point is the analysis of current and potential competition.

Depending upon your choice of specialization, there are generally two types of competition in the life insurance business.

The first is what I call *atrophied*. These are all of the mature markets, in which most practitioners who have established themselves are earning a comfortable living. The competition has paid its dues and, perhaps, has grown a little complacent. Examples of this abound in long-established business insurance markets, such as pensions and profit sharing and executive bonus.

This type would also include the traditional family market and financial planning market. The overall penetration in these markets has diminished in recent years, relative to the level of demand. As previously mentioned, time-tested formulas will produce consistent, predictable and very rewarding results for the agent willing to put forth a little extra effort. The reality is that in the established markets, there is no serious competition from other agents; the real competition comes from downward pressure on compensation and the self-destructive practice of companies willing to outillustrate one another. In other words, the competition is product illustrations and compensation give-backs. The strong agent with a well-thought-out business plan can overcome these obstacles early on.

Agents practicing in these markets must deal with competition head-on. They must convince their clients that they are worth what they are being paid for their services and that the company they recommend will deliver on its promises.

In established markets, it's back to basics. The competition is visible, manageable and beatable. The markets are generally fairly wide open for the well-prepared, well-qualified professional.

The second form of competition is the *innovators*—those who develop new solutions to old problems. *Product* innovations such as interest-sensitive whole life were most common in the 1980s. Today, we see *concept* innovations, such as accelerated death benefits, pension maximization and executive bonus plans.

Innovative competition is very healthy and very real. If you are operating in a market where innovative concepts are hot, you will want to be involved.

Before you plunge head-first into the latest iteration of zero net outlay life insurance, I cannot overemphasize the importance that you do your due care on the concept and its viability. Above all, review every sales concept, illustration and all support documentation with your company's compliance officer.

As to specific competition from other agents, it has been my experience that the time spent fending off the other agent we occasionally encounter on a case is a waste of energy. Be a friend, a colleague and a professional to other agents. The occasional case you may lose to them is insignificant when compared to what you lose by engaging in brinkmanship.

Establishing Profit Margins

We may no longer be able to mandate profits in our business, but we can still have target profit margins. It is important today that agents look at their business from the standpoint of net revenues. Many producers think in terms of commission dollars generated, which historically may have been a good measure of success. However, there are considerable expenses involved with building a successful practice, and one would hope that you would invest a significant amount of your commissions back into your business. The secret is to manage that investment based upon standards you set for yourself. We will go into more detail on this subject in Chapter 8.

Determining Who You Will Be in the Marketplace

The best advice I can offer to anyone in the midst of building a business is this: *Make all important decisions by moving yourself down the road five years.*

When you decide to build your practice around a primary market or area of specialization, you should create a blueprint of what you would like your practice to look like in five years. At this point, I'm not talking about a five-year plan or a business plan, but rather about an overall vision or result. How do you want to be thought of in the marketplace five years from today? As the most prominent? The best? The biggest? Will your practice be centered around your community or state, or will it be nationwide?

You also should profile the typical client you will serve. Age, income, profession and net worth are all things you should have a vision of with regard to the clientele you wish to build. And decide what your educational and certification objectives will be.

I recommend that you sit down and write a narrative describing your overall practice five years from today: who you are, who you serve, how you operate and how people perceive you both within and outside of the industry. Also, it should all be written in the present tense, as if it has already occurred.

This is not a document with numbers or goals; that will come later. Instead, this is the overall result—the essence of what you have built. It is your personal statement of an important plateau in your career. Put this narrative in an envelope, seal it and date it five years from today. Keep a copy to revise periodically, as needed. Compare the two at the end of five years.

A Word to the Wise

No matter which area of specialization you choose, that market offers a variety of prospects ranging from the marginally successful to the highly affluent. All other factors being equal, things usually work better for agents who focus on more affluent prospects. With this in mind, I think it makes good sense for agents to build their practice with an eye on the wealthier end of their market.

MARKET ANALYSIS

Once you have a clear understanding of your choices, the next step is to compare the opportunities offered by those markets that interest you. Remember, *we measure success by the gap between your achievements and your potential.* You will be best served by picking a market that utilizes your strengths, yet still requires you to stretch. Only then will you grow.

After you have narrowed your choices down to the two or three markets that hold the most appeal for you, I recommend the following exercises:

Examine the Learning Curve   Ask yourself "What must I learn to master this market?" Start by doing your own research. Visit with company managers, home office officials and successful agents. Read company and industry materials available on the markets you are considering. Prepare yourself mentally to take some time on this decision. If it's made correctly, you'll be doing it for a long time; if not, it could take you out of the business. Find out what it takes to attain true expertise in the markets you're considering. Then, think about what you have in the way of aptitude for each market. Define expertise by listing the qualities, talents and credentials your research tells you are important to success in a market. Then score yourself on each of these qualities. Use a scale of 1 to 10 (10 being total mastery).

For example, if you are considering estate planning:

What It Takes	*What I've Got* (On a scale of 1–10 where 10 = mastery)
1. Comfortable working with people over age 50	6
2. Educational qualifications (CLU, ChFC, CFP, NASD and college degree)	7
3. Access to prospects socially and professionally	9
4. Work well with CPAs and attorneys	8
5. High level of understanding of tax law	4
6. Ability to spend months developing each case	5

$$\frac{\text{What it takes}}{\text{What I've got}} = \text{Potential success factor}$$

If the result is much greater than 1 (meaning it takes a lot more than you have), you may be reaching too far. (The factor in this example is 1.54.) If the result is too close to 1, you might be underachieving, since before even entering the market you are already close to the optimum.

On the other hand, even an objective exercise such as this leaves significant room for subjectivity. For example, newer agents in the business may not currently score high on educational qualifications. They may be working on several and believe that they have good potential and comfort level with other issues, such as mastery of tax law.

Consider Demographics for Your Area Some markets are great but narrow. They may not work within certain geographic, cultural or economic environments. For example, estate planning is usually done for those in their 50s, 60s and even beyond.

For an agent new to the business or fresh out of college, the estate planning market may look glamorous, but it may not be a realistic choice.

Despite the enormous potential of the international market, it would not be the best primary choice for an agent who wished to live and work in Des Moines or Omaha.

Use the "Ben Franklin" Approach to Strengths and Weaknesses of Each Market List the advantages and disadvantages as you perceive them for each market you are considering.

Be objective but realistic. For example, proposed legislation may have a terminal effect on a given product, as it did with single-premium whole life in the 1980s. On the positive side, while it lasted, the advantages were a bonanza for agents and their clients. (Perhaps too much so, in that aggressive marketing was perceived by some as an abuse that contributed to the product's demise.)

Weigh the advantages against the disadvantages.

Estate Planning

Pros	*Cons*
1. Large average case	1. Purchase is for benefit of others rather than insureds.

2. Easy-to-find premium dollars

3. Easy to sell: "Pay kids or pay the IRS."

4. Persistency is excellent.

5. Can lead to business sales and sales to kids.

6. Good work will bond me to the attorney.

2. Older prospects have insurability problems.

3. Congress could change laws motivating sale at any time.

4. Involves working with attorneys and accountants.

Layer the Results Over Personal Strengths and Weaknesses

Once you feel you have the right potential to succeed in a market (learning curve), you have considered environmental factors (demographics) and you have looked objectively at the pros and cons (Ben Franklin), it's time to choose.

First, list your personal strengths and weaknesses (as you see them) and compare them to your analysis of each market. This is an attempt to take subjective data and lend some element of objectivity to it. The point is not to be scientifically accurate, just objective. This is difficult for many of us in sales, because we often let our emotions rule us. We think about what we'd like to do and who we'd like to be, instead of what we are able to do to become the best person we can be.

Personal Strengths

1. I love tax law and complex cases.

2. I relate well to affluent people.

3. I have access to a lot of high net worth individuals.

4. I perform well in the presence of attorneys and accountants.

Drawbacks

1. I am impatient and lose interest in a prospect who is not motivated.

2. I cannot afford to go a long time between sales.

3. I like to have a victory every day (a sale or something good).

5. I am very comfortable
   with older prospects.

None of these exercises is designed to give you the answer. Rather, by going through them thoughtfully and systematically, you are inputting data that your subconscious mind will eventually digest and analyze in its own way. I truly believe that life's important decisions are rarely successfully arrived at by analysis alone. Instead, we pour the ingredients into our mental data bank through exercises such as these, and we wait for the answers to reveal themselves. If we push ourselves too hard, it's like pushing a rope—we just get tangled up.

Go with Your Instincts   After your analysis, I suggest you turn to the human element for additional input.

Seek the counsel of those who know you: spouse, managers, fellow agents and your mentor (providing you have one).

If possible, seek out agents who are active in the markets you are considering. Ask them to let you accompany them on a few calls. Most successful agents welcome the opportunity to show their peers how to do it right. Watch and learn. Then think about it.

From all of this, you will eventually develop a gut feeling—an inclination and instinct about the market that is best for you.

When you believe you're ready, make a choice; then go with it. If it's a good choice, chances are you'll be doing it for quite a while. On the other hand, it's not a choice for life unless you want it to be. Many of us switched majors in college. Others of us went into businesses completely different from the one our degrees prepared us for, but our general education prepared us for it all the same.

It's the same in our business. If you work at it, you will learn the basics regardless of the field of play on which you practice. The real secret in our business is mastery of the principles of successful life insurance selling through mastery of the sales process itself. These things are the same no matter what your area of specialization. That's why changing areas of specialization later is so much simpler for life insurance people than it is for other professions. The rules are the same—it's just a different league for us; for other professions, it's usually an entirely different game.

THE CHOICE IS YOURS

There are many areas of specialization in the life insurance industry. We have looked briefly at a few of the more attractive ones, but new markets are appearing every day. This is one of the amazing things about our business. There is and always will be more markets and opportunities within those markets than there are qualified agents to fill them.

Many years ago, in the 1930s, the introduction of Social Security was thought by some to bode ill for the life insurance industry. In fact, some predicted it spelled the end for life insurance salespeople. Then agents, seeing how inadequate Social Security was as the sole provider for Americans, developed a simple program to fill the huge spaces left by Social Security upon premature death or for retirement needs. Social Security awakened the need for the average American to address the issues of dying too soon, living too long or becoming disabled along the way. Therefore, it turned out to be an asset. It protected against abject poverty, so agents could get clients excited about using their money to plan for comfort and prosperity!

Since the 1930s, Congress has gone through various social benefit programs, each of which was perceived by some as a threat to our industry. Always, our fears turned out to be largely unfounded. As it turns out, Congress has been the silent partner of the life insurance industry, always stirring the pot to stimulate agent creativity—always digging one hole to fill another. I should add that these social reforms were created out of good intentions, and many have, indeed, been beneficial to our citizenry. Social Security is one good example. So, whatever changes the future holds in store for us will create new market opportunities—new choices for the agent to specialize in solutions that help the public accumulate and conserve its wealth.

3

Carrier Selection

"I ain't nearly so interested in the return on the money as I am in the return of the money."

—Will Rogers

The subject of due diligence, due care and carrier/agent liability is one of the key issues facing our industry today. Like it or not, today's agent needs to know more than a little about the financial analysis of a life insurance company and the integrity of the products he or she sells.

It has become a common and well-founded complaint that we live in the most litigious society on earth. This unfortunate condition has long prevailed at the home office and claims levels of our business. Now these problems are finding their way to the point-of-sale arena. Today's agent must be ever-conscious of the fact that every statement made at the point of sale, every piece of information left behind and everything communicated or perceived should be handled as if they were someday going to be reviewed in a court of law. This is the world in which we live. We will deal with actual point-of-sale conduct in Chapter 7.

Now, and in the next chapter, we will look at two other areas with which agents must concern themselves: the companies they represent and the products they sell.

The work involved in carrier analysis is not as difficult as some may think. Yet it is probably more important than most believe it to be. The key is to understand a few basic concepts in the construction of a carrier's financials and the products it sells. Once you understand the basics, you can then do a great deal of research and comparison on your own. After all, ultimately you are the one who must be satisfied with what you sell. However, qualitative analysis is only the first step. In my view, it's the subjective analysis that can make the real difference in carrier selection.

Remember, too, that you are not expected to be a recognized expert in the due diligence field, only a responsible professional or prudent man, if you will. This is why it is important to always use the term *due care,* as opposed to due diligence. *Due diligence* is a term reserved for the securities industry that implies some sort of stamp of approval. Never expose yourself legally by using the term due diligence, but do your best to practice it all the same. Due care is our term for a best effort at looking out for our clients with regard to what we sell them.

The advice on carrier selection that follows should be viewed as opinion, not gospel. It is based upon my 25 years of experience as an agent and marketing officer. My views are those of a salesman who was required to learn the technical side of carrier analysis and who sought to develop ways to communicate what I learned to agents and policyholders. I don't claim to know everything about carrier analysis, but what I do know, I know well; I learned it when the top 15 company I worked for collapsed around me and all who represented it.

What I do consider myself qualified to discuss are those aspects of carrier selection that the financial analysts do not address: instincts, common sense and managerial competence. Perhaps, between their views and mine, the reader can draw his or her own best conclusions.

My view of carrier analysis consists of measuring strength and performance in three key areas: financial strength, capital strategies and management performance.

FINANCIAL STRENGTH

Chances are you are already with the right company. That's a big statement, but the fact is, despite recent adverse events, the vast majority of the companies in our industry are sound, solid and safe. There has been a lot of overreaction to some well-publicized failures in recent years that has caused some to view our industry to be financially troubled. This is simply not the case. Granted, there have been some notable failures, and we should always remember that life insurance policies are only as good as the company that stands behind them and, to a degree, the industry that stands behind the companies. But on balance, that has been awfully good!

To my knowledge, no death benefit has ever failed to be paid, and, although sometimes delayed, every policyholder in a failed company has eventually received his or her principal, usually with interest or some equivalent. The life insurance industry owes no apologies to the public for its performance over the past 200 years. I know of no 200-year-old, 100-year-old or even 50-year-old industry that can claim a better track record. You can be very proud of your industry's performance for policyholders.

Despite the relatively outstanding record of the industry, life insurance companies do, on rare occasion, fail. So, we must deal with the due care issue. After all, the only system that guarantees against failure collapsed a few years ago over in Eastern Europe from the weight of its own idealism.

What companies are expected to do in a free-enterprise system is to guard against disaster, against culpable activities by management and against inequity toward the policyholder in a failure situation. When a company fails to perform in these areas, we have the additional checks and balances provided by the industry through organizations such as NOLGA (National Organization of Life Guarantee Associations) and NAIC (the National Association of Insurance Commissioners).

Given what the agent usually has at stake, it should be obvious that he or she would want to do the most responsible job possible in choosing a carrier, regardless of what the legal obligations may be.

Measuring the financial strength of a life insurance company has historically been an inexact science. As much as we would all like to rely on a quick reference that was reliable and consistent, such as a rating from one of the rating agencies, this is simply not enough. From my experience, which has included both the success and the failure of companies with which I have been associated, I recommend looking at three broad categories: ratings, key ratios and investment performance.

The rating agencies have distilled the process of carrier selection down to a simple numerical or alphabetical scale. This is both good and bad: good in the sense that if you understand that the rating agencies are a quick reference or a starting point rather than the final determining factor in the evaluation process, they are invaluable; bad in that if you think or tell your prospect that these ratings are all-encompassing assurances of performance or even the key consideration, you may be very disappointed.

With this in mind, let's briefly look at four of the major rating agencies to better understand their criteria in evaluating life insurance companies.

A.M. Best

Assignment of Best's Ratings and Financial Size Category is made in the spring of each year shortly after the company has submitted its annual financial statement (due March 1). Official notification by letter is sent to the chief executive officer of each company.

A++ and A+ (Superior)—Assigned to companies that, according to A.M. Best's established standards, have achieved superior overall performance. A++ and A+ (Superior) companies have a very strong ability to meet their policyholder and other contractual obligations over a long period of time.

A and A- (Excellent)—Assigned to companies that, according to A.M. Best's established standards, have achieved excellent overall performance. A and A- (Excellent) companies have a strong ability to meet their policyholder and other contractual obligations over a long period of time.

B++ *and* B+ *(Very Good)*—Assigned to companies that, according to A.M. Best's established standards, have achieved very good overall performance. B++ and B+ (Very Good) companies have a strong ability to meet their policyholder and other contractual obligations, but their financial strength may be susceptible to unfavorable changes in underwriting or economic conditions.

A.M. Best Company
Ambest Road, Oldwick, NJ 08858-9888
1-900-555-2378 for rating information
908-439-2200

Standard & Poor's

A Standard & Poor's insurance claims-paying ability rating is an opinion of an operating insurance company's financial capacity to meet the obligations of its insurance policies in accordance with their terms.

Claims-paying ability ratings are divided into two broad classifications. Rating categories from *AAA* to *BBB* are classified as "Secure" claims-paying ability ratings and are used to indicate insurers whose financial capacity to meet policyholder obligations is viewed on balance as sound.

AAA—Insurers rated *AAA* offer *superior* financial security on both an absolute and a relative basis. They possess the highest safety and have an overwhelming capacity to meet policyholder obligations.

AA—Insurers rated *AA* offer *excellent* financial security, and their capacity to meet policyholder obligations differs only in a small degree from insurers rated *AAA*.

A—Insurers rated *A* offer *good* financial security, but their capacity to meet policyholder obligations is somewhat more susceptible to adverse changes in economic or underwriting conditions than more highly rated insurers.

BBB—Insurers rated *BBB* offer *adequate* financial security, but their capacity to meet policyholder obligations is considered more vulnerable to adverse economic or underwriting conditions than that of more highly rated insurers.

Ratings below *BBB* are considered to have "Vulnerable" claims-paying ability.

Standard & Poor's Corporation
25 Broadway, New York, NY 10004
212-208-1524

Duff & Phelps

The insurance company claims-paying ability (CPA) service provides purchasers of insurance company policies and contracts with analytical and statistical information on the solvency and liquidity of major U.S. licensed insurance companies, both mutual and stock.

The CPA ratings are based on the same scale as the Duff & Phelps bond and preferred stock ratings. However, reflecting the difference between an insurance company's ability to meet its claim obligations and an obligation to service debt, the insurance company CPA rating scale utilizes different definitions of safety. The first ten CPA rating categories *(AAA* to *BB-)* fall within a range that is analogous to the widely recognized regulatory investment-grade category.

AAA—Highest claims-paying ability. Risk factors are negligible.

AA+, AA, AA-—Very high claims-paying ability. Protection factors are strong. Risk is modest but may vary slightly over time due to economic and/or underwriting conditions.

A+, A, A-—High claims-paying ability. Protection factors are average and there is an expectation of variability in risk over time due to economic and/or underwriting conditions.

Duff & Phelps Credit Rating Company
17 State Street, New York, NY 10004
212-908-0200
or
55 East Monroe Street, Chicago, IL 60603
312-368-3131

Moody's Insurance Claims-Paying Ratings

Moody's rating symbols for insurance claims-paying ratings are identical to those used to show the rating quality of debt securities. The system of rating securities was originated by John Moody in 1909 and was applied to insurance companies for their policyholder obligations for the first time in 1986.

Rating gradations are broken down into nine distinct symbols, each symbol representing a group of ratings in which the quality characteristics are broadly the same.

Moody's Insurance Claims-Paying Ratings are opinions of the ability of insurance companies to repay senior policyholder obligations and claims punctually. Moody's employs the following designations to indicate the repayment ability of insurance companies:

Aaa—Insurance companies that are rated *Aaa* are judged to be of the best quality. Their policy obligations carry the smallest degree of risk.

Aa—Insurance companies that are rated *Aa* are judged to be of high quality by all standards. Together with the *Aaa* group, they constitute what are generally known as high-grade companies.

A—Insurance companies that are rated *A* possess many favorable attributes and are to be considered upper-medium grade.

Baa—Insurance companies that are rated *Baa* are considered as medium grade; their policyholder obligations are neither highly protected nor poorly secured.

Ba—Insurance companies that are rated *Ba* are judged to have speculative elements; their future cannot be considered as well assured.

B—Policyholder obligations of insurance companies that are rated *B* generally lack characteristics of the desirable insurance policy.

Moody's Rating Service
Corporate Rating Desk
212-553-1653
Moody's Investor Service
99 Church Street, New York, NY 10007

Note: In addition to the information provided by the rating agencies, there are independent services that merge information from the rating agencies into a single comprehensive report. The best known of these services is VitalSigns, offered by United Systems Corporation, 20537 Sidewinder Drive, Park City, UT 84060, 801-649-5300. For a more detailed example of the VitalSigns Analysis, see Appendix B.

I like to think of rating agencies as being similar to the sports physicians who check out athletes before a contest. They give you the statistics and their opinions on the strengths and weaknesses of their subjects. They weigh, measure and run analyses. They tell you the condition of their subjects at a given point in time. They warn of the possible effects that past injuries or mistakes may have on future performance. They even may have opinions on the outcome of a given contest in which the athletes compete. Their opinions are, unquestionably, of critical importance. Yet when the athlete goes onto the field of play, the team physician stays in the locker room and watches the game with everyone else.

The information provided by the rating agencies is certainly valuable. Indeed, it is the first of the three key elements we look at. However, ratings can only go so far in telling you what you need to know. They can only tell you and your client what the situation is at the "opening gun" of the contest. We call that the point of purchase. There is an inherent problem with stopping here, however, which I call the Rating Agency "Flaw": *The condition of your life insurance company when you buy a policy is not nearly as important as it is when you have a claim or want your money back . . . and that can be years or even decades down the road.*

You see, just as a team physician cannot measure the intangibles of heart, determination and second effort in an athlete, neither can rating agencies determine these qualities in a life insurance company—nor should they be expected to, although, to their credit, they try all the same. Most rating agencies attempt an analysis of the intangibles, but it simply is not their strength. I was intimately involved with a company that went from having the highest rating available from the top two rating agencies to no ratings at all in just six short months! Interestingly, the rating agency team visited that company regularly and pored over it like an army of ants. They understood a lot, but not the human element. This is nothing against the rating agencies, just a fact about their limitations.

The management of a life insurance company is being paid to perform for policyholders, and that means taking some acceptable risks. Think of our athlete again. If the physician's report says there is no evidence of an injury of any kind and, in fact, there's not even any evidence of physical contact, does that elevate our confidence in the athlete if things get a little rough out on the field of play?

I'll take my chances with a warrior as opposed to a perfect specimen every time. If a company has only the highest ratings, it is important to ask how they were acquired. Were they won over a long period of solid growth and steady performance for policyholders and agents? Is the company committed to its distribution systems—that is, have its agents been given what they needed to compete in good times and in not-so-good times? Some companies have won good ratings by sitting on the sidelines, while others tried to move with the current environment. Now those companies have awakened from their slumber with high ratings stamped on their foreheads, and they don't even know how they got there!

Although good ratings are good news and a solid indication of strength, don't assume that a highly rated company is automatically one you or your clients will be happy with. Clients should understand that it should not be necessary to sacrifice performance for safety. Company management is paid to invest policyholder funds and deliver acceptable results at minimal risk. A portfolio that is all investment-grade or all government securities can be assembled by a child. This is not what responsible portfolio management is about. Any authority on the subject will explain that the key is to reach for yield while avoiding unreasonable risk. To avoid *all* risk is a formula for an unhappy policyholder down the road. After all, the sizzle of most sales today lies in the living benefits provided by our product. While granting the importance of paying claims, responsible companies realize that the vast majority of clients use life insurance for its living benefits.

Fortunately, as the apparent trend toward variable life and equity-based products continues to build momentum, much of this argument is becoming moot. Any analysis of the choices made by purchasers of variable life will support the notion that policyholders have a healthy tolerance for risk when it comes to the portfolios backing their life insurance policies. This doesn't mean they want to gamble with their life insurance dollar, but it does mean they expect their life insurance company to deliver performance on funds entrusted to them.

CAPITAL STRATEGIES

The second thing we should look at in the financial analysis of a carrier is its strategic use of capital. Capital and surplus are essentially the net worth of a life insurance company—the source of the funds a company uses to grow its business.

In the case of mutuals, this is the money left after all obligations to policyholders are met. Technically, this surplus account is owned by the policyholders in a mutual, but for purposes of this discussion it can be viewed as a retained earnings account set aside for contingencies, growth plans or other opportunities, including, of course, dividend distributions to policyholders. In the case of stock companies, capital and surplus consist of balance sheet items such as retained earnings and shareholder equity.

Although I am deliberately leaving the discussion of balance sheet analysis to those who are more qualified to discuss it, capital strategies is one issue that must be considered here. The availability of and strategy for using its capital are probably the most important considerations in life insurance company management decisions. This is because the availability of capital and a company's plans for its use are the key factors in determining the company's plans for growth. Financial analysis aside, the reason an agent must understand these issues when selecting a company has to do with sales performance. All other things being equal, it's a lot easier to grow with a company that wants to grow than it is to grow with a company that wants to slow down.

Today, many companies cannot or will not grow as fast as they once did due to shortages of capital or other choices for its use than the writing of new business. To attain a more complete understanding of this vital issue, we are going to have to make amateur actuaries out of you. *If you read the next few pages carefully, you will have an advantage over many of your fellow agents in your understanding of one of our industry's most important issues—surplus strain.*

To get started, most businesses require initial capital that is in excess of their revenues. Put simply, they start off in the hole and use the initial investment of the owners as start-up money until revenues create a positive cash flow. Usually this money is borrowed from banks (debt financing) or investors who buy stock in the company (equity financing). Theoretically, when the business is up and running, the investors get appreciation on their stock plus dividends, or the bankers get their money back plus interest, and everyone is happy.

Life insurance companies operate under an entirely different set of rules. The cost of putting a life insurance policy on the books usually far exceeds the first-year revenues, not just in the beginning stages of building the business, but on every policy they ever sell. Thus, there is no positive cash flow in the early years with which to reward owners and investors, nor do you reach the point where cash flow on new sales becomes positive because the initial revenues exceed the initial outlay. Instead, there is, by design, a significant negative cash flow that can take years before turning into a profit to owners. The best way to understand it is to view a life insurance contract as a long-term installment purchase on which you make annual payments over many years—as few as seven or eight large premiums, or much lower premiums that continue over your lifetime, depending upon which type of policy you choose. This logic no longer applies just to accounting. Because of the new, unbundled insurance products sold today, it is also true from a consumer perspective. The company and the consumers are partners over the life of the policy, sharing in results that will vary from year to year. As the industry has learned, the results can vary a great deal from the projections used in the point-of-sale materials.

There has been a change in recent years that is difficult even for life insurance companies to understand. We now know that the consumer no longer simply "buys a life insurance policy." Rather, he or she is buying the life insurance policy over a protracted period of time. The performance of the company's investment portfolio, its expenses, its persistency and its mortality experiences are all a moving target that can be periodically adjusted, either directly or indirectly. For the customer, the results of his or her purchase will vary from year to year based upon a series of factors built into the contract.

When a new policyholder makes that first installment on the purchase of a life insurance policy by paying the first year's premium, the cash flow is not adequate to cover the company's expenses. For example, in the case of a $250,000 life insurance policy purchased by a man at age 40, the cash flow might look like this:

Initial premium	$2,500
Agent commission	$2,000
MGA compensation	500
Underwriting expenses	400
Miscellaneous expenses	100
Total expenses*	$3,000

*For purposes of illustration, taxes and similar considerations are omitted.

So, there's a shortfall of $500. To make the sale, we must then tap into the corporate equivalent of our shareholder equity, which, in a life insurance company, is called capital and surplus. Unlike a manufacturer, who can go to the well for an initial capital infusion to prime the pump to get his or her business going, a life insurance company must keep going back to the well every time it makes a new sale. The more successful the company, the more drain on its capital and surplus base. True, industrial companies, when they reach certain plateaus, must raise capital to build new plants and buy more equipment, but not to sell each and every product. In fact, the opposite is true: As they reach certain levels of critical mass, their costs diminish on a per-unit basis and their profits increase.

In an insurance company, eventually profits do begin to emerge on older policies because, although the premiums remain the same, the expenses are dramatically reduced in later years. For example, in the policy we cited, the expenses in years two through ten might be about $300 per year, including renewal commissions to agents and policy administration costs. Of course, any death claims would go straight to the bottom line, but that's what the mortality charges are for. If claim experience is as expected, there will be a profit left over from the mortality charges after all claims have been paid. Further, most of the remaining value that accrues is passed on to the policy-holder—at least, that's the way it has been in recent years, thanks to the changes in new products we have seen. Historically, insurance companies' accountants, by using generally accepted accounting principles (GAAP), allowed them to amortize (spread out) certain expenses by deferring policy acquisition costs over the expected life of the policy. But these helpful practices are quickly drying up, and the once-dramatic difference between GAAP accounting and STAT (statutory—required by the NAIC) accounting is narrowing. A company can still defer its acquisition costs, but now it must also defer the profits it books on the piece of business in question, which greatly diminishes the benefit of cost deferral and affects the design and attractiveness of the typical life insurance policy offered today.

In addition to the fact that it costs more on a cash-in/cash-out basis to write business, life insurance companies must also satisfy the insurance regulators to be sure they have planned properly to meet their obligations. The regulators do this by requiring companies to set aside additional reserves beyond those expenses associated with putting the business on the books.

These additional reserves have to do with the values and benefits the insurance company is guaranteeing to policyholders. Because all future benefits are based on assumptions, there is, obviously, a margin for error. Life insurance companies tend to assume that they will be right part of the time and wrong part of the time, but that things will work out in the long run about as expected. Thus, the insurance companies make their best guess at what claims experience, expenses, persistency and investment performance will cost each year over the expected life of one policy. They then use present-value tables to back into an annual premium they can charge that will be both fair to the insured and profitable to the company.

As regulators whose sole interest is the protection of the policyholder, the NAIC tends to assume that the life insurance companies will be wrong most, if not all, of the time. This is as it should be. It is their job to assume the worst-case scenario, and recent times have demonstrated that the industry needs the perspective of the regulatory bodies.

It's perfectly OK for the insurance company to assume it can earn a given rate of interest on invested policyholder funds, provided it puts aside extra money based upon the more conservative assumptions used by the regulators. These extra reserves belong to the insurance company, but they are tied up or pledged against future policyholder obligations. During the course of the policy's life, the company may prove to be right about its assumptions, but it still can't recover its extra earnings until all obligations are met. This regulatory safety valve is called the market interest adjustment, or MIA.

So where do these additional reserves come from? The insurance company has two choices: Charge a higher premium or go back to the well and pull the necessary funds out of surplus. Charging a higher premium would potentially cost the company business. Because competitors will use surplus to fund their shortages, most companies wanting to stay in the game will do the same. They have already made up a cash shortfall due to current expenses exceeding revenues on a new policy; now they must put up more in anticipation of a possible future shortfall. Unfortunately, it doesn't end there.

In addition to the actual cash drains when a policy is sold and the reserves that must be put up in anticipation of possible future interest-earning shortages, the insurance regulators have another major issue they must deal with.

So far, the issues we have studied with regard to pricing have concerned initial expenses and earnings on premiums collected. If the interest and investment earnings assumed by the insurance company are more aggressive than those the regulators want to assume, the company must put up the difference in the form of a reserve. The next question the regulators have for the insurance company is "What are you planning to invest these premiums in that causes you to believe you will get this yield?" The answer from most insurance companies is that they plan to have a well-balanced portfolio of bonds, real estate and securities. The issue for the regulators is now the *return on* the money. In other words, policyholders must be protected against investments that go sour by either being "underwater," meaning their market value is less than their original cost, or by defaulting altogether, such as a nonperforming mortgage on vacant commercial real estate.

Here again, the regulators must, in their view, take a worst-case view and assume that whatever *can* go wrong *will* go wrong. If they think there is a potential for default in a given category of investment, they will require an additional contingency reserve called an Asset Valuation Reserve, or AVR. In other words, the value of an asset can be based upon what was paid for it or what the current market would yield should the company have to liquidate it to meet current obligations. If the regulators believe that an asset is worth less than the amount paid for it (book value), they may require an additional reserve (AVR) to be put aside.

All of these surplus strain and reserve issues can be confusing and frustrating to the agent who is trying to make an intelligent, comfortable choice regarding which company to represent. Let's take a step back and look at the big picture by using an analogy with which most of us can identify.

If, instead of a life insurance company's capital base (capital and surplus), we were talking about a life insurance agent's capital base (net worth), many of the issues would be similar. Let's say, for example, that you wanted to buy a new home. Assume the purchase price was $300,000 and, after the mortgage company qualified you, it required a 30 percent down payment. The numbers in the transaction would look something like this:

Purchase price	$300,000
Down payment	90,000
Home mortgage	$210,000

Once the bank approved your loan, you would reduce savings by $90,000 and increase home equity by the same amount. Your assets would increase by $210,000, while your liabilities also would increase by $210,000. Your net worth would not change, but your liquidity would. Liquid savings would be transferred to less liquid home equity.

This is roughly what happens when a life insurance company writes new business. It is required to make a "down payment" of sorts on its new business. Just as the mortgage company wants to have a margin for error should the homeowner default and it has to take the house back and sell it, so the regulators want a margin for error should the insurance company have to liquidate an asset below its book value and, thus, not have enough to meet its obligations.

Insurance regulators have one big advantage over mortgage companies: They can change the rules after the transaction has been completed. If the regulators believe that the value of certain assets has slipped, they can require an increase in the down payment *retroactively!*

To continue our mortgage example, if the market value of your home were to decrease from $300,000 to $250,000, you might not be that concerned. After all, if you don't intend to sell the house and you are making the payments on time, you could live with this "underwater" condition for as long as you needed to.

Suppose, however, that you had a special kind of mortgage that allowed the mortgage company to require periodic increases in your original down payment to reflect decreases in the market value of your house. Now the adjusted $250,000 market value of your house would have the following effect:

Home value	$250,000
Required equity (30%)	75,000
Current equity	40,000
($90,000 original equity reduced	
by $50,000 decrease in value)	
Shortfall	$ 35,000

In such a situation, you would be required to pony up another $35,000 of equity or face the possibility of losing your home. If you had the liquid assets needed to meet this additional requirement, you would reduce savings another $35,000 and increase home equity by this same amount. If you continued to carry your house on your balance sheet at the price you paid for it (book value), this transition would have no effect on your assets, liabilities or net worth. What it would affect is your liquidity. Funds you may have had earmarked for other things, such as investing in the growth of your insurance practice, would now be tied up and unavailable until your mortgage was paid off. At that time, the real estate market may or may not have recovered and you could wind up realizing either a gain or a loss on the sale of your house.

This is pretty much how it works for life insurance companies. They have to put up what amounts to a down payment on their book of new business. They call it a surplus strain. The amount of this down payment is determined by all of the factors we discussed: the cost of putting business on the books, standard reserving requirements based on company estimates, extra reserves due to the difference in assumptions between the company and the regulators, and special reserves, such as Asset Valuation Reserves, required as a hedge against riskier investments. All of this adds up to surplus strain. Years later, after all policy obligations are met through claims, maturities or surrenders, these reserves are freed up as those obligations are met. If more than was needed to meet the obligations is there (which is almost always the case), it goes straight to the insurance company's bottom line. This is why it is a popular practice for knowledgeable suitors to acquire insurance companies and close them down or consolidate them into a larger entity. Liquidation of an insurance company can free up a bonanza of unrealized gains in the form of reserves that are in excess of what is needed to meet policyholder obligations.

The difficulty encountered by many companies is that they determine how they wish to invest their capital based upon their desired returns, or "hurdle rates," as they call them. The main reason that the life insurance business offers an attractive choice for the investment of surplus has to do with leverage; in other words, the down payment on their book of business.

Going back to our home mortgage analogy: If you pay cash for a house and eventually sell it for 20 percent more than you paid, you have received a 20 percent return on your investment. If you put only 20 percent down on the house and sell it for the same gain (ignoring the cost of money for the 80 percent loan), you have received a 100 percent return on your investment! Thus, the higher the down payment you must make, the lower the return will be on your investment. So it is with life insurance companies. The more surplus they have to put up to cover expenses and reserving requirements, the lower the leverage on their return on invested surplus becomes.

It's all a bit more complicated than I make it sound, but if you grasp the home mortgage analogy, you pretty much have it in a nutshell.

So far, in our actuarial lesson, we have covered surplus strain (the fact that it costs more than a dollar in the first year of a policy to put a dollar of premium on the books) and reserving requirements (the way regulators protect policyholders by requiring the companies to put aside extra funds in case their assumptions are too inaccurate).

Next is the issue of capital strategies, meaning how a company arrives at a plan for using its working capital with regard to the mix between risk and yield and with regard to return on investment (ROI).

As we have learned, to put a new piece of business on the books, a life insurance company must dip into its capital and surplus account to temporarily cover expenses. Before a company decides to take such action, it must analyze the factors that determine the expected outcome. Obviously, the outcome the company wants is for profits to emerge eventually on the products it sells. In order to justify the choice of investing surplus in the writing of more business as opposed to other investments, the company must look at the risk/yield issues.

THE MANAGEMENT OF RISK

In the general insurance industry (including the casualty and health business), there are basically four risk categories:

1. *Catastrophic events* that may never happen, such as an earthquake

2. *Noncatastrophic, but nonmanageable events,* such as an automobile accident

3. *Fluctuation events* that are likely to happen, but the timing is uncertain and the frequency varies, such as sickness or disability

4. *Events that will happen,* with predictable timing for large groups, such as death

In the life insurance business, we insure against the inevitable: death. The last time I checked, the death rate in America was still one per person. And, if the actuaries and underwriters do their jobs, our policyholders will die right on schedule. Thus, we generally know how much the claim will be and when it will occur.

What this really means is that when we narrow risk management down to the life insurance business, we quickly see that it tends to be more *financially* focused than *event*-focused. The real issue has always been not when the claim will occur or how much it will be, but what the company will do with policyholder funds between the time it receives them and the time of a claim or surrender. In other words, in life insurance the biggest risks have to do with investment yields on invested capital, not claims.

The actuaries have categorized the various risks involved in this issue into four classifications. These are the considerations they look at when deciding what assumptions should go into the design of a product you sell. These assumptions then determine things like premium rates, surrender charges and surrender values at various policy durations.

Actuarial Risk Categories

1. C-1   Asset default/yield impact

2. C-2   Premium inadequacy

3. C-3   Interest-rate change

4. C-4   Business/management risks

Asset Default/Yield Impact (C-1)   The key issue here is the drive for yield. Those companies whose investment strategies reach for yield must pay the appropriate risk charge for access to a higher yield. As we have already discussed, for certain riskier investments, a life insurance company does that through special reserves such as the asset valuation reserve. So when a company reaches for yield, it must factor the price of the possible default rate into its expected net yield.

Premium Inadequacy (C-2)   Premium inadequacy is simply the validity of experience assumptions. The assumptions used by actuaries to determine how much premium is needed to meet morbidity or mortality charges in an insurance company are based on fairly predictable events so far as disability and death are concerned. However, one must take into account such factors as the business environment at the initial pricing of the product, and monitor results to consider repricing the existing books of business.

One of the powerful tools used by life insurance companies of which the consumer is generally unaware is the fact that companies can adjust for premium adequacy, even though the actual premium on a whole-life policy does not change. They do so in mutual companies by increasing or reducing the dividend they pay, based on mortality and/or persistency and expense experiences. In stock companies, they do it by adjusting the credited interest rate and/or the mortality charge levied on the contract. In either case, the companies can, in the current regulatory environment, use sales materials that illustrate results beyond current experience. Then, once the policy is on the books, if they fail to achieve projected results, they can adjust the mortality or risk-rate charges up or down based upon actual experience. They also can adjust the credited interest rates. This is all well and good, but in reality I believe that in most states we need more effective regulatory restrictions that require policy illustrations to be based upon actual experience.

Interest-Rate Change—Product Design Impact (C-3) This is the risk that occurs when, due to an environment of higher interest rates, certain assets in the portfolio are discounted on a mark-to-market basis due to perceived decline in value. For example, in a 10 percent interest-rate environment, a 6 percent bond in the company's portfolio would trade at a discount from its carrying value should it have to be liquidated to meet an obligation of the company.

If assets and liabilities in the company are properly matched, then the underwater issue is not so damaging, because in theory the company can hold the asset to maturity and receive its full carrying value before it becomes necessary to meet the obligation. However, assumptions about the duration of liabilities can often be incorrect due to unexpected events that can create a run on policyholder funds.

Business Risks (C-4) These risks are not actuarial or financial by design, but simply have to do with the choices and decisions executives make in running the company. Sometimes these can just be matters of bad judgment, such as going into markets for which the company is ill-prepared. Poor expense management would probably be the most common of C-4 risks; in addition, we should mention lawsuits over management performance. Historically, some of these risks seemed remote. Today, the suits piling up against those who set the investment strategies of a number of top companies are a painful reminder of the fiduciary responsibility that companies have for the policyholder funds entrusted to them.

Obviously, in addition to the C-1 through C-4 risks, there are other factors that affect the profitability of a life insurance company. Some of these items include experience fluctuations, inflation, regulation, tax laws, competition, production projections, sales processes and assumption mismatches. All these factors affect how a life insurance company develops its book of business and manages its assets and liabilities.

The Psychomedia Risk

To all of these considerations, I would suggest to the industry's actuaries and investment officers that some recent adverse industry publicity has demonstrated that there is yet another risk—one not factored into their strategies. Most companies were responsible about the C-2, C-3 and C-4 risks. The C-1 risk, which is the asset default risk, is covered by the NAIC through its heavy mandatory reserving requirement. What the insurance companies have historically not counted on was a fifth risk, which we will coin the *C-5 risk, or psychomedia risk.* C-5 is the risk that even though you do everything right, something unexpected will happen that creates the perception of failure although the facts don't support it. When this occurs, the actual facts become subordinate to the perception. The result is a crisis in confidence, which leads to a run at the bank or, in this case, an avalanche of policy surrenders. It is this psychomedia risk (created by the media) that many companies—especially more aggressive ones—have significantly underestimated in the past.

The psychomedia risk has its origins in the media, which promulgate notions and perceptions that move like electricity through our computerized financial services industry and can create a crisis in confidence overnight. This modern technological phenomenon of the instantaneous communications environment has advanced dramatically over the past decade. I believe the C-5 psychomedia risk may be the most difficult challenge for senior management in the future. This is why our third consideration in carrier selection is so important.

MANAGEMENT PERFORMANCE

Now, our analysis of carriers goes outside of traditional bounds and into the realm of opinion—my own opinion, but one I hope you will share. The issue here is identifying the key qualities you should look for in the management of a company you wish to represent and measuring candidates against them. Beyond that, you cannot be expected to control or predict the way management will behave. Just as you cannot control the behavior of every prospect, you cannot be sure your judgments about company management will always be sound. That's the unknown or "X factor" you simply must live with.

Historically, management of a life insurance company was a somewhat custodial job with regard to the financial side of things. In the 1960s and 1970s, the investment committees of most major life insurance companies met quarterly to put their rubber stamps of approval on the latest choices of the chief investment officers. Today, these committees typically meet weekly in hard-hitting, "no non-sense" discussions of strategies, yields and risks in the portfolio. It's a different world. Some companies are up to the task, some are not.

Exactly how you evaluate management is something I can't give you a lot of help with, because for every rule there is a notable exception—except one: Generally, in today's environment, those who started out as life insurance agents don't make good CEOs of life insurance companies. I wish it weren't so, because it was my lifelong ambition to rise from my beginnings as an agent to run a substantial life insurance company as CEO. However, almost to a person, those who have been selected to move through the ranks from agent to CEO have failed.

How, then, do we evaluate top management in a life insurance company? Well, the rating agencies have a scientific and very credible procedure, which they explain in their sales materials. The regulators have their own method, and for those involved with stock life insurance companies, the securities analysts have excellent experience and good track records in management evaluation. I suggest that agents go to all of these sources and garner whatever information they can on companies they are considering. However, before you draw your conclusions, you should consider a big dose of input from the person whose livelihood may depend on the choice at hand. If you have much aptitude for this business, you probably have good instincts. In the carrier selection process, your instincts may, in fact, be your greatest asset.

I'm not talking about the aura of dignity that exudes from the CEO when he or she walks into a room or gives a speech, nor do I mean some type of karma that draws you together. I'm talking about common sense and good judgment. Here are a few things to look for.

Background   Our business is about as arcane as it gets. The only way to learn it is to experience it. Few outsiders have been able to learn the life insurance business well enough to succeed over the long term. In most cases today, the noninsurance person doesn't have the luxury of time or resources for on-the-job training.

So, rule number one in management evaluation is to ask yourself, "Do I have the sense that the company CEO is truly an insurance person?"

Aptitude   American business lives in a very different world from the one it lived in a few years ago. Change, challenge and quick response are the conditions we must deal with. The management of today's life insurance companies must be poised for the unexpected and ready to act with decisiveness in an ever-changing environment. The problem is that the culture of our industry has not been conducive to developing this type of executive. Instead, much of our industry's old guard is populated with avuncular custodians who view their role as more that of a shepherd than a leader. I, for one, enjoyed the old warm, fuzzy leadership I grew up with in the industry, but that is not the world of the year 2000. We need bold, assertive leaders who can look beyond the horizon, make tough decisions and lead us toward their vision.

Pick a company with a CEO who has aptitude for the job at hand. You will have to make your own call. Trust your instincts.

Imagination   Our world is changing at different rates for different people. The ability of most people to change lags behind that of the world of technology. Those who will prevail are those who can respond to the seemingly overwhelming successive waves of change in a way that brings order out of chaos. The quality required is imagination.

In evaluating company management, I have noticed two things that should be observed as they relate to imagination. The first is obvious. How have they responded to change? With enthusiasm and a sense of vision of what could be, or with resistance and denial? We have had more than enough change in our industry for you to research this subject and draw your own conclusions.

The second is more subjective. What perceived changes have management chosen to respond to? Have they historically shown vision and picked the right trends? Have they resisted the false alarms and Trojan horses that have led some companies down a dead-end road?

On the other hand, don't be too hard on management that has tried something that didn't work. You want your company to be a factor in the marketplace and, as such, it should be trying new concepts and ideas. All the same, you will want to hitch your wagon to a star, not to a flash in the pan.

Judgment Closely related to imagination is the crucial quality of good judgment. I consider this the single most important quality that separates the mediocre CEOs from the outstanding CEOs. Once again, it is not something I can show you how to measure, but if you are vigilant in your evaluation of top management, you will know what to look for.

Successful CEOs know how to distinguish between the merely pressing and the important. They know how to draw on every available resource in making important decisions. They also tend to make the right choices. How they do it seems sometimes to be as magical as Peter Lynch picking a string of successful stocks, or Barbara Streisand choosing to perform in concert. Though we may wonder at the process, we all applaud the result. Look at some recent choices made by the company you are considering. Look not only at its traditional successes, but also at the more recent ones to which the CEO lays claim.

People Skills I pointed out earlier that the best leadership of a life insurance company today probably should be provided by a financially oriented person. Some life insurance agents fear this means they must sacrifice their need for a people-oriented CEO. This is clearly the case with some great financial people, but I believe it need not be the case with those who lead a life insurance company.

At the distribution level, ours is a people business—agents caring for clients, managers caring for agents and all of us in the distribution segment caring for one another. I believe that the CEOs of leading companies must love life insurance for what it does for the customer and must love life insurance agents for what they do for the company. Above all, the CEOs who succeed into the year 2000 must love people.

Incidentally, in looking at this issue, don't judge your CEO by your own standards. Many agents mistake salesmanship, hoopla, charm and glibness for sound evidence of a person's integrity and love of people. If this were so, our greatest leaders, from Mahatma Gandhi to Abraham Lincoln, would never have led their followers to triumph. Avoid CEOs who exhibit the disease of egotism at all costs, no matter how clever they may seem.

People skills come in many personality styles. Look more for the caring and thoughtfulness than the delivery style. Above all, look for wisdom. It has its genesis in the love of mankind and the belief in subservience to a purpose. Again, this is something on which you will have to trust your instincts.

Leadership As the legendary Lee Iacocca puts it, "Lead, follow or get out of the way!" In the years to come, the life insurance industry will be dominated by leaders who lead. I have read everything I can find on leadership, but the best thoughts I have encountered came from my friend, Warren Bennis, the brilliant University of Southern California professor and business school dean who has devoted much of his life to the study of leadership and has written several books on the subject. Here is some of what Warren has to say:

> The first basic ingredient of leadership is a *guiding vision.* The leader has a clear idea of what he wants to do—professionally and personally—and the strength to persist in the face of setbacks, even failures. Unless you know where you're going, and why, you cannot possibly get there. . . .
>
> The second basic ingredient of leadership is *passion*—the underlying passion for the promises of life, combined with a

very particular passion for a vocation, a profession, a course of action. The leader loves what he does and loves doing it. Tolstoy said that hopes are the dreams of the waking man. Without hope, we cannot survive, much less progress. The leader who communicates passion gives hope and inspiration to other people. . . .

The next basic ingredient of leadership is *integrity*. I think there are three essential parts of integrity: self-knowledge, candor and maturity.

"Know thyself" was the inscription over the Oracle at Delphi. And it is still the most difficult task any of us faces. But until you truly know yourself, strengths and weaknesses, know what you want to do and why you want to do it, you cannot succeed in any but the most superficial sense of the word. The leader never lies to himself, especially about himself, knows his flaws as well as his assets, and deals with them directly. You are your own raw material. When you know what you consist of and what you want to make of it, then you can invent yourself. . . .

Maturity is important to a leader because leading is not simply showing the way or issuing orders. Every leader needs to have experienced and grown through following—learning to be dedicated, observant, capable of working with and learning from others, never servile, always truthful. Having located these qualities in himself, he can encourage them in others.

Integrity is the basis of *trust,* which is not as much an ingredient of leadership as it is a product. It is the one quality that cannot be acquired, but must be earned. It is given by coworkers and followers, and without it, the leader can't function. . . .

Two more basic ingredients of leadership are *curiosity* and *daring*. The leader wonders about everything, wants to learn as much as he can, is willing to take risks, experiment, try new things. He does not worry about failure but embraces errors, knowing he will learn from them. Learning from adversity is another theme that comes up again and again . . . often with different spins. In fact, that could be said of each of the basic ingredients." (Warren G. Bennis, *On Becoming a Leader,* Addison-Wesley Publishing Company, Inc., Reading, Mass.)

CEOs who are also leaders are probably the easiest management to identify, once found. On the other hand, finding life insurance CEOs who are leaders today poses more of a challenge. That doesn't mean there aren't a goodly number of them, because there are. However, our industry boasts of some 1,200 companies active in the marketplace. The number of companies with true leaders is probably somewhat less than that.

How does an agent responsibly research these qualitative issues? Well, it isn't easy. There is no quick reference or numerical scorecard that will give you a complete answer. The answer, like most important answers in life, lies within you—you and those who have walked where you would walk. This is your final reference source in company evaluation—the policyholders and community with which the company you are considering does business.

Most reputations are earned and, as such, they can be our greatest asset or the bane of our existence. Talk to agents, managers, policyholders and home office employees. Find out what the reputation and perceptions are about the company you are considering. Check with those who have led and those who have left (under favorable conditions only). If you learn enough, you will learn both good and bad. Deduct the bad from the good and make your decision on what's left.

THE X FACTOR

In the world of selling, some of the agents I've worked with have coined a term to refer to situations when the prospect doesn't buy even though all the necessary conditions were present—there's need, money, motivation—and the agent has conducted a well-prepared, well-delivered selling interview. Every base has been touched. Yet the prospect doesn't buy. My friends write these instances off to the "X Factor." What they mean is that something they were unaware of or could not control killed the sale. Maybe the client wasn't candid enough about all of the facts and thus the premise of the sale was inaccurate; or perhaps bad chemistry existed between the client and agent; or maybe some outside factor wasn't uncovered early on, such as a brother-in-law in the business. Whatever the reason, the sale is dead and needs to be written off so the agent can get on with business. The key to using the X Factor to help you is to acknowledge that you did everything that could and should have been done to make the sale. Only then can you "write it off" to experience.

In carrier selection, you can only do so much in the way of due care. You hope you had access to all of the pertinent facts, but you can never be 100 percent certain. Things can happen that never could have been anticipated and over which no one has control. Remember, you are responsible for due care, not due diligence. You can only do your best.

Remember also to point out to clients that you are putting your reputation and perhaps your entire career on the line for the carrier you choose to do business with or be employed by. If you get clients to think about it this way, they will realize that you have a lot more reason to be concerned about the right choice than they do. That doesn't mean the company you work for won't ever have problems; it probably will from time to time. It just means that given the information you had to work with at the time, you made the best choice you could for yourself and your clients. That's responsible behavior.

I like to explain the difference between a prospect's commitment to a company and an agent's commitment with the old "chicken and pig" story. The prospect's commitment to an insurance company compared to that of the agent is like a chicken's commitment to a bacon and egg breakfast compared to that of a pig—one is significant, the other is total!

4

The Three-Legged Stool: *Product, Service and Compensation*

The traditional agent criteria for measuring a company, the "three-legged stool"—of product, service and compensation, are still an important part of the process. We have seen that the company's financial strength, capital strategies and management are, today, almost prerequisites to the three-legged stool. Without them, it is about as valuable as a milking stool without a cow! However, once the cow is in position, the stool is as important as ever. Let's look at the product leg first.

What is it that we sell? Do we sell protection? Do we sell investments? Do we sell savings? Over the years we have sold all three with varying degrees of emphasis, depending upon the prevailing economic winds. To understand more fully what it is we really sell requires a look at our industry's history.

In the very beginning, life insurance was sold as pure protection; the only benefit was the death benefit. Companies charged annual premiums that they felt would be adequate to cover the expected claims of those policyholders the actuaries told them would die in a given year. It didn't work very well. The only people who consistently renewed their policies were those encountering health problems. Eventually, most of the early companies lost a lot of money. Many went broke.

Later companies developed the level premium concept, by which policyholders would pay a little extra in the early years, which, if prudently invested by the company, would grow to an amount in later years that would offset the need to increase premiums. These advance premium accounts eventually became cash surrender values, which were available to those policyholders wanting to quit before death. Thus, life insurance became a product with a dual purpose: protection and savings. Of course, it's more complicated than that, and the responsible agent should take the time to understand how whole life really works. My associate, perennial Top of the Table agent Guy Baker, has put together a wonderful booklet titled *The Box,* which explains the workings of permanent insurance in layman's terms. *The Box* is not only an educational piece, it's a due care piece. If you review it and leave it with a client, you can feel pretty certain that the client can never accuse you of not explaining what you sold him or her. A detailed discussion of *The Box* is provided in Appendix C. I believe that this is a tool all agents should use on all sales to assure they are "practicing safe selling."

During the post–World War II era, the idea of life insurance as a savings vehicle really took off. We had a product that was a panacea: live, die or quit. We had all of the bases covered. Then, in 1978, the Federal Trade Commission published a study that hit the industry like a thunderbolt. In essence, it claimed that, based on its research, cash value life insurance was a rip-off, paying yields as low as $1\frac{1}{4}$–$1\frac{1}{2}$ percent.

In those days, our industry had no formal mechanism in place to defend itself. We made a few isolated efforts, the most notable of which was when NALU president and industry great Tom Wolff went on the "Phil Donahue Show" to defend us. This and other efforts met with moderate success, but by and large the genie was out of the bottle. The low yields of our product were, in fact, a partial truth. We were back in the protection business by the late 1970s, selling huge amounts of low-margin term insurance and trying to figure out how to get back into the savings business.

In the early 1980s, just when things were getting pretty tough, the universal life/interest-sensitive revolution hit. This time we didn't go from the term business to the savings business, as we had a few years earlier. There were other dynamics in play in the 1980s— namely, high inflation coupled with runaway interest rates (prime eventually hit 22 percent!). With these kinds of yields available, many companies forgot about the savings approach and designed products that were sold more like investments. All of a sudden, life insurance agents not only had something to sell, they had a tiger by the tail! Ours was arguably the best combination of yield and safety available for the consumer savings dollar in the 1980s. Or so it appeared.

During the 1980s and early 1990s, the life insurance industry learned that what goes up must come down. The idea of taking a period when interest rates spiked through the roof and extrapolating those results over the life of a long-term purchase, like life insurance, proved to be irresponsible. Eventually, the industry came out of orbit and reconnected with its core values. In the process, our products were completely revamped, most would argue, for the better. Also, our better agents began to learn about how life insurance really works and how life insurance companies operate. From the human side of the equation, it was a period of incredible growth and expansion. Many mistakes and much learning occurred.

So, what *do* we really sell? Protection? Savings? Investment? In the past we've sold all three, and if we manage our practice carefully and pay attention to the rules, we will continue to be permitted to do so. If that is the case, we are at the beginning of a great and opportune era in the life insurance industry. However, the key to our continued freedom to offer sound choices to our clients lies in responsible, professional sales practices. All of this reminds me of the quote that, for so many years, has been on the first page of *Forbes* magazine: "With all thy getting, get understanding." Today's agents must understand that once they have chosen a carrier to represent, the basis of their relationship with their company will revolve around what the industry has traditionally referred to as the three-legged stool: product, service and compensation.

The surest way to practice due care with regard to the first leg of the stool—product—is to be certain that you understand what you are selling. When litigation resulting from misrepresentation, fraud and deceptive practices occurs, it is appropriate and justified. Litigation resulting from misunderstanding, faulty communications and mental laziness is an unnecessary and costly burden to the insurance industry, taxpayers and the free-enterprise system. For your part, it's your responsibility to know your business well enough to be comfortable so that you can defend your professionalism and integrity, if need be, under the most challenging of circumstances. We will examine the crucial issues of sales practices later. First, however, let's look at our product from a couple of fresh perspectives. The first task is to understand the basic ingredients and assumptions that go into a life insurance policy; only then can we be sure we are selling it correctly.

WINNING THE ILLUSTRATION GAME

It's no mystery that some companies can outillustrate others. The real issue is not promises, however; it's performance. Permit me to state the obvious: *The funds available to your clients at retirement, death or upon surrender will not be generated by the illustration shown them at the point of sale.* They will be generated by company performance and nothing else.

   If you look at it objectively, all we really sell are configurations of numbers on a piece of paper. Computerized illustrations have been both the boon and the bane of our industry in recent times. How does an agent analyze a company's products to determine their competitive strength? If you simply look at the illustrations and compare them to those of competitors, you are making a big mistake. Illustrations are projections based upon assumptions. They are never 100 percent accurate. Just as the initial course charted by NASA when it aims a rocket for the moon must be constantly adjusted during the journey, so must the assumptions about a life insurance policy's ultimate loads and values be adjusted during the insured's journey. There is no shame or apology necessary in this fact, just understanding. Most individuals who buy life insurance, and many who sell it, do not understand that its cost and benefits are a moving target.

   The life insurance industry sells *the only product I know of that is as good as the company selling it says it is!* In some extreme cases, it's as if the owners of a fast-food restaurant could, based upon their own evaluation, declare it a Three-Star Michelin Award-winning restaurant and charge appropriate prices—that is, if you believe that the illustrations of the companies trying to woo your business are based upon fact rather than estimates.

Our first rule in evaluating product is to look at the assumptions behind the illustrations. Promising is easy; performing is quite another matter. It is your job to understand how any company you represent goes about arriving at the point-of-sale information you show to your customers. After all, you will be held accountable by clients for the quality of your recommendations. This is a very big due care issue and one you should rely upon no one else to handle— not even your company. *You are the one who should believe in the numbers you illustrate.*

The basic thing that must be thoroughly understood in product analysis is that there are four, and only four, variables or assumptions that go into building a life insurance policy, and they are the same for every company: *persistency, mortality, expenses and investment earnings.* Remember, when you look at an illustration that outperforms those of the company you represent, illustrations are based upon assumptions about company performance in these four key areas. If one company makes more aggressive assumptions regarding persistency, mortality, expenses and investment earnings than another, it can generate a more attractive illustration. This begs the question about the facts behind those assumptions. Does the company have actual experience in these four key areas that supports its assumptions? If it does, you can feel a bit more comfortable. If not, then you should be aware of it. Remember, it's a level playing field; every company has the same four ingredients to work with, nothing more. If one company uses more aggressive assumptions than another, you will want to understand why. Is it because of superior past performance in these areas, or is it just gutsier guessing?

Companies should be willing to provide the evidence behind their assumptions. If not, you can research it. Every product a company sells in your state must be filed with and approved by the state department of insurance. Assumptions are a matter of public record. Look behind the numbers in company illustrations. There's a reason for everything, and if you understand where the numbers come from, you can make intelligent choices for your clients.

Persistency   Company persistency is available from many sources, including most of the rating agencies. Assumptions about how long a company expects a policy to stay on the books can dramatically affect its expected profits and, therefore, the ways in which it illustrates its products. In most instances, the longer the client keeps his or her policy, the easier it is for the company to recover those acquisition expenses that are amortized over the expected life of the policy. Also, if the company can assume that it will have the asset in the policy (cash value) to invest over longer periods of time, it can afford to tie up policyholder funds in longer-term investments, which, traditionally, have been higher yielding than short-term investments.

However, in today's creative world of innovative illustrations, even the correlation between good persistency and good policy values can be turned upside down. Some companies actually assume poor persistency so they can design policies that have lower than typical value in the earlier durations (policy years) and much higher values in the later years. The theory is that if the policy is generally mediocre except for those who keep it to the end (e.g., age 65 or 70), there won't be many policyholders left to pay off in the end, so the company can promise them much more. Of course, the logic of this approach is flawed in that, if the payoff is so much better than for other policies, consumers could surprise the company by keeping their policies in much greater numbers than expected. Should this happen, the company could get whipsawed into a massive default on its promises. The other problem is one of ethics. It assumes most people won't be aware enough to take advantage of the opportunity. This "tontine" approach is as old a trick as there is in the bait-and-switch game. These are the types of facts behind persistency assumptions about which agents must be aware.

Mortality   Mortality is mostly a function of underwriting. If one company's mortality assumptions are lower than another's, the agent should expect that company to have tighter underwriting standards. As discussed earlier, the life insurance business is more investment-focused than it is event-focused. If the actuaries and underwriters in a company do their jobs, the policyholders will die pretty much on schedule.

Life insurance companies generally illustrate mortality based upon three sources of data: current mortality, or that which they are currently experiencing; contractual mortality, meaning the maximum they are permitted to charge according to the policy provisions; and projected mortality, which is an educated guess based upon past experience and assumptions about future experience.

Even though mortality is fairly manageable, there is one aspect of it the agent should watch out for. Over the past 30 years or so, companies have experienced dramatic and continuing decreases in their mortality experience. It's no secret that, due to the many advances in medicine, people are living a lot longer. However, in recent years these trends have been less dramatic, and some companies have seen mortality expenses actually exceed their expectations significantly. Thus, if a company is projecting historically lower trends in mortality into the future, you will want to understand the company's reasons for doing so. Most current medical evidence does not support this practice.

In my opinion, mortality assumptions should not be prospective. They should be based upon experience and perhaps cushioned a bit for the unexpected. If properly managed, mortality should be a fairly predictable variable in the product design process and not a tool for manipulating illustrations.

Expenses Expenses are those costs of doing business that the life insurance company allocates to every policy sold. Rather than list all of these allocations, let's just say that, if done properly, they should include every expense that would *not* be incurred if the company did not write a new policy. This includes such items as sales, marketing, data processing, underwriting administration and, of course, commissions. Far and away, the biggest expense in most life insurance products is the cost of its distribution system. In companies using independent distribution, most of these expenses are variable and paid to layers of wholesalers and agents in the form of commissions. In career agency companies, some of the expenses are allocated to training, financing and developing the agents as well as housing and servicing them and providing fringe benefits.

The term *low-cost provider* has become a buzz phrase in our industry in recent years. In evaluating a company's products, it is important to try to understand how expense assumptions are arrived at. Is the company really a low-cost provider based upon experience? Or, is it assuming that its aggressive illustrations will result in so many new sales that it can reduce its per-policy expenses? Is the company being realistic, or is it hoping for a self-fulfilling prophecy? Here again, the agent must evaluate the validity of the assumption that stands behind the illustration.

Investment Earnings Investment performance is the variable that has had the greatest impact on performance for policyholders in recent years. After deducting their expenses from premiums collected, insurance companies turn the balance of funds collected over to their investment departments for safekeeping until they are needed for policyholder claims or surrenders. The investment department has three major responsibilities with regard to managing the portfolio:

1. Yield—The return on the money

2. Safety—The return of the money

3. Liquidity—Payable as needed for benefits or surrenders

From the policyholder's perspective, this means that the policy guarantees are there no matter what. The policy projections are expected to be met, or at least be within a reasonable margin for error, and all that was promised for claims or surrenders should be available upon demand by the policyholder.

Well-managed life insurance companies can provide agents and policyholders with understandable materials describing their investment philosophies and showing their track records. Safety comes first. It is the company's responsibility to look beyond the ratings assigned to the securities in which it invests, just as it is your responsibility to look beyond the ratings those same agencies assign to the companies themselves. The investment strategy, as it pertains to safety for a life insurance company, must look beyond the ratings, too. The worst nightmare of an investment officer is to buy a credit that is rated investment-grade (e.g., *AAA*) by the rating agencies, and then have the investment downgraded, perhaps to the junk-bond level. Safety is a starting point, but it should not be the only value. As I previously pointed out, companies are expected to take reasonable risks or they will not justify keeping policyholder funds. Poor yields can lead to surrenders, which, in turn, can adversely affect policyholder performance even more. Of course, excessive risk will also lead to poor yields and create the same undesirable result with regard to surrenders. The secret is balance.

The third issue, liquidity, has to do with matching assets and liabilities. The investment department must know how long the actuaries expect a policy to stay on the books in order to meet their assumptions. The expected duration of the asset (time to liquidation) into which policyholder funds are invested must parallel the expected duration of the corresponding liability (time before a surrender or claim). Historically, the duration of policyholder liabilities has been predictable and consistent. Recent industry events have changed all of that. A while back, when interest rates went to 20 percent and beyond, there was an avalanche of loan activity at many companies. A policyholder could borrow money out of his or her life insurance contract at 6 percent or so and put it in a certificate of deposit at 12 percent or more. Meanwhile, the life insurance company had the policyholder funds tied up in illiquid 7 percent or 8 percent 30-year mortgages. Many companies had to go to the bank and borrow money at 16 percent so they could lend it to policyholders at 6 percent! The whipsaw effect obviously created a great deal of long-term stress in insurance company portfolios. This was the first liquidity crisis in the history of the life insurance industry. It wasn't long before we saw a second, even greater one.

During the second half of the 1980s, we saw a different kind of liquidity crisis. Due to the seemingly "once in a lifetime" rates of the day, some companies reached too far for the high yields available and ignored the risk factors. The resulting defaults led to panic among policyholders, which, in turn, led to a crisis in confidence and massive policyholder surrenders. Some companies got into serious trouble and others were seriously weakened. The alarm these crises caused throughout the industry had a paralyzing effect on many.

As previously mentioned, I can address this subject from first-hand experience. I was the senior marketing officer of a major company that got into serious financial trouble during the 1980s. My advice is to be sure your policyholders understand that you don't want to represent the company with the highest yields or the most aggressive illustrations. Tell them you choose not to compete on the basis of outpromising the competition. Life insurance is a long-term purchase and does not lend itself well to fads or hot streaks. If you err in evaluating a company's investment strategy, err on the side of caution. If you explain this correctly to your policyholders, they will accept your less aggressive sales illustrations as a sign of your company's strength and integrity. This is the true answer to winning the illustration game. Turn lemons into lemonade by helping prospects avoid the most aggressive companies.

To gain perspective on the importance of illustration integrity, let's look at a couple of examples in the financial services industry that demonstrate the significance of our superior latitude over other products with regard to consumer trust.

Who's Really Regulated?

Once a policy is on the books, life insurance is among the most regulated American consumer products. We have stringent regulatory reserving requirements, prudent investment guidelines and reams of statutes and codes protecting the interests and rights of the policyholder. Once you are a policyholder, it seems your consumer interests are protected, monitored and reported upon with considerable regularity. On the other hand, what an agent can say to a prospect to induce him or her to become a policyholder in the first place is relatively a matter of choice. As I said before, we sell the only product I know of that's as good as we are willing to say it is. However, many believe that is all about to change as we approach the year 2000.

When we look at the current regulatory issue as it pertains to the point of sale, I like to compare us to the casualty insurance business. If the company underwriting your automobile insurance decides it needs a rate increase to cover claims experience, does it just send you a premium increase? Of course not. The company must attain regulatory approval for any across-the-board rate increase. Sometimes companies must even band together and go to their state legislature for an approved rate increase. Yet, when you think about it, if you don't like the premiums on your auto insurance, you can take your business somewhere else. There are no exit penalties or losses from loads or the like. You even get a refund of any unearned portion of premiums paid.

Now, what happens if your life insurance company wants to increase premiums or create an equivalent effect by reducing projected benefits? It can decrease dividends, increase mortality charges or reduce credited interest rates, all of which have the same effect as a premium increase, and (in most cases) with no regulatory approval.

Yet if you want to change life insurance companies because you're unhappy with policy charges, it's a lot tougher on you than it is with car insurance. There are usually surrender charges or the loss of loads paid that now must be repaid on the new policy. You'll be older and, therefore, probably have to pay a higher premium on the mortality portion of the contract. And, of course, your health and insurability may have changed. Clearly, we must be sure we sell our clients policies they will want to keep for a long while.

WOULD YOU BUY THIS MORTGAGE?

Many Americans today have variable- or adjustable-rate mortgages (ARMs). To give another perspective to the way life insurance can be abused, let's apply our products rules to a home mortgage. We all understand that an adjustable-rate mortgage asks the mortgagee to assume the risk of an increase in long-term interest rates. If rates go up, so does your house payment. Conversely, if they go down, your house payment goes down. It's a fair gamble. Now, suppose your adjustable-rate mortgage could cause your house payment to fluctuate under any of the following circumstances:

- Change in market interest rates

- Increase in operating expenses at the mortgage company

- Defaults that occurred among other mortgages that were higher than expected

- Changes in tax laws or accounting practices as they affect the mortgage company's profits

- Adverse legislation or social reform affecting the profitability of the mortgage industry

Would you buy such a mortgage? Not likely. Yet our product can be, in the broadest sense, subject to pricing changes after it is purchased due to any or all of these factors. These may not be the reasons given for changes in credited interest rates, mortality charge increases or dividend scale reductions, but they may, in fact, be key considerations in the policymaking decisions regarding pricing changes.

The issue is not that life insurance companies have this freedom, but rather that the agent feels comfortable that the company he or she represents is responsible and fair in exercising these trusted powers. Clearly, the vast majority of companies have performed in exemplary fashion in the area of responsible pricing behavior. However, not every company has always done so. And before an agent brokers a case or considers a change in company loyalties, careful research should be undertaken.

What do we sell? We sell configurations of numbers on a piece of paper. We sell a combination of promises, commitments and educated guesses. This means the agent's integrity and reputation are in the balance of every sale. Be prepared to put your reputation on the line for your company. Do your homework so you can feel confident that you have discharged your responsibility to do the best you could for your client.

What do our clients really buy? Well, when our clients buy life insurance policies, they make a mistake if they think they have "bought" anything at all. Rather, we are "buying" life insurance. It is an installment purchase the price of which can and will change from time to time over the payment period. The price of life insurance is a moving target. Every policy is the result of assumptions about the same four ingredients: persistency, mortality, expenses and investments. No one has any magic dust to add to his or her company's formula. If someone tells you otherwise, run, don't walk, to your next choice.

So how do you win "the illustration game"? You win it the way you win most things worth winning in life: with knowledge, preparation, skill and truth. If you represent a quality company with quality products, you should never—and I do mean never—lose a sale because someone was willing to "outillustrate" you. If you do, you didn't get outillustrated, you got outsold!

Agents should know enough about their company and how it designs its product to win with the facts. Because everyone operates under the same four assumptions, if we line up ten companies and one outillustrates all the rest, we need to know why. A company's integrity at the point of sale is a good indication of what we can expect later on. If a company is the best at projecting, then it's easy enough to check how it has performed relative to the competition in the past. If it can't substantiate its performance, then by knowing the facts, you will prevail. If it can substantiate its performance, back away, congratulate the prospect and move on. You can't win 'em all, but if you do your homework, you'll win your share.

SERVICE

To take care of our clients, we must look at a company's financials, products and management. Then we must go further and look for a company that takes care of the agent. Otherwise, he or she won't be there to take care of the client.

The most important aspect of your relationship is how your carrier treats you. This is true for both you and your clients, for the company's treatment of policyholders is a direct reflection on you.

The three key areas to look at in service are *people, resources* and *systems.* You can tell a lot about a company by the kind of people they hire. Conversely, you can tell a lot about the people who stay.

Companies have cultures that permeate their home office and overflow into their field force. If you've been with a given company any length of time, you know how it feels about you by the way you're treated and the importance the company attaches to the relationship. Whatever it is, it is; you won't change it. On the other hand, the company may change it. Happily, in recent years we have seen the rebirth of an attitude by many companies that the agent is their customer. I think this is important and I believe it will continue.

People are the number-one ingredient in a company's ability to deliver good service. It has been my experience that FIRST-RATE LIFE INSURANCE COMPANIES HIRE AND RETAIN FIRST-RATE PEOPLE, WHILE SECOND-RATE LIFE INSURANCE COMPANIES HIRE AND RETAIN THIRD-RATE PEOPLE. To put a new spin on an old cliché, *just as you can tell a lot about people by the company they keep, so you can tell a lot about companies by the people they keep.*

The people in the home office of the company you represent are to a life insurance agent what the kitchen staff of a fine restaurant is to a waiter. You can control the relationship with the customer, make recommendations and do your best to give good service, but on each issue the people in the kitchen can make you or break you. If they blow it, they still get paid, but your income, like a waiter's gratuity, can be significantly affected.

If the company you represent has good products and good people, it will be within your control to deliver exceptional performance to policyholders. To get the job done, you will want to build strong trusting relationships with every home office employee with whom you have regular contact. The underwriting department, for example, must know you under the most favorable terms possible. They must know you as a true field underwriter who gives them all the available information they need to do their jobs and who delivers good risks and quality business. If you give this consistently, just when you need it most, they will give you the benefit of the doubt that saves an important sale. So it should be with each company department that can help you succeed: commission accounting, policyholder service and advanced underwriting.

Most important, remember that, just as you appreciate first-rate people in the home office, they appreciate first-rate agents in the field. Warmth, courtesy and, above all, patience toward all home office employees pay bigger dividends than most agents ever imagine possible. On the other hand, I have, time and time again, seen a short-tempered and rude outburst by a frustrated agent (whether justified or not) cost that agent in ways he or she never even knew about. Believe me, a good rating with the rank and file of your home office can be worth a fortune over your career.

The second area to which the management of a company must be willing to dedicate attention is the marshaling of adequate resources to support their field force. Items such as advanced underwriting, sales training, casework and product training used to be taken for granted. Today, the cost of all of these things must come directly from the product we sell. This means that companies can no longer afford to put everything upfront in hopes that the business will come. They are more likely to allocate resources only to those agents who are getting the job done and are loyal to them. This is the world we live in. I think that's fine, so long as the resources are available for those who perform. Here are some things to look for.

There is usually competition for the resources of a life insurance company. As we have already discussed, the scarce resource of capital is always in demand. Other resources, such as sales promotion, advertising, advanced underwriting support, sales training schools, point-of-sale materials and 800 customer service lines, all take time, money and commitment to provide. Performance in each of these areas will tell the agent how committed a given company is to good service.

Another area where resources are crucial concerns a company's ability to bring new products to market. Today, the cost of new-product development is at an all-time high, while the shelf life is shorter than ever. Yet when solid new markets appear, the leading companies must respond to the opportunities posed if they wish to hang on to their sales force. Just as important as actual responsibilities is choice. No company can jump on every new product idea. The good ones tend to choose the right products to develop and avoid those that involve fads or loopholes. Stated differently, a key resource in the product arena is the resource of good judgment.

The third resource to consider is data-processing systems. By and large, the life insurance industry missed the data-processing revolution of the 1980s, except for the point-of-sale illustrations. We were very sophisticated in computerizing the sale of a policy, but we were in the Dark Ages when it came to servicing the new universal life and interest-sensitive policies we sold. Things are gradually improving, but agents need to understand that the more sophisticated the sale, the harder it will be for the company to administer.

Given some of the liability issues we face today, it is to some degree incumbent upon the salesperson to be reasonably certain that, in a more complicated sale such as deferred compensation or split-dollar, the company can service what it illustrates. These types of problems have a way of sneaking up on us. For example, many policies sold to accumulate cash at retirement illustrate a series of policy loans—or rollouts, as they are called—that are free of income tax under current law, provided the policy retains the minimum values needed to stay in force until death occurs. However, if the illustration goes only to life expectancy, what about those who live beyond this point? What about changes in the tax law that might invalidate the assumptions used to sell the policy? The forward-thinking agent will want to know that the company has the systems in place to monitor its in-force policies and alert policyholders to changes that could affect illustrated performance.

Data-processing problems can bring a company to its knees about as quickly as anything imaginable. You are not likely to be enough of an expert to know everything about life insurance data processing, but you will want some assurances of the capabilities of the companies that will be monitoring the policies you sell.

Evaluating Compensation

When looking at compensation, consider all factors. As you weigh the higher commission contracts in the marketplace, you must remember that there are many trade-offs to be considered.

In today's environment, companies with long-established, well-known names can bring significant benefit to the point of sale. On the other hand, some lesser-known companies that focus on your market can make a good case for being dedicated to the things that matter to you.

Sales conventions and trips are often overlooked as an important part of agent compensation. At most companies, the cost of these trips is factored right into the agent commission schedule. Other considerations we will discuss elsewhere include fringe benefits, renewals, production bonuses and equity participation programs.

So how does an agent evaluate the all-important compensation leg of the three-legged stool? Here are a few thoughts to guide you.

First of all, commission schedules alone do not determine your level of compensation. If they did, then those companies paying the highest level of commissions as a percentage of premiums sold would be doing the most business. This, of course, is far from the case. *It is performance that determines compensation, not commission schedules,* and performance is a function of many things. What we all want is the proper balance among those ingredients that determine our level of performance given the same level of sales activity. Product, service, company reputation and sales support are a few considerations. Of these, product becomes more important as the agent grows and enters more advanced markets. It doesn't matter how high the commissions are if you don't make the sale. Commissions do, after all, come directly out of the product. In the big-case market, where competition exists, things like dividend history of the company will be compared. All other factors being equal, the company with the lowest distribution expenses will have an advantage here.

It is not that commission schedules are not an important part of the equation, it's just that they are the easiest for a company to deliver! The other elements take skill, talent and resources. Commissions are simply what a company can afford, or is willing to pay, after it has provided all it can to differentiate itself from the competition.

Most life insurance companies that provide quality, competitive products allow a realistic percentage of the first-year premium for commissions and distribution expenses. This is one assumption about which they have sound information from past experience. The percent assumed is often remarkably similar from one company to the next. Because everyone has the same dollar to work with, it's more a matter of how they stretch it.

Of course, a company can always diminish a product's competitiveness to increase compensation to agents and managers. However, with the ever-increasing demands of consumers for good value, few companies will succeed in the long run if they pay more than it takes to get business on the books while meeting the competition's illustrations. Eventually, something must give.

Company performance, on the other hand, is that dynamic that makes all the difference. By performing in areas such as expense management, agent productivity and net investment yields, companies can deliver a superior product and still pay a fair commission. Herein lies the key to agent understanding of the commission issue. As a rule, companies that can perform with product for the customer and training, support and service for the agent will never pay more than a fair commission. They don't need to and, in my opinion, they should not. When you hear the term "top commission dollars," you must understand that life insurance companies pay what they need to pay, and no more, to get your business. They get what they pay for, and you pay for what you get—or don't get. If you take commissions over other benefits, it's a simple trade-off. Just be sure that the extra points are worth as much or more than you are giving up. That doesn't mean you shouldn't weigh commission schedules heavily in your selection process; just don't assume you're getting something for nothing.

PHILOSOPHIES ON COMPANY/AGENT RELATIONSHIPS

The subject of the three-legged stool cannot be concluded without considering the seat of the stool, which is your overall relationship with the company you represent. My advice is to approach carrier selection and related considerations the way one might want to choose a mate. If you pick the right person in the first place, you solve a lot of problems before they arise. Then, when they do occur, you're usually comfortable that you will be dealt with, if not with total fairness, at least in a consistent and predictable way. Like mates, life insurance companies are never perfect, but an underlying sense of compatibility is essential to a successful relationship. When we are attracted to a company by compensation and product illustrations alone, the chances are we will eventually leave it for the same reason.

So, if you're tempted to stray from your primary carrier relationship, be mindful that if a company offers a "better deal," you had better understand why. That's not to say that one carrier can't legitimately woo your business from another with better value for you and your client. Some probably can. But be sure that value is measured in performance, not promises.

Carrier selection and product analysis (as opposed to the three-legged stool) are a relatively recent dynamic in the composition of a successful practice. Yet they may be the most important elements at which to excel.

I do not believe that a life insurance agent is, or should be, expected to be accountable beyond reasonable due care on these issues.

After you have done the best research you can, look at your relationship with your current carrier and decide what your definition is of a good relationship with a company. For me, the answers are more intuitive than scientific. I have developed five questions for agents to ask about their companies. Grade each question by assigning a number from one (lowest score) to ten (highest score). If your answers to these questions are more positive than negative, it's a good indication that you are with the right company.

1. *Am I the main event in my company's life?* Is the company committed to putting ever-increasing amounts of quality business on the books through your efforts and those of your distribution system?

2. *If I wanted to invest my money in a life insurance company, would I pick the one I represent?* You cannot ask your clients to put their money where you would not put your own.

3. *How has my company performed on its illustrations in the past relative to the competition?* This is your company's credibility index. If it doesn't stack up to the competition, you have much to lose.

4. *Does my company have the capital to grow and the desire to lead in the fiercely competitive global environment of today?* Understand your company's capital strategies and how those strategies affect you.

5. *Does the senior management of my company have a clear vision of who they are and where they are going, and are they equipped to compete in our new global economy?*

Without confidence in the leadership, a meaningful commitment from the agent is not possible.

The life insurance business is a long-term business. Companies do not tend to think along the same first lines as do their agents. Their views, values and perspectives may vary greatly from those of the agent. That's neither good nor bad—just fact. Don't confuse your carrier's point of view with any negative feelings toward you. Don't let ego cloud your judgment as a businessperson. Agents tend to react emotionally; companies tend to react logically. That doesn't mean they can't be partners. On the contrary, once a mutual understanding of both points of view is accomplished, many of the perceived differences between the field and home office vanish.

I have said all I can about what I value in a carrier. Once that decision is made, the real work begins—making your choice the right choice. Let's look at six tips on how to build good relationships with your company. After all, if you have a company with superior people, resources and systems, you will want to be able to use these assets to your advantage.

Tip #1 *Foster a relationship with a champion in the home office.* If you're good and have a bright future in our business, someone in an important senior role in the home office would like to be a mentor to you. Seek out a person whose experience and knowledge of the business you respect. During a home office visit, ask that person to lunch or dinner. Solicit advice and guidance on the issues you are struggling with in your career. Successful and prominent life insurance executives are truly honored and excited when given an opportunity to mentor an up-and-comer in the company. Such relationships will stay with you throughout your career.

Tip #2 *Identify a key person in the technical area of the company with whom you can build a trusting and mutually beneficial relationship.* The purpose isn't political; rather, you want a genuine connection to the home office technician who helps you understand the company and how it runs, the products and how they work, or the financial strategies. Unlike the mentoring relationship, this friendship will be tutorial in nature. The person will likely be an actuary, lawyer or investment officer.

Tip #3 *Don't ask for exceptions and favors.* This is an abuse of the relationship and only leads to problems and questions about your motives. Never use relationships or friendships as leverage to bend the rules to your advantage. If you build valued relationships with your mentor and tutor, they will see to it that more than your share of breaks comes your way.

Tip #4 *Be your client's representative to the company and your company's representative to the client.* Today the customer is king, but the company is your long-term partner. As important as they are, our clients will come and go. In fact, in a successful practice the departure of no single customer should ever cause permanent damage. Companies are another matter. Your demeanor, the quality of your business and your reputation as an agent can be sullied only once with most companies. Once it is, it's time to move on and hope (probably in vain) that the cause of your problems doesn't follow you.

　　We are not talking about the importance of putting your clients' interests first here; you should always do that. What we are talking about is being a true field underwriter on behalf of your company. In the long run, it will pay big dividends and will serve the best interests of your clients as a group.

Tip #5 *Revisit your commitment to your carrier periodically, and then close the book until the next review.* Today we cannot commit to "forever" unconditionally. Things change. When they do, you have the right—indeed, the obligation—to evaluate those changes relative to your commitment to your company. Having said that, I would encourage you to reevaluate your company affiliation as infrequently as possible. It is a very disruptive process and should not be undertaken without tangible reasons for doing so. Then, when you make your decision, don't look back.

Tip #6 *Never slam doors behind you.* If you must leave your company at some point, remember that at some time in the future you will probably encounter most of the key people, and you will want to be proud of the way in which you left. Negative or acrimonious behavior must be avoided. Such activities serve no useful purpose and can come back to haunt you.

If you do leave your company, do whatever it takes to close that chapter of your life with a happy ending for all involved.

The three-legged stool of product, service and compensation has changed over the years in that the interrelationship among the three has become more obvious. If you fatten up one leg of the stool, you most likely will have to whittle one of the others down. The seat of the stool is the relationship between you and your carrier, and it can be well cushioned without weakening the legs. After a balanced look at product, service and compensation, I urge agents to use their character and integrity to build a relationship with their company founded on trust and respect.

5

Habits of Success

*"Everyone is, in reality, two persons: He [or she] is the one
he's familiar with and he's the one he could be if he
narrowed the gap between his habitual way of performing
and his potential."*

—Earl Nightingale

The business of sales training and sales management within our industry is a huge industry in and of itself. Now we will focus on the key issues of work habits and related disciplines and see how they provide the framework for success.

Each company has its own sales training program, or, if you're with a large agency, management will have a procedure in place to teach you how to sell. Furthermore, books by legendary life insurance master salesmen such as Ben Feldman and John Savage are available for the "how to" aspect of selling. However, the next two chapters will be devoted to those sales tools that I have had the most success with and that will, I hope, complement those you are currently using. Let's set the stage with a discussion of the universal habits of successful salespeople, because they provide the foundations for agents to effectively use those tools.

The old formula—knowledge, attitude, habits and skills—is still pretty much on target as the formula for sales success for the year 2000 and beyond. However, to it we add the business of packaging the agent, or image building. Good habits and a good image are the cornerstones of a successful life insurance practice. The fact is, ours is a simple business if we follow the road maps drawn for us by others.

The path we are about to show you in this and the next two chapters is known by many but practiced by few. If you wish to become successful in life insurance selling, you must become one of those few.

By now, you know what you're going to do (your area of specialization) and you know whom you're going to do it with (carrier). All that remains is to do it!

First, let's dispel a myth. Knowledge is *not* power; it is only potential power. It is worth something only if you habitually apply it every day in everything you do. Success in life insurance selling is nothing more than putting together a very long string of successful days. This means the forming of good work habits that allow you to apply all of your knowledge and skill every day. The hard part about that statement is "every day."

DEVELOPING A BUSINESS PLAN

Every business should have a written plan explaining how it is going to succeed. As a sole proprietor, you will want to put together a plan that is integrally involved with your personal goals. Still, you must step back and view your practice as a business like any other.

If you managed a large corporation, the management or owners would insist on a detailed business plan to be sure you were giving them what they wanted and were paying for. As a sole proprietor, don't you have the same responsibility to yourself? There are many sources to draw upon at any bookstore for guidance in writing a good business plan, but most of the framework for your plan will be in place by the time you finish this book. You will also find a number of helpful tools for developing your business plan in the appendix.

The key ingredients of your business plan will include the following:

- *A mission statement.* What overall accomplishment do you strive for in your practice? What is your vision for your practice? Example: The mission of the XYZ Insurance Practice is to profitably distribute quality life insurance and financial services products to the health-care professionals in

Midtown, U.S.A., and to be known as a low-cost, service-driven provider of those products.

- *A summary of purpose.* What is it that you bring to the table for the insurance-buying public? Example: The purpose of XYZ Insurance is to become well and favorably known as the premier and most knowledgeable provider of insurance and financial products to small businesses in Midtown, U.S.A. Our image will be built around quality, value and service.

- *Persistency goals, achievement and credential goals, and timetables.* To meet your mission and purpose objectives, you will need to establish standards of performance and quality that support these values.

- *Budget and profit objectives.* Plan your expenses and the target profits you expect to garner from your practice. Understand that you must run your business as any other. You will want to establish a procedure for measuring your results and planning your expenditures.

- *A pro forma projecting when and how results will occur over a period of time.* Quarter by quarter, plot out your cash flow and expenses. Keep the score, report the score and the score will improve.

- *The long-term plan for capitalizing (selling) your business.* If you build it right, you should someday be able to sell it. However, this will only happen if you carefully plan for it.

When you complete your business plan, share it with the important people in your life and career. Give copies to your spouse, your manager, your mentor and anyone else who has an interest in contributing to your success.

Above all, keep a copy in a prominent place at the office and at home for regular review and revision. Make a review of your business plan part of your quarterly and annual review process.

Historically, most sales tracks we learn in our business try to move our prospects to action because of vignettes such as the "100-man story," which points out that by age 65, most Americans are either dead or dead broke. We close with the lamentation that "they didn't plan to fail, they simply failed to plan!" Like so much of what we do in our profession, our advice to clients applies to us, too. Put your business plan in place now and you will not be an unhappy statistic down the road.

FOCUS ON ACTIVITY AS A PRIORITY

Calvin Coolidge said it best: "Activity is the key to all growth. And activity means work."

Most good things that happen in your practice will happen because you make them happen. To be a success in life insurance sales, you must focus on those activities that only you can perform and delegate all of those activities that can be performed by someone else. This is a philosophy that must permeate every corner of your professional life. The key is to identify the activities that you must focus on. And this is exactly what successful agents do: *They identify those activities that are essential to their success, and then they habitually do what it takes to become very good at them.* This is a simple concept to comprehend, but a difficult concept to implement consistently. Let's take a quantum leap on this critical habit by identifying those key activities.

There are six key activities agents must be good at if they wish to reach their potential:

1. Prospecting
2. Getting appointments
3. Opening cases
4. Presenting cases
5. Delivering cases
6. Prospecting

Prospecting

This is where it starts. This is where it ends. Prospecting is the linchpin that drives all of the other activities. We list it as both the first and the last activity, because it is the key activity that closes the never-ending circle. As such, it is twice as important as the others. How you prospect is not our main subject here, but let's share three thoughts on it that will help you grasp the priority it deserves.

First, when an agent says, "I'm not a good prospector," it's like a baseball player saying, "I can't hit a curve ball." If you can't prospect, you can't play the game. It's that simple. Prospecting is an agent's lifeblood. You don't have the luxury of being a "poor prospector" any more than a surgeon can say, "I'm not handy with a knife," or a preacher can say, "I'm not much for prayer." By definition, a successful life insurance agent is a successful prospector.

Second, most agents who are not good prospectors are really saying that they don't give prospecting the priority it deserves. If prospecting is the one thing that gets done before everything else, every day, no matter what, then guess what? You will be a good prospector!

Third, prospect by any means necessary, no matter how crude, until you can prospect by the only means that makes long-term sense. Cold call in shopping malls. Do direct mail followed up by a telephone solicitor. Work orphan policyholders. Call newlyweds and births listed in the local newspaper. Do whatever it takes to get in front of people who can and will buy life insurance.

Then become as good as you can at getting referrals. Referrals are, ultimately, the center of the prospecting effort in any practice. If you do a quality job for your clients, they will refer you to others. If they won't, you'd better examine your selling practices. Referrals are an indication of a job well done. The lack of referrals from a new client doesn't bode well for when the next premium is due. In the next chapter, we will share ideas on the "how to" of prospecting. These ideas will do you no good, though, unless you understand the priority of prospecting.

Getting Appointments

Nothing happens until an appointment is set, and only you can do that. Like prospecting, getting the appointment is something at which you don't have the luxury of being mediocre. You simply must work at developing your skills in this discipline until, when you hang up the phone, you can honestly say, "If the appointment could have been gotten, I would have gotten it." If you are building your practice with the One-Card System (see Chapter 7) or a comparable process, you will be assured of a second chance at appointments missed.

The great thing about developing telephone skills in the area of getting appointments is that it is a relatively simple, learnable task at which almost anyone can become competent with a little focused education. There's no need to learn to be an arm-twister or an obnoxious pest when developing appointment skills. In fact, skills in these tactics are a waste, because an appointment gained under duress will often not be kept. Stand-ups are very costly, and you should minimize them with the fall-back position offered by the One-Card System. Some suspects must become friends first, through a series of callbacks, before they can become prospects. Let nature take its course in such situations. Our purpose here is to be certain we communicate the importance of being good, *very* good, at the learnable skill of getting appointments under favorable conditions.

Opening Cases

We "open a case" when we have a successful initial or fact-finding interview in which six things occur:

1. *Trust and empathy.* We succeed in building a rapport and gaining the prospect's trust level in us and our company as the kind of people he or she would like to do business with.

2. *Hot button and need.* Through a series of strategic questions, we uncover a need(s) for life insurance and prioritize that need as the problem the prospect would most like to solve.

3. *Motivation.* We gain a response to our questions about that need *that convinces* us that we can motivate the prospect to act.

4. *Ability to buy.* We document the availability of funds for the purchase of life insurance and obtain a money commitment.

5. *Commitment to process.* We obtain the prospect's approval to analyze his or her needs and prepare recommendations.

6. *Stage set to buy.* We set an appointment to make our presentation under favorable conditions with all decision makers present.

Only when all six of these steps are completed with a favorable result have we opened a case. These steps are not optional or desirable; they are bases that must be covered before a sale can be made. These steps are not only important to your material success, they are also important to your psychological success. You cannot waste time second-guessing yourself; it will destroy your confidence and, with it, your mental attitude. You will always want to know that you did your part. That's why it is important for you to touch every base every time. Then you don't have to look back. You know when you go to the next step that you will be doing so under the best possible conditions.

Presenting Cases

Over the years, this step has been referred to as the "close," the "buying interview" and various other euphemisms for "the agent's payday." The truth of the matter is that case presentation should be the easiest and smoothest step in the sales process. In the Kinder organization, where I was trained, they used to refer to it as the "mechanical close," meaning that the real sale is made on the initial interview, where those six critical steps are completed. If you do your job upfront when the building blocks of a successful sale are being laid, the solution to a nagging problem will be provided by the welcome relief of writing a check and signing an application.

It's interesting that so much energy in the sales training arena is devoted to closing. The real masters I have been privileged to observe have shown us that the pivotal point is the uncovering of problems that matter. The solutions are the easy part.

All the same, the close is when the agent asks for the check, so it must be viewed as a great occasion, which is prepared for, rehearsed and presented with all of the intelligence and conviction necessary for the prospect to make a buying decision. You might look at it like a great case being tried in a court of law. The closing argument must be dramatic and convincing, but the verdict will be based upon the previously presented evidence and facts. Few lawyers will win a weak case with a strong closing argument, but some have lost a strong case with a weak closing argument!

Delivering Cases

The policy delivery is an important step in the sales process—important enough to be included in this short list of activities that are crucial to your success. This is for three reasons:

First, the client deserves one interview when the pressure is off, during which you can validate the wisdom of the purchase and make the official transition from salesperson to counselor and friend.

Second, a well-executed policy delivery not only affects the persistency on your business, but it also sets the stage for the next sale. In the course of reviewing why clients bought, you will remind them of other needs that they chose not to address at this time. The annual reviews will be the moment of truth on these needs.

Third, we must close the circle and continue the never-ending chain of prospects necessary to sustain our practice through the gathering of referrals. Referrals aren't the only method of prospecting, but they beat the daylights out of whatever is in second place! You'll never have a better chance of getting referrals than you will upon the delivery of a policy. Make the most of it on every occasion.

GOALS: THE UNIVERSAL HABIT OF SUCCESS

Becoming and Staying Goal-Oriented

> "Cheshire Puss," she began rather timidly . . . "would you tell me, please, which way I ought to walk from here?" "It all depends a good deal on where you want to go to," said the cat. "I don't much care where," said Alice. "Then it doesn't matter which way you walk," said the cat.

So go the memorable lines from *Alice In Wonderland.* Many sales careers go afoul because the agent doesn't know where he or she is going. You must plan your career conscientiously and know where you are going if you are to achieve the success that can be yours. This encourages disciplined activity. *Planning is the first step toward developing a focus on desired results.*

Now we are going to look at a proven process for setting goals and fixing a plan of action. Then we will learn about the most powerful strategy in all of business—the mastermind principle. You'll find that goals are the springboard for making you a consistently effective agent—this year and every year.

First, a word about the importance of setting goals. I know of no life insurance agent regarded as genuinely successful who is not committed to a regular regimen of setting goals and monitoring the results of those commitments. This is an important point, especially today. Unfortunately, in the world we live in, there seems to be a cynicism about some of the core values of the free-enterprise system. Sadly, some of this cynicism may have its basis in incidents where trust and belief by consumers or company employees were abused and betrayed. Certainly, this has been an occasional condition in American business in recent years. However, such highly publicized incidents have been the exception, not the rule. The fact is that commitment to honest, intelligent goals is the very essence of achievement in almost every culture. We need goals if we are to realize our potential.

Setting Goals

An agent without goals is like a ship without a captain. The ship may be seaworthy and have the finest equipment, but without a captain to take command and guide it to a designated port, it goes nowhere.

The key is *direction* and *focus*. An individual with specific goals will display determination and drive. Effectiveness and productivity will be greatly multiplied by determination and drive. They will be greatly multiplied again when you have a definite purpose. Tunnel vision is good when your target is clearly identified. Remember, goal setting is the cause; success is the effect. This is how goals become motivators.

With this understanding of the importance of goal setting, here are four important guidelines to keep in mind:

1. *Your goals must be achievable.* Why push and strive toward a goal when you know it's beyond your reach? Set your goals high, but be sure they are realistic and attainable by determination and hard work.

2. *Your goals must be believable.* This is closely related to the first point. Goals must reflect realism, not idealism. Goals must be something you are convinced you can reach.

3. *Your goals must be measurable.* Think about your favorite athletic event. Would you still find it interesting if there was no way of keeping score? What makes football exciting is knowing what the score is and how much time is remaining. It's the same with your goals.

4. *Your goals must have deadlines.* Few people know what they want; still fewer know when they want it. Time is your most precious commodity. It can never be replaced. If you are to use your time most productively, you must commit yourself to a plan of action and you must give that plan a deadline for completion.

Thus, the four pillars that will support your goals are achievability, believability, measurability and firm deadlines. The great salesman, Ben Feldman, put it well when he said, "We need goals and

Figure 5.1 Goal Setting

Well-Conceived Goals	Poorly Defined Goals
Stated numerically in terms of end results.	Stated in terms of adjectives and adverbs.
Achievable at a specific time.	Are never fully achievable; no specific target dates set.
Definite as to what is expected.	Ambiguous as to what is expected.
Realistically high and practical.	Theoretical or idealistic.
Precisely stated.	Too brief and simplistic or too long and complex.
Limited to five or fewer areas.	Written with many areas of concentration.

deadlines—goals big enough to be exciting and deadlines to make us run."

There are two chief cornerstones that support success: a sharp *focus* on your goals and *a plan of action* to get you there. In this chapter, we will show you how to evaluate yourself and determine what your dreams are so that you can specify your goals and establish a plan of action to achieve them. Figure 5.1 will help you see the difference between well-conceived and poorly defined goals.

The more thought and analysis you put into your goals, the more real and achievable they become. At one end of the spectrum, we have people who think they are defining goals by setting their sights on some result such as the Million Dollar Round Table, 100 paid cases or, even worse, some vague generality like "success" or "happiness"—which, of course, are not goals at all.

Goals such as the Million Dollar Round Table or 100 paid cases are merely the starting point in the goal-setting process. The real work

Figure 5.2 Analysis of Last 200 Sales

Source	Sales	Lapses
Personal observation	_____	_____
Policy owners	_____	_____
Cold calls	_____	_____
Referred leads from policy owners	_____	_____
Referred leads from contacts	_____	_____

Occupation		
Attorneys	_____	_____
Business owners	_____	_____
CPAs	_____	_____
Religious institution–related personnel	_____	_____
Doctors and dentists	_____	_____
Executives and professionals	_____	_____
Other professionals	_____	_____
REALTORS®	_____	_____
Salespeople	_____	_____
Spouses and children	_____	_____
Miscellaneous	_____	_____

Time the Sale Was Made		
Day	_____	_____
Night	_____	_____
Weekend	_____	_____

Ages Accumulative	Sales	Percentages	
Under 30	_____	_____%	_____%
30–34	_____	_____%	_____%
35–39	_____	_____%	_____%
40–44	_____	_____%	_____%
45–49	_____	_____%	_____%
50–54	_____	_____%	_____%
55–59	_____	_____%	_____%
60–64	_____	_____%	_____%
Over 65	_____	_____%	_____%

Figure 5.2 (Continued)

Annual Income	Sales	Percentages	Accumulative
Under $50,000	_____	_____%	_____%
$50,000–$75,000	_____	_____%	_____%
$76,000–$100,000	_____	_____%	_____%
$101,000–$125,000	_____	_____%	_____%
$126,000–$175,000	_____	_____%	_____%
$176,000–$250,000	_____	_____%	_____%
Over $250,000	_____	_____%	_____%

Professionals—
- are good and know it.
- critique their own performance.
- keep on getting better.

begins when we determine what we must do to attain our goals and then develop an action plan to follow every day. As one of my favorite Top of the Table agents likes to say, "You cannot manage results, you can only manage activity!" With this in mind, let's look at a recommended goal-setting process.

Client Profile Fundamental to the success of every business is a detailed understanding of its customer. Before you decide whom you're going to sell to next year, take a good look at those you've *been* selling to. I like the approach in Figure 5.2.

After you have built the detail on your last 200 sales, the next step is to review your overall performance over the past year and look at your expectations for the next year. The five-step process in Figure 5.3 is a good tool for guiding you through this procedure.

Looking at Me The next step in goal preparation is to take a good look at yourself. Earlier in our market selection discussion, we introduced this formula:

$$\frac{\text{What it takes}}{\text{What I've got}} = \text{Potential success factor}$$

Figure 5.3 Performance Review

Step I. Review of Activity and Results

  A. Where are your markets?

      1. Occupations _____

      2. Age group_____

      3. Where are new clients originating?

          Existing clients?_____

          Referred leads? _____

          Centers of influence—e.g., CPAs, attorneys, etc.? _____

          Direct mail? _____

          Office leads? _____

          Others?_____

  B. What are you selling?

      1. Life insurance (Mix? Permanent, term, universal, interest-sensitive, etc.) _____

      2. Disability income, group, pension, annuities, medical care, etc. _____

      3. Equity products _____

  C. What are current earnings, net after expenses?

      1. First-year commissions _____

      2. Renewals _____

      3. Other_____

Step II. Preparation for the Next 12 Months

  A. General objectives

      1. Review career path programs.

      2. How much do you need to earn? (Review personal and business budgets.)

      3. How much do you want to earn?

  B. New-business objectives

      1. Improve method of maintaining a continuous flow of new names and contacts. Set minimum number of new contact calls each day. Improve social mobility—improve contact consciousness.

Figure 5.3 (Continued)

2. Maintain a sense of urgency about achieving key results.
3. Manage time effectively.
4. Be responsive to follow-up items—e.g., applications and other requirements.
5. Keep abreast of product and/or procedure changes.
6. Budget the most effective use of business expenditures.
7. Maximize repeat sales among current clients.
8. Maximize use of computer support.
9. Forecast results.
   Monthly income
   Monthly volume
   Persistency objective
10. Update "Weekly Effort Formula."

Step III. Administration and Policy Owner Service Improvements

A. Make greater use of form letters.

B. Employ a "calendar signaling system." This will bring to your attention those clients who pay premiums by dividends or policy loans or both and, in addition, to those clients who require notification of PS 58 figures and other information involving pension plans.

C. Train secretary to keep records and fulfill certain service obligations.

D. Make greater use of policyowner reviews. This brings clients up to date and provides premium resources for new sales.

E. Make greater use of Million Dollar Round Table (MDRT) Information retrieval filing system.

Step IV. Professional Enhancement Objectives

A. Attendance at programs, seminars or institutes.

   1. American college institutes
   2. College-sponsored learning experiences, such as those at Purdue
   3. Speech, self-improvement, Dale Carnegie courses, etc.

Figure 5.3 Performance Review (Continued)

B. Make better use of reading and cassette libraries.

C. Develop one new habit that will make a significant difference in your professional and/or personal growth.

Step V. Expectations

A. What specifically do you expect of *you* next year?

_____

_____

_____

_____

_____

_____

_____

_____

_____

_____

_____

_____

_____

_____

_____

_____

B. What specifically do you expect of *management?*

_____

_____

_____

_____

_____

_____

_____

_____

_____

Your success in selling can be predicted and measured with mathematical precision and will come to you in the exact degree of the effectiveness with which you live each day.

Figure 5.4 Business Self-Assessment

The proficiency checklist below serves as a self-inventory of your skills and abilities. Its purpose is to determine the performance/potential gap in your selling job.

SELF-ASSESSMENT
(1 is low, 5 is high)

1. Displaying professional presence	1 2 3 4 5
2. Setting reachable goals with established guidelines	1 2 3 4 5
3. Planning time and activities for the next day	1 2 3 4 5
4. Prospecting in nests	1 2 3 4 5
5. Preapproach effectiveness	1 2 3 4 5
6. Skill in fact-finding and probing	1 2 3 4 5
7. Sales presentation persuasiveness	1 2 3 4 5
8. Meeting objections	1 2 3 4 5
9. Closing skill and strategy	1 2 3 4 5
10. Obtaining referred lead introductions	1 2 3 4 5
11. Use of weekly report to determine "dollar value" of each selling activity and progress being made toward my goals	1 2 3 4 5
12. Involvement of specialists in joint selling	1 2 3 4 5
13. Efficient office administration, including computer literacy	1 2 3 4 5
14. Secretarial, telephone, facsimile and mail services	1 2 3 4 5
15. MDRT and NQA qualification, CLU, ChFC and NALU presentation	1 2 3 4 5
16. Staying active in business, civic and religious activities	1 2 3 4 5
17. Reading, cassette listening and video viewing	1 2 3 4 5
18. Physical fitness programs	1 2 3 4 5
19. Managing personal financial affairs	1 2 3 4 5
20. Personal planned self-improvement programs	1 2 3 4 5

Total possible score   100

This year's score   _____

Performance/potential gap in my sales job (100 – score)   _____

(Last year's score)   (_____)

"Know thyself" was the inscription over the Oracle of Delphi.
And it's still the most difficult task any of us faces. But until
you truly study, assess and know your strengths and weaknesses,
you can't succeed except in the most superficial sense of the word.

Figure 5.4 Business Self-Assessment (Continued)

1. To be successful, you must _____.
   A. look at the bottom line
   B. build a quality business
   C. look to the future
   D. all of the above
2. Quality business means _____.
   A. good persistency
   B. high income
   C. college degree
   D. none of the above
3. Goals are _____.
   A. specific
   B. measurable
   C. directly related to activities
   D. all of the above
4. The _____ is used to analyze your past performance.
   A. My Past Performance worksheet
   B. Preparations for the New Year Ahead worksheet
   C. My Objectives worksheet
   D. none of the above
5. Once you have calculated your _____ for each sales activity, you can use those figures to plan the activity you will need to meet your sales goals.
   A. activity quotient
   B. activity per sale figures
   C. new leads
   D. net worth
6. Schedule _____ time first.
   A. training
   B. selling
   C. management
   D. personal

Figure 5.5 Sales Personality Evaluation

Name _____ Date _____

	Evaluation				
After you consider each question carefully, draw a circle around the figure in the rating columns that represents your evaluation on each of the seven dimensions.	Poor	Weak	Average	Good	Super
1. GOAL DIRECTED To what extent are you focused on definite goals—more paid cases and increased commissions. Are these goals in writing? Are you emotionally committed to their achievement?	20	40	60	80	100
2. PROACTIVE To what extent have you earned the reputation for thinking right, selling right, studying right and living right? Are you a product of decisions or conditions? Active or passive?	20	40	60	80	100
3. EFFECTIVE To what extent do you know where your time goes? Do you plan your sales day the day before? Do you demonstrate a sense of urgency? Do you focus on the critical sales activities that are "high payoff"?	20	40	60	80	100
4. CONFIDENT To what extent do you make your enthusiasm contagious? Do all three of your "sales companions"—enthusiasm, preparation and profes-sionalism—show up with you on all interviews? Does your enthusiasm for your product add interest and power to all you say? Do prospects feel your self-confidence?	20	40	60	80	100

Figure 5.5 Sales Personality Evaluation (Continued)

	Evaluation				
After you consider each question carefully, draw a circle around the figure in the rating columns that represents your evaluation on each of the seven dimensions.	Poor	Weak	Average	Good	Super
5. COMPETENT To what extent are you resourceful? Do you know your products and your competition thoroughly? Have you formed the habit of being well informed and current? Do you prepare in advance to meet situations likely to come up in interviews? Is your technical competence always improving? Do you have a true service attitude toward prospects?	20	40	60	80	100
6. CONSISTENT To what extent are you convincing in your contacts with prospects? Do you have prospects' interests uppermost in your mind during your contacts with them? To what extent do you express absolute, unshakable loyalty to your agency and your company? Do you have the reputation for being a person with a strong sense of responsibility?	20	40	60	80	100

Figure 5.5 (Continued)

	Evaluation				
After you consider each question carefully, draw a circle around the figure in the rating columns that represents your evaluation on each of the seven dimensions.	Poor	Weak	Average	Good	Super
7. BALANCED To what extent does your reputation in the community precede you? Does your appearance attract prospects? Do you treat clients as you would like to be treated if you were in their place? Are you a good manager of personal finances? Do you schedule "quality time" with the members of your family on a regular basis? Do you display staying power?	20	40	60	80	100

Add the circled numbers to get your Sales Personality
Evaluation

Average rating of present Sales Personality
 (Divide the above number by 7)

The same approach applies to goal setting. I like the Business Self-Assessment (Figure 5.4) and Sales Personality Evaluation (Figure 5.5) materials that were developed by Jack and Garry Kinder.

The last piece of preparation has to do with productivity. Before you set a production goal, you must understand the level of activity it will take to attain it and then distill those numbers down to the lowest common denominator: daily appointments. I would hope you are already familiar with this process and are using a program such as the One-Card System, which converts activity to a simple daily point system. Whatever system you use, you will want to have a clear understanding of *your numbers* before setting production goals. There are four key activity ratios you will need to know:

1. Number of contacts to get an interview:

$$\frac{\text{Contacts}}{\text{Interviews}} = \underline{\hspace{2cm}}$$

2. Dollar value of each contact:

$$\frac{\text{Commissions}}{\text{Contacts}} = \underline{\hspace{2cm}}$$

3. Number of interviews to make a sale:

$$\frac{\text{Interviews}}{\text{Sales}} = \underline{\hspace{2cm}}$$

4. Dollar value of each interview:

$$\frac{\text{Commissions}}{\text{Sales}} = \underline{\hspace{2cm}}$$

Now that you have taken a long, hard look at yourself and your results, you can set goals that have some real teeth in them. You can start with the desired result, then back into the monthly, weekly and daily activities it will take to get there. For example, if your goal is to pay for 100 cases next year, you can start with the result, 100 cases, and back into the activity:

100 Paid cases = 115 Submitted applications
115 Submitted applications = 250 Case presentations
250 Case presentations = 400 Fact-finding interviews
400 Fact-finding interviews = 500 Successful approaches
500 Successful approaches = 1,500 Qualified referrals

If you're going to work 50 weeks, then you must get two paid cases each week (100 annually), which means 30 referrals and 10 appointments. On a daily basis, that's six referrals and two appointments. That's it! Remember, you can only manage activity. The results will take care of themselves.

Once you understand that two things must happen every day—six referrals and two new appointments—your goals take on new meaning. You simply go to the plate and swing. Every day, six and two.

One last thought that is central to achieving our goals: How do we discipline ourselves to do our number-one job, prospecting and getting appointments, every day? The secret is to decide to do it, then never revisit the issue. It's simply not subject to negotiation.

My favorite story about the quality of doing your job day in and day out comes from baseball legend Ted Williams. Toward the end of the season in which he became the last player ever to hit .400 for the year, the Red Sox were playing a doubleheader. The first game, Williams went 0 for 4, thus weakening his chances of establishing what has since become baseball's most impressive Major League record. His manager told him, "Ted, it's a doubleheader. If you're having an off day, there's no reason for you to play in the second game and jeopardize your chances for a .400 season. Let me put someone in for you." Williams thought for a moment and then replied, "Coach, either I'm a .400 hitter or I'm not." He played the second game and went 3 for 4.

Once you know your goals and what it takes to reach them, you either are a 100-case producer or you're not. You either are a Million Dollar Round Table producer or you're not. You either are a convention qualifier or you're not. The choice is yours. Make it once and the rest will take care of itself.

OTHER HABITS OF SUCCESS

Balanced Lifestyle

There are a lot of reasons to build your personal and professional life around a commitment to balance. Physical, social, spiritual and intellectual balance make for a happy life. And there's a business benefit to a balanced life, too.

According to an old Chinese proverb, "He who plants a tree loves someone other than himself." The purchase of life insurance is like the planting of a tree. Life insurance is, in the final analysis, a character purchase. People buy it out of prudence, love, foresight and a sense of responsibility. So, logically, they prefer to buy it from someone who cultivates values similar to their own. Let's briefly look at those values.

The importance of being physically fit has finally become a concern of almost every responsible American's daily life. The real issue is to develop a philosophy around the two general areas that affect physical health: diet and exercise. There are a lot of opinions on these two subjects. You need only drop by your favorite bookstore to browse through the volumes of literature on both subjects.

I have a simple approach that is at the core of my beliefs about fitness and that dictates my actions on these subjects: Maintain a low-fat, low-cholesterol diet and get a good aerobic workout at least four times per week. To do this, you will have to read enough about fat and cholesterol so that you know by memory what foods to avoid. You will also have to know enough about aerobics to know how to get yourself to the desired pulse rate for at least 30 minutes four times per week. That's it. All that remains is to do it. Given the payoff we are now seeing in longer life expectancy for the physically and nutritionally fit, the incentives couldn't be greater. There are literally hundreds of books on the subject. If I had to recommend one out of the dozens I have read, it would be a simple primer titled *Fit or Fat?,* by Covert Baily. It tells you all you need to know on both subjects in about 150 pages.

Your social life is probably more important than you think. I'm not talking about cocktail parties and country clubs. Those things are fine if you want them, but they do little to add balance to your life. What I mean by social life is the nurturing and cultivation of important relationships and socially relevant activities. Family, real friendships, community activities and the love of one's fellow man are the elements of social balance in your life. Caring, involvement and personal sacrifice are what it takes to be a good dad, mom, spouse, friend, benefactor and citizen. Contrary to popular perception, we are not born with these qualities; like every other aspect of balance in your life, they must be worked at and cultivated. And like the others, once they are fully developed, the personal rewards are great.

The real satisfaction we get in life comes from what we do for others. To be sure, much of this is why we came into the life insurance business, but for that good deed we are handsomely paid. Become involved with those whom you can help solely for the benefit to them, and it will awaken in you a joy that will carry over to all aspects of your life.

Today, unfortunately, any specific discussion of spiritual balance may evoke an objection from one group or another. So let's just say this: Know what you believe and practice it every day. Let people know what you stand for and what they can expect from you as a result of your beliefs. Let it be known that you are serious about your spiritual beliefs, regardless of what those specific beliefs may be. Use your spiritual beliefs as armor, not as a cloak, and they will serve you well.

Intellectual balance is what separates you from the pack. Do whatever it takes to learn all you can about people, life, business, happiness, success, relationships and love. This is the foundation on which successful life insurance practices are built. Become passionate in your desire to understand, to grow, to learn.

If you have a high "need to know" level in your personality, you are much more likely to succeed in our business. A genuine curiosity about people—their problems, hopes, dreams and aspirations—is at the center of the personality of every successful life insurance agent I have worked with. Work to understand and love your clients. Work to learn what it is they want out of life and how they can attain it through your products and services.

It's great to be in a business where growing and developing your personal qualities contributes directly to your performance. This is probably true of other businesses, too, but none so much so as life insurance sales. To the person to whom family values and personal development are important, our business fits like a glove. If you have true balance in your life, the people who are naturally drawn to you will also be the people who are the best prospects for your services. And that's a pretty sweet feeling!

Family

Today's family is a moving target. Heads of households and insurance buyers vary in origins, lifestyles and values. What never changes is the cement that holds the family unit together: love. Love is what will make your family work, regardless of its composition, and sound values are what will cause it to last.

Never allow your career to become so important that it eclipses your family as the most important thing in your life, or you will wake up someday to discover that your life has lost its importance. Remember the old joke about workaholics: "No one ever said on their deathbed, 'I should have spent more time at the office!' "

Community Activities

Just like any corporation that believes it benefits by being a good corporate citizen, so will your life insurance practice benefit by you being a good corporate citizen. Granted, you can't have your own public-relations department, but you can do certain things that are good for your image in the marketplace and the community. This is one of those areas in which you must do serious soul-searching. In general, businesspeople become good corporate citizens for two reasons: It's good for business and it's good for the soul of the businessperson. Be sure in the choices you make that both needs are met.

The term "be a joiner" has negative connotations, and clearly you shouldn't join an organization just for the sake of joining. What you should do is pick a good organization in each of the arenas in your life and join it with a commitment to making a genuine difference. This would include church or temple, civic, social and professional organizations. A word of advice: Become known in each organization as a contributor and a leader. It will be good for your community, good for you and good for business. If you are not prepared to eventually pay the price of being a leader in the community activity you choose, you may want to pass. Instead, pick a cause or service that motivates you to go the extra mile.

An idea I love to promote is to develop a really first-class presentation, complete with slides and handouts, on some aspect of the life insurance business or your personal area of specialization. Then make sure everyone in the community knows you are available to make your presentation to appropriate groups.

You'll be surprised at how quickly the news of your expertise will travel. The work you do has great benefit to the community you work in. After all, life insurance is a socially relevant product, the benefits of which undeniably accrue to the entire economy of your city or town. Let your community know that the work you do contributes to the solutions they seek. Let them know you have a worthwhile story to tell about your services and that you tell it in an entertaining and informative way.

Personal Annual Review

I hope every life insurance agent reading this book sits down at least annually to review goals and performance and to set objectives for the next year. That's pretty basic. Yet I fear that it is not the case in some instances. So let's spend a few minutes on those elements that are so essential to your success.

I recommend an in-depth annual review to be conducted by you on all aspects of your performance for the year. The tools discussed earlier in this chapter will do an excellent job at helping you with your personal annual review. Whether you use this recommended procedure or one adopted by your company, I urge you to do an annual review. Our approach is a bit different from most in that I suggest you do as we did when I was part of a Fortune 500 financial services company: Do an actual "annual report to shareholders," complete with a profit-and-loss statement. Give yourself the luxury of being treated as if you were a shareholder in a publicly traded company, the primary business of which was your insurance practice.

This annual report approach allows us to step back and remove much of the subjectivity we introduce into our own self-evaluation—primarily excuses! As a guideline, take a look at the annual report of your own company. It starts with a message to shareholders (or policyholders, in the case of a mutual), then proceeds with a breakdown of the numbers and other results. Tell the truth as you see it about what occurred last year. Then map out your specific plan for next year. Be specific about sources of revenue, expenses and profit margins on goods sold. I believe this experience will have an awakening effect in a very positive way for most agents.

The Habit of Doing It Right

Management guru Peter Drucker says, "Good managers do the right things right." This is especially true for those managers and agents who plan to succeed in the year 2000 and beyond. They:

Live Right	and set an example in their community.
Sell Right	to be sure they protect their reputation of integrity with clients.
Study Right	to create the competitive edge only competence can give.
Choose Right	with an eye on what's right and fair.

The rule of thumb I advocate in any situation or circumstance is, when offered a choice, ask yourself, "In what way will the action I am about to take contribute to my success, my goals and my self-esteem?" Your answer will direct your behavior and form your habits.

6

Selling Skills

"Every insurance agency or individual practice should be built around one simple credo: 'We are a sales organization'."

—Roger G. Molski, C.L.U.

Above all, you are a salesperson. Master your craft and you will be forever secure.

This is not a book on salesmanship. The objective is to guide the agent in the task of being a good businessperson in the life insurance business, a crucial part of which is being a good salesperson. One hopes the reader has already acquired basic sales skills. However, there are several philosophies about developing and sharpening sales skills that must be covered to complete our discussion of what it will take to succeed in the year 2000 and beyond.

BECOMING BRILLIANT AT THE BASICS

The ultimate goal of every agent desiring to build a successful practice should be to become a master salesperson. To become a master, we must first love to sell, but also we must have some aptitude for selling. This is a subject that has been of concern to me throughout my management career. There is a tendency in the world of sales training to view salesmanship as a skill that is acquired through education alone. This is a mistaken belief. Yes, you must learn selling just as you would any other profession, but to learn it in a way that gets superior results, you must also have some aptitude for it. Unfortunately, many in the motivation and hype field ignore this obvious truth and tell their audience, "Anyone can do it if he or she has the desire." I guess this broadens their own prospect li⸴t, but in my view it can cause people to have a bitter experience attempting to learn something that cannot always be taught.

Another way of putting it is to say that the selling skills that deliver lasting results are "caught, not taught!" We learn them, then apply them by intermingling them with our own personality and style. It is the leverage that aptitude for sales work brings to the equation that makes the difference. Without it, those merely aping the skills taught by the masters eventually fizzle out. Am I saying that great salespeople are born, not grown? Not at all; but to deny that greatness begins with potential, aptitude and, yes, talent is naive. Without some aptitude, no amount of hard work and training will do. With aptitude, hard work and coachability, success may occur.

So, how do you measure aptitude for selling? The industry has been looking for a valid test or set of criteria for decades. I can't tell you how to measure your talent for life insurance work, but I can tell you what I have learned to look for. Tests and profiles are a bit like trying to measure the talent of an actor through an interview. You seldom can learn much of value. However, when the curtain goes up or the silver screen lights up, the abilities of a talented actor become self-evident. This is one reason I am such a relentless supporter of joint fieldwork. It lets both the performer and the understudy observe each other on center stage.

Here are ten traits and qualities. If they come naturally to you or at least are learned with relative ease, you probably have an aptitude for life insurance selling.

1. The ability to build rapport with strangers with whom you have little in common

2. The ability to cause most people to like you and to find a way to like most people

3. A high level of energy coupled with a high level of need for accomplishment

4. Close, loving relationships with family members and other key people in your life

5. A past pattern of envisioning your dreams and putting forth exceptional effort to realize them

6. The ability to stay focused on the people, activities and things that you perceive to be important

7. A strong belief system anchored in values that reflect the American work ethic and the free-enterprise system

8. A sense of urgency about activity, results and personal achievement

9. The ability to sustain a positive attitude in a generally negative environment

10. A capacity to find joy and inspiration in those simple things in life that many people take for granted

These character traits are hard enough for those who possess them to foster. They are next to impossible to measure in any way that determines aptitude for our business. Yet in my experience, they are omnipresent among the industry greats. If you believe you possess most of them to one degree or another, then you probably have an aptitude for our business. Just how much aptitude will be demonstrated only after a few hundred curtain calls. In other words, the best evidence of potential is still past performance.

Finally, in addition to aptitude and education, we must add yet another noble quality to our criteria. If we want to be master salespeople, we will have to work at it *with a passion.* Nothing else will do.

Michelangelo put it this way: "If people only knew what I had to do to attain mastery, the end result wouldn't seem so great at all."

I learned a long time ago that I can neither endow an agent with aptitude nor instill him or her with passion. I will leave that to the infomercial hypesters to peddle on Saturday morning TV. What professional management can do is create an environment where the qualities we have discussed here may flourish. For me, it all starts with pointing agents in the right direction. Here are a few places you can garner the knowledge of the masters:

Books No matter what your level, you should read a good book on sales, business, marketing or finance at least quarterly. My favorite books on life insurance selling are those that have withstood the test of time (available from Dearborn Financial Publishing, 155 N. Wacker Dr., Chicago, IL 60606, 800-629-9621): *High Touch Selling,* by John Savage; *The Feldman Method,* by Ben Feldman; *The Selling Heart,* by Jack and Garry Kinder; and *How to Make Money Tomorrow Morning,* by Sid Friedman.

We are fortunate that our industry has produced so many great talents who are willing to share their secrets and also remind us of those principles we learned but may have forgotten.

Sales Training Courses, seminars and continuing education offerings are all a necessary part of your ongoing development.

As company budgets shrink, it is becoming more important that agents become aware of the industry-sponsored and independent sources of this type of training. Through the Million Dollar Round Table, Life Underwriters Training Council (LUTC) and other industry organizations, you can learn about the opportunities to attend seminars in your area.

A good place to start for newer agents is the Dale Carnegie Sales Course and the frequent sales seminars conducted by organizations like Kinder Bros. & Associates and those of your local life underwriters' association. These types of meetings provide an excellent foundation on which to build. Information on them should be available through your local life underwriters' association.

Joint Work The forgotten gold mine.

Sermons We See

I'd rather see a sermon than hear one
any day.
I'd rather one should walk with me
than merely show the way.

The eye's a better pupil and more willing
than the ear;
Fine counsel is confusing, but example's
always clear;
And the best of all the preachers are
the men who live their creeds.
For to see the good in action is what
everybody needs.
I can soon learn how to do it if you'll
let me see it done.
I can watch your hands in action, but
your tongue too fast may run.
And the lectures you deliver may be
very wise and true;
But I'd rather get my lesson by observing
what you do.
For I may misunderstand you and the
high advice you give,
But there's no misunderstanding how
you act and how you live.

—Edgar A. Guest

There simply is no substitute for joint work. You will discover your own greatest talents while sitting in the presence of those who have mastered the art of selling life insurance. Find the best in your area of specialization and ask them to help you with a good, strong case. If you don't want to go to a competitor, go to another state and, through the Million Dollar Round Table or by reputation, find the best performer. Ask him or her to work on a case with you. It will be the best sharing you ever did, because the skill shared with you will be far more valuable than the commission you share.

Mentoring—The Key to Personal Insights Few who build a successful practice do so without a role model, an example, a teacher that they look up to and try to emulate. Once you have gone through the exercise of selecting your area of specialization, seek the guidance of someone you respect in building your business plan. This may be your sales manager, your agency manager, an agent or a company official you respect.

Being mentored and then eventually mentoring someone wishing to learn from you are among the most gratifying experiences in life.

A great deal of work has been done in this area by my friend Richard McCloskey of Newport Beach, California. Dick, an industry great in his own right, has developed an outstanding program in his agency by which established agents can team up with neophytes to build sales results that are truly synergistic. Many believe that mentoring programs such as those of Dick McCloskey will solve the industry's problem of cultivating enough new talent in a cost-effective way.

The value of mentoring was explored in a recent study of 2,400 career agents conducted by Life Insurance Management Research Association (LIMRA). It compared the performance of those who had someone they considered to be a mentor for their career with the performance of those without a mentor. The results clearly indicate that if you don't have a mentor, you should obtain one. Those in the survey who had a mentor experienced a paid case rate of 17–25 percent higher and had a 10–15 percent better chance of surviving in the business. In addition, they gave their management and trainers significantly higher grades for their performance. (Anthony T. Dalessio, "Does It Work?", *Managers Magazine,* January 1993.)

Industry Meetings   Ours is the most caring and sharing industry in all of American business. The forums for these habits of sharing are well known: local life underwriter meetings, Million Dollar Round Table, American Association of Life Underwriters and a host of study groups and sales caravans sponsored by agent organizations all across the country.

For me personally, attendance at local life underwriter meetings early in my career, where I was able to sit at the feet of the likes of Norman Lavine, Tom Wolff and Al Granum, made the difference between just survival and real success. Our industry's great performers cannot make you great, but they can bring out the best in you, which may include greatness.

Pick the meetings you think you will most benefit from and form the habit of regular attendance.

KNOWLEDGE: THE FAIREST FORM OF SEGREGATION

They can outillustrate you, they can undercut your compensation and perhaps they can even outsell you. But the one thing the competition can never do is outsmart you, unless you let them pass you on the never-ending learning curve of life insurance knowledge. Your knowledge about your business is your most important selling skill and usually the hardest won.

As we stated earlier, knowledge is not power in and of itself. You must habitually apply it to benefit from it. My definition of knowledge for our business is: *Knowledge is the dynamic in life insurance selling that takes us up the pyramid of competence to a place where the competition cannot easily reach us.*

$$\text{Activity} \times \text{Selling Skill} = \text{Results}$$

This is a truism. But look what happens to the equation when we add the additional K Factor:

$$\text{Knowledge} \times \text{Activity} \times \text{Selling Skill} = \text{Results}^3 \text{ (the third power)}$$

LEARNING IS EXPONENTIAL!

In your quest for knowledge, you will acquire the symbols of knowledge along the way: CLU, ChFC, CFP, LUTC and various licenses with the NASD. These credentials are important to a successful career in that they build prestige and let others know you are qualified to practice your chosen discipline.

But to build a truly successful practice, you can never stop at designations. Designations help to *open* doors, but knowledge and skills are what keep those doors open.

In addition to the pursuit of professional designations, industry study groups are essential for the top-producing agent. Study groups are formed in various ways. Some are groups of producers at various stages of development, while others are more homogeneous, containing all advanced producers or all developing producers. Some study groups consist only of agents within a given company, while others are subgroups of agents belonging to an industry organization such as the National Association of Life Underwriters or the Million Dollar Round Table.

The primary purpose of most study groups is to obtain hands-on working knowledge of advanced underwriting concepts, both new and old. The thing that distinguishes study groups from academic or classroom learning is that the knowledge is usually obtained from real-life cases that pay big commissions, rather than textbooks or third-party re-creations of cases. This tends to have a significant impact on the participants' ability to absorb the material studied. It has long been believed that commission dollars are the greatest catalyst to help agents climb the learning curve. If applied knowledge is power, then the most logical way to acquire it is from those who know how to apply it. Sales results are the best indicator of the ability to apply knowledge, so listening to the successful practitioner is the best way to learn, except for being out on the actual case while it is being written.

Study groups will also help you meet and become friends with people who are leaders or aspire to leadership. People who are dedicated professionals and people who want to grow and do better are all you will find in a study group. You can find a mentor, too, or become one, as well as develop new friendships and locate good sources for joint work. The benefits you will acquire in addition to the knowledge are worth the involvement in a study group all by themselves.

THE JOURNAL: YOUR WINDOW INTO PERSONAL INSIGHTS

The building of a successful practice is an important event in your life and in your industry, and it should be recorded. The story of building your practice need not be a literary masterpiece. But taking a few minutes at the end of each day to record events, observations and facts is not only good therapy, it's good business.

I recommend that you create your journal by simply writing in the back of your monthly planner. The Franklin Planner™ is one of several good products in the market that provide space for a journal. Examples of the types of things you will want to record in your journal/planner include

- a critique of each selling interview.

- a record of important telephone conversations.

- thoughts and philosophies encountered along the course of the day.

- devotions.

- ideas for improved performance.

- lessons learned.

- affirmations.

We are the sum total of our experiences. Yet our experiences are our best teachers only if we remember them.

Creative Time

Selling is a creative process, and great salespeople are creative people. Distill the complex concepts of your specialty down to simple solutions. Selling is like writing a poem. You decide what you want to say by writing it out in as many words as are necessary to communicate your idea. Then you prune, cull and refine the words until the concept is stated as concisely and simply as possible but still with a lot of punch. This "wordsmithing" process should be a labor of love to which you devote literally hundreds of hours in your spare time.

The job of the master salesperson is to tell a story, sell the problem and offer the solution, in progressively fewer words. If we read the works of our industry's greatest salesmen, we find they learned to speak in aphorisms. *The Feldman Method* by the late, legendary Ben Feldman, is a classic example of how to communicate complex concepts in very few words. Spend time building your skills in this critical area. Be a poet, not a peddler!

Don't reinvent every wheel; instead, learn to build a better wheel. No sales concept is ever finished. They are always evolving. For example, key-person retirement insurance became split-dollar; split-dollar became reverse split-dollar; reverse split-dollar led to the insured retirement plan. All of these innovations came from the minds of agents who wanted to improve on already good ideas.

Some agents resist sales tracks or structured sales procedures, such as Financial Need Analysis or the One-Card System, because they want to create their own techniques. This is OK if it works, but it can be a big mistake. When I say you should refine and perfect, I don't necessarily mean you have to reinvent. Rather, the creative opportunity lies in improving upon your performance of the sales material you use or are being trained with. Think about the great actors. They don't rewrite their lines, they simply perfect their performance through hard work. The work of Shakespeare cannot be improved upon, yet over the years performances have varied dramatically based upon the actor's interpretation of the Bard's script. The creative opportunity, then, lies not in inventing your own sales track, but in developing your unique interpretation of the material. This is one of the subtle truths of our business that so many sales trainers and agents seem to lose sight of.

Write out your sales presentation in longhand. Before we introduce the new, we must first master the old. Before impressionist artists could create their surrealistic, sometimes childlike paintings, they first had to learn to paint with the skill and realism of the Dutch masters. This is the step many newer agents miss when they decide to put their own spin on the sales tracks with which they are being trained.

Find new or better ways to sell the problem. *People don't buy life insurance; they buy solutions to problems*—problems the agent has framed in a way that burns! The proposal is simply a welcome relief to the discomfort created by the agent's presentation.

Many of those who sell life insurance have become enamored with the outstanding value our competitive products bring to the consumer today. Some become even more excited about the elaborate computer-generated proposals showing comparisons of life insurance to other investments, such as CDs or government bonds. They develop point-of-sale charts with vividly colored, high-density graph-

Figure 6.1 Greed-Based Selling

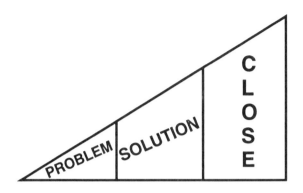

ics. Their focus seems to be on how this wonderful product is just too good a deal to pass up. For these agents, the sales process looks like the graphic in Figure 6.1.

The assumption is that the product is such a great deal, anyone would want it. The only challenge is to present it in such an attractive package that other savings and investments will pale by comparison. All you need to succeed is to be a stronger closer! This approach doesn't work in today's environment—or at least it shouldn't.

Today's superior agents are continually working on finding new ways to help prospects understand the problem—not just intellectually, but emotionally. Needs-based selling has long been the foundation of the great careers in our industry. In recent years, some factions have slipped away from this core value and, in so doing, caused life insurance to become more like a commodity. Whether this is in the consumer's best interest or not remains to be seen, but there is no question that a commodity perception of our product does not bode well for the agent.

The ability to uncover needs and awaken prospects to problems that are best solved by life insurance is what makes life insurance agents necessary. For those who understand and are skilled at needs selling, the sales process looks like the graphic in Figure 6.2.

Figure 6.2 Needs-Based Selling

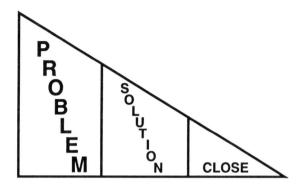

When people buy life insurance as the best solution to a problem they have resolved to fix, they defend their purchase to would-be critics and competitors.

As I stated earlier, this is not a book on salesmanship. We do, however, want to point you in the right direction. There is a lot of training in salesmanship available, including some of the systems mentioned here. Never stop taking some time to sharpen your sales skills. As we climb the knowledge curve through education and development, there is a real danger we will lose sight of the basics, which can lead to many problems. Just keep in mind that to accomplish big things, we must be *brilliant at the basics!*

BUILDING THE RIGHT IMAGE

Great life insurance people are known for who they are, what they believe and how they perform for their clients and the companies they represent. So, before we leave the subject of selling skills, we need to discuss the most important sale you will ever make: YOU. Until the prospect buys you, he or she will buy nothing from you. So you'd better know how to make this sale every time.

In building your practice, you have at least *three distinct publics.* Each requires specialized attention.

Public #1: Your Clients

This is the area in which you will want to be overt and direct in your public-relations effort.

The most valuable public-relations piece I know of for clients is the quarterly newsletter. Typically, the letter should point out problems and provide solutions involving life insurance. Of course, general matters of interest about financial and tax issues should also be included.

There are virtually dozens of services available that provide customized newsletters for you to send to your clients on a personalized basis. Most of them advertise in industry trade journals. Typically, the cost of sending a quarterly newsletter to 200 clients, customized to your practice, will run from $400 to $500 per year. That has to be one of the best investments an agent can make.

Also, be sure to pass on all accomplishments by you, your agency or associates and your company to your clients. They should be reminded, in a positive way, of your presence in their lives as often as possible.

Public #2: Your Prospects

Have a regular mailing list consisting of those in your community you have identified as candidates for your services. We call this our reservoir prospect list. It contains the names of all of those we have talked to or would like to talk to. Eventually, those people will probably buy insurance. When that time comes, we want them to think of us. Of course, your One-Card System, which we will discuss later, will give you the ideal vehicle for staying in touch with prospects on a prescribed basis. Still, you may wish to do even more by including this group in things like your quarterly newsletter.

Public #3: Your Community

As we have previously discussed, it is important to maintain a professional presence in your community. A well-done presentation on a topical aspect of life insurance is a valuable investment of your time. Avail yourself as a speaker to local trade and professional organizational meetings.

Today there are virtually unlimited ways to become involved in community activities that will help you make a contribution while becoming well and favorably known. I suggest you pick several organizations that represent a cause or purpose in which you have an interest. It may be humanitarian, such as care for the elderly or abused children, or it may be entertaining, such as a ski club, a cooking class or a barbershop quartet. It may be local, such as a library or an historical society, or global, such as ecological or international cultural exchanges.

The key is to find an interest to pursue or a cause to champion. Commit yourself to making a difference and business will come your way from surprising sources.

Establishing Your Presence

Image Brochure Another important investment you should make in your practice is a first-class printed piece that describes you and your services. Be careful not to make your image brochure an "ego trip." Emphasize what you can do for the prospect with understatement about yourself. Refer to your practice in a way that will memorialize *it,* rather than you. If you have a staff, mention them to help create the feeling of an ongoing entity.

People like to deal with those who are successful. An image brochure can elevate the prospect's comfort level with regard to your worthiness of his or her business. The objective is to sell yourself and your services with as little fanfare as possible. It's worth investing in a good local advertising firm to counsel you on the development of this piece.

Sales and Marketing Clubs Cultivate centers of influence whenever possible. An excellent way to do this is to join the sales or marketing clubs in your community. They typically meet for breakfast monthly for the purpose of sharing ideas and exchanging leads.

If you don't have access to a sales and marketing club, start one. It's easy enough to go to local real estate, business machine, stock-brokerage and other offices that have salespeople to get the ball rolling. It will be a lot of fun and has proven time and again to be a real win/win situation for those involved.

Industry Work   The life insurance industry is going to give you a lot over your lifetime. Giving back to the industry will help you in more ways than you might think. Here are some ways to do that.

- Become an LUTC instructor.

- Teach a CLU course.

- Develop a powerful motivational talk to give at industry meetings.

- Make yourself available for mentoring agents who are new in the business.

- Become involved with the Million Dollar Round Table.

- Join your local life underwriters' association and be an active member.

Personal Appeal   It's no secret that your overall personal appearance and the impression you create have a great deal to do with whether people do business with you. Employers are not permitted to discriminate against prospective employees because of personal grooming, weight, ability to communicate, language barriers, life-style or habits, such as smoking or chewing gum. This is fine, but it has nothing to do with the rules of life insurance buying.

Prospective buyers of our product can and will discriminate against you at their pleasure for any reason they wish. They can choose not to buy without giving any reason at all. And you can rest assured that if your personal appearance or habits are a turnoff to prospects, they will never tell you.

My recommendation is that you take an objective look at yourself with regard to such items as appearance, grooming, habits and vocabulary. If there is something about you that you can change that could cost you a sale from time to time, you have a choice. But at least be aware of the opportunity available through improvements in personal areas.

When I started out in the business, the company I went to work for used a selection tool called "The 1,000-Point Man." It assigned a numerical value to various traits that included, among others, "married, good physical condition, serious about his religious beliefs and comes from or belongs to at least one club or organization." The idea was to look for the person whose score added up to 1,000. Well, today such criteria would be laughable beginning with the title, which assumes the ideal candidate is a man! Yet the concept of measuring a person's suitability to a profession is still valid. I believe the 1,000-point person is not something others should measure against their own criteria, but it could be something we can measure against *our* own criteria. Think about the person you would most like to be as a life insurance agent. Then break the criteria down to qualities with assigned values totaling 1,000 points. This is the person you want doing the selling for you. To demand of yourself that you become that person is not discrimination, it's determination!

The Skill of Caring

A lot of things are not necessarily good for business but are good for you, which is even better. Call them habits, skills or virtues, the important thing is that the agent who is emerging as a success will cultivate them.

Be good to those who care for you and fair to those who don't. You're not a missionary. You don't have to convert every prospect or acquaintance to your beliefs. I have sometimes heard it implied that to succeed as an agent, he or she must have "the religion of life insurance." In the broadest sense, those of us committed to the business sometimes tend to describe our calling with a religious or missionary zeal, but this can be dangerous. Life insurance is not a religion, it's a business. If you don't succeed at it, your worth as a human being is not in doubt. If people don't buy from you, it is not an indictment of their character or yours. Don't overreact to those who reject you. They are still prospects, and situations do change.

Keep your perspective and be fair to everyone you deal with, giving the benefit of the doubt to those who exercise their right not to buy.

Remember your beginnings. We all start in this business from ground zero. Remember and savor every moment of challenge and even defeat. We come into this world alone and we leave it the same way. The bell curve in between, which we call our lifetime, will vary from one individual to the next, but in the end we must all be measured by our deeds toward others.

If you make it a habit to put something back into your business on a regular basis by teaching, mentoring or just taking the time to stay in touch with those who touched your career along the way, you will avoid the disease of ego, which can destroy even the finest of careers.

Look after the support people. Every home office or agency employee has the potential to contribute to your success. But to do so, they have to be on your team. Let them know they are important to you. Treat them the same as you would any good prospect.

The really outstanding agents in our business do not differentiate in their treatment of business associates by rank, station or income. Time and again I have been warmed by looking on, unobserved, as a high-producing agent waiting in the agency reception area visited pleasantly with company employees. The interest in the goings-on in the staffers' lives, careers and families has always served as a reminder to me that the superior-performing agent is almost always an undiscriminating lover of people. This frequently shows on a home office visit, and it comes back to that agent in ways he or she might never imagine.

Do some good for your fellow man. Whether through involvement with charities or anonymous activities, do something for your community that has absolutely no potential business purpose. And make it something that takes your time rather than your money, like being a Big Brother or Big Sister.

The biggest dividends from charitable and community activities are the positive changes you can make in the lives of others. There is no greater reward in life than to make a difference for the better.

Becoming brilliant at the basics of selling skills requires aptitude first; then attitude; and, finally, discipline. All are essential to the mastery of your craft. The aptitude can be enhanced, but the basic talents for high performance must first be present. The attitude can be created and maintained through sales training, mentoring, joint work and industry functions. Discipline is what you must draw upon for the acquisition of knowledge and the building of a healthy image.

You now have the framework to move to the next step in our blueprint—thinking right and selling right.

7

Philosophies That Win, Systems That Work

"He never really knew who he was."

—Arthur Miller, *Death of a Salesman*

Sales performance is closely related to what we believe and how we behave. This includes our philosophies of life, our personalities, our sales practices, our attitudes and our skills. It can be stated many ways, but it all boils down to this: We must know what it is we believe and who we are; we must know what it is we want to accomplish and have a way of accomplishing it. The great management consultant Garry Kinder calls these tandem qualities "philosophies that win and systems that work."

DECIDE WHAT YOU BELIEVE AND LIVE BY IT

Throughout this book, we have referred to the importance of your various values, beliefs and attitudes as they relate to your success in selling life insurance. It's no coincidence that virtually every speech or article written by industry leaders on the topic of success begins with a discussion of these aspects of the agent's personality. Ours is a mental-attitude business, and your attitude is dictated by your philosophies of life.

Without the armor of a good self-image, a positive mental attitude and a desire to win, we would soon be overwhelmed by the daily rejection and setbacks our industry deals out in generous portions. These qualities—image, attitude and desire—are the first of our three categories of a winning philosophy. To understand how we develop these sound mental habits, we must first understand the process our mind goes through when life deals us a card.

Victor Frankl, the great psychologist, taught us that we have three central values in life: the experiential, or that which happens to us; the creative, or that which we bring into existence; and the attitudinal, or our response in difficult circumstances, such as when we face rejection or defeat. Frankl, who survived the death camps of Nazi Germany, observed that it was not so much what happened to people that determined whether or not they survived as how they reacted to those events. He found that deciding to survive was the key to survival. He made his observation while surviving the most horrifying of human experiences—seeing his loved ones, including his own family, ruthlessly murdered for no reason. He chronicled the behavior of those who survived physically and how they reacted psychologically to seemingly imminent death. He found that many gave up and died on their own before their brutal assassins could murder them, while others chose not to give in to anything. As Gandhi put it when his tormentors attempted to break him and his followers, "They cannot take away our self-respect if we do not give it to them." Selling life insurance will never require us to draw on the unbelievable strength of character Frankl and Gandhi had to reach for, but the principle is the same.

We must first decide what we believe about our business, our practices and our experiences. We can decide what we believe and choose how we are going to respond. We cannot control our prospects and their responses, so we should waste no energy on how they respond to our attempting to sell them life insurance. What we can control is how we respond to their attitude. If we believe in our product, the value of the work we do and the sincerity of our intentions to help people, then no negative response to our efforts can create a negative feeling within us. Sometimes this is easier said than done, as I found out early in my career.

When I was 23 years old and new in the life insurance business, I had an experience that taught me in a relatively microcosmic way the importance of understanding Frankl's experiential, creative and attitudinal principle values.

I had driven all the way across town on a particularly bitter cold, snowy evening to a closing interview. Upon exiting my car, I slipped and fell in the snow, dropping my proposal, which became wet and illegible. When I got to the door, the house was dark, and it became obvious after a few rings of the doorbell that no one was home.

This came on the heels of a very tough day and an even tougher week. It was one of those times we all experience sooner or later, when we ask ourselves that unthinkable question, "Am I going to make it?" Driving home that night, I wanted to run, I wanted to hide, I wanted to quit. I wanted to leave the life insurance business—or at least I thought I did. That's when it happened. I found the secret to handling rejection and defeat.

As I thought about quitting, some inner wisdom revealed itself to me and told me that I should not let the person I was today make the call. It was too important. Instead, I should let the person I would someday be decide what I should do. The person I had envisioned so many times in my mind was successful, prosperous, respected and established in the life insurance business. He was well known and liked, and a person from whom others sought advice, counsel and guidance. I, too, would now seek his guidance.

I had created this person so vividly in my mind that I felt obligated to let him choose how I was going to respond to my seemingly abysmal circumstances. After all, it was he who was going to have to look back from some future time on how he behaved when the going became unbearably difficult. It was the person I would someday be who would have to stand at a podium or write an article about how he handled defeat and rejection.

Oddly enough, I had no problem letting down the guy I was at 23. After all, a brief, misbegotten foray into life insurance sales at this point in my life would be a soon-forgotten blemish on my résumé. But the man of 20 years later would know better. Him I couldn't let down. And I didn't. At least I haven't yet, because I still am becoming that person—a person I never want to disappoint.

I went back to work the next day more determined to succeed than ever and armed with a new, winning philosophy. I called it "vicarious detachment": the ability to have a kind of "out-of-body experience" or detachment and allow the "ideal you" to view the "actual you"; vicariously, if you will. Then to let the person you plan to be help you make choices that will contribute to making this envisioned personality a reality.

What all of this taught me was what Victor Frankl had already figured out. I had this sign printed and hung on my wall:

OUR MEMORIES OF TRYING TIMES ARE NOT
FOCUSED SO MUCH ON THE EVENTS AS THEY ARE
ON HOW WE RESPOND TO THOSE EVENTS.

This, then, is the first winning philosophy, and it will help you to deal with what happens to you in life.

The next philosophy is more complex; it concerns how you make things happen in your life as opposed to waiting for them to happen to you.

BECOMING AND STAYING MOTIVATED

The motivation business is a subindustry of the sales profession. There are hundreds of books, seminars and tapes available on the subject. Many of them are very good. However, few of them can, by themselves, motivate you in a way that will make a permanent difference in your performance. The only lasting source of motivation comes from within. In a world where everyone seems more and more in want of a quick fix for every problem—quick weight loss, radio psychotherapy, faxed answers to every inquiry and a communications superhighway—there ought to be a shortcut to becoming highly motivated. There are a number of "infomercials" on Saturday morning TV that claim they can deliver a motivated, happier, more productive you by selling you a six-video package. Forget it! A lot of changes will occur by the year 2000, but a shortcut to motivating salespeople is not among them.

You see, motivation—like a fit body, a well-schooled mind or a good marriage—is one of those things in life that can occur only with a sustained focused effort over a period of time. It is the result of a philosophy, a belief system, a way of life. Becoming and staying motivated can never be induced externally; rather, motivation is the external manifestation of your values—values centered around your perceived needs. To become motivated, then, you must understand your own needs and how setting the right goals can satisfy those needs. This is why you will sometimes hear or read about goals becoming motivators. This is true, but only if those goals are accurately tied to your needs.

This is most graphically illustrated when we look at our most visceral needs. If, while sitting in your favorite armchair and reading a book on motivation, you suddenly found yourself at the North Pole, you would become highly motivated to find warmth and shelter and would not need to consult the book further for inspiration to begin your search. Or, more realistically, if while reading the same book you were munching on an apple and a piece of it became lodged in your throat, you would again become highly motivated, this time to get some air into your lungs. In both instances, your only motivation would be survival. Because you now have shelter, warmth and air, these things are not motivators for you. But what about your psychological needs?

The satisfaction of these needs can, in some ways, be as critical to your emotional survival as food, shelter and air are to your physical survival. When you understand your specific psychological needs, you will hold the key to unlocking the secret of becoming and staying motivated.

There are certain psychological needs that are present in nearly all of us. The need to be loved, the need to be touched and the need to be communicated with are *primary* needs we all crave for psychological survival. There are also *secondary* needs, such as the need for affirmation, the need to be understood, affiliation needs and the need to be appreciated and respected. It is understanding these secondary needs that will lead you to self-motivation as it pertains to success in selling.

Think about those psychological needs that seem to be most important to you, and try to identify the values that correspond to those needs. Values are those things that we perceive to be the road map to satisfying our needs. Understanding your values and identifying the corresponding needs is the key to becoming and staying motivated.

Values can differ dramatically from one person to the next, even among people with the same need. For example, say two children have a need for affirmation. One child may value academic achievement, so the goal might become to win the school spelling bee. The other might seek affirmation but value aggression; therefore, the goal might be to become the schoolyard bully. Same needs, but different values, which lead to very different behavior.

Thus, we learn that false values such as aggression, power and materialism can lead to goals and behavior for which there is no payoff. You reach the goal—smashing the opponent, gaining revenge on the enemy or owning the biggest house in town—but the need is not satisfied.

This is not because the need is inappropriate; it's just that many people choose the wrong road map to fill their needs. They go over and over the same old road, hoping that this time it will lead to a different place. Of course, it never does, because it's the wrong path. Instead, all they get are bigger and bigger doses of false values: more power, more control, more money and bigger titles. Goals based on such values are like drugs and, as such, can never satisfy the need, so it doesn't matter whether the goal is met or not, because it is founded in a false value. The victories are always empty, the triumphs unfulfilling.

The toughest thing of all about this human circumstance is that our values seldom change. Unless we have some type of life-changing experience, such as a near-death encounter or a religious conversion, our values tend to remain pretty much the same throughout our lives.

The good news is that most of us are neither cursed with all false values nor blessed with all virtuous values. Instead, we have some of each. I sincerely believe in the human struggle between good and evil. For me, it is as graphic as the proverbial devil on one shoulder and angel on the other. For others, it may be more subtle, but the point is that we always have a choice. We must try to meet our needs by focusing on our higher values so that, when we set a goal and achieve it, we will feel fulfilled in our needs and will be satisfied with our performance.

For example, if you have a need for affirmation, you might think about how you value status and recognition as opposed to how you value winning. As a result, your goal might be accomplishing membership in the Million Dollar Round Table instead of beating the agent down the hall who is currently outproducing you. Both goals are motivators, but one will satisfy your need through the gaining of a valued credential, elevating your self-esteem, while the other will be an empty victory, leaving you looking for someone else to beat and still feeling inadequate.

The need is affirmation, the value is recognition, the goal is membership in the Million Dollar Round Table. The motivation is the mental image of how the recognition of being an MDRT agent will make you feel. The behavior is to make calls, and the result is a very positive affirmation of your worth by the accomplishment of MDRT performance. The feeling of becoming a member of the MDRT is a very self-affirming one. When it appears on your business card, it will evoke a positive affirmation every time you look at it, which will be several times daily, even if you only notice it subliminally as you hand your card to a prospect.

On the other hand, beating the agent down the hall may have taken the same or an even bigger sales performance. Yet it will not satisfy your need to be affirmed in a healthy way, and you certainly wouldn't want to print this achievement on your business card! So there's no meaningful payoff.

One might argue that if the "beat the other guy" approach gets as good or even better results, who cares about meeting your psychological needs? After all, aren't the results our final judge? Well, that's not how it works. Results come in two flavors: those for everyone else and those for the person who achieves them. They may look similar on the outside, but they are not. The results that others judge us by don't take our needs into account. They judge us by their own frame of reference or their own needs, if you will. The results we judge ourselves by are based solely upon our needs gratification.

Yes, the results are our final judge, but only we can measure those results in a way that counts—namely, by how far they go in satisfying our needs. When they go a long way, we then can look to satisfying other needs on our hierarchy. As we satisfy more needs, we move up the need hierarchy toward that point that psychologist Abraham Maslow called "self-actualization." We become complete and fulfilled human beings. Moving up the need hierarchy is far more motivating than being stuck in the same place time after time, chasing the same elusive rainbows and reaching farther for the same brass ring. Both approaches may get increasingly better external growth, but only one will lead to internal growth.

This is why there often seems to be a bifurcation among those agents the industry judges as being highly successful. One may be a professional success by every external measurement but a failure in both business and personal relationships, while another views his or her accomplishments as a natural by-product of a notable success in business and personal relationships.

Motivation is, then, the result of several dynamics that, when blended under the right conditions, can be ongoing. To become and stay motivated, we must understand the process by which motivation occurs. Once we accomplish this, we can create an environment conducive to motivation. This is where the selection of the agency or associates we choose to work with comes into play. It is true that others cannot motivate us, but they can provide an environment in which motivation is more likely to occur.

For example, an agency with an atmosphere of high achievement is likely to provide recognition programs and awards that appeal to your need to be appreciated. They may provide field training programs that deliver results through joint work, which meet your need to validate your choice of the life insurance business as a career. The manager may be empathetic and a good listener, helping to meet your need to be understood. The agency may be a leader in the company or in the life insurance community, thus satisfying your affiliation needs.

When we are in an environment that has the capacity to meet our needs, we are more likely to become motivated. We can see a clear path to satisfying results.

All that remains is to be sure that the values of the environment are similar to our own. If they are, we have found a fit we should never abandon. On the other hand, I have seen high achievers leave an agency or working relationship because their values were in conflict. Under these circumstances, leaving is the right choice, because, as I stated earlier, values are not likely to change on either side.

The subject of human motivation is complex. I'm not sure any one psychologist has it figured out, and I know most of the so-called motivational speakers haven't, either. Nor have I, but I have picked up bits and pieces over my career and, in the process, developed a formula that works for me:

Need + Value = Goal
Motivation + Behavior = Result

If we understand our needs and appeal to our *higher values,* we can, in the right environment, become motivated to behave in ways that move us toward obtaining satisfying results. This, then, is the second winning philosophy.

ATTITUDES AND BELIEFS

The third winning philosophy has to do with our attitudes and beliefs.

Attitudes are our way of looking at things we encounter in life. Beliefs are our perceptions of reality.

We all know that ours is a mental-attitude business, but have you ever thought about how this conclusion was drawn? Well, it is based on the belief that the life insurance business is one of those experiences in life that is a constant and ever true to our perceptions. It is a business of numbers and of consistent, predictable results for those who know how to work with those numbers. It is a business of available knowledge, learnable skills, acquirable habits and manageable activities all of which, when pulled together, deliver predictable results.

Knowledge × Skills × Habits × Activity = Results

This means that the only other dynamic that can affect performance is our interpretation of these realities, or our attitude.

What many of the motivational speakers fail to point out is that a good attitude can make a difference only if it is applied to a valid belief. When we predicate our behavior on a mistaken belief, it doesn't matter how hard we work or how good our attitude is; we will fail all the same.

If, for example, we believe that the world is flat, no amount of effort or positive mental attitude will allow us to drive our enemies over the edge. There is no edge.

On the other hand, if we believe we can succeed in the life insurance business by following time-tested systems and procedures that have worked for others before us, our attitude can make the vital difference, because it is being applied to sound beliefs. When we have sound beliefs, we tend to become "right-thinking" people, which leads us to a good attitude. The following are examples of some of the beliefs you can comfortably embrace about the life insurance business:

- BELIEVE that the modern-day, client-oriented life insurance contract is the single best instrument for providing a complete and balanced hedge against the twin economic dangers that confront every prospect: living too long or dying too soon.

- BELIEVE that financial products and services, properly sold, are of considerably more value to your buyer than any commissions you can possibly earn.

- BELIEVE that you are your most important customer. You must be sold on your job, your products and your ability to perform.

- BELIEVE that you should set realistically high goals and achieve them on schedule.

- BELIEVE that time is money and that learning to manage your time productively will be one of your most profitable achievements.

- BELIEVE in the law of averages and in the wisdom of knowing the dollar value of each of your primary activities—the telephone contact, the fact-finding interview and the closing interview.

- BELIEVE that honest, intelligent effort is always rewarded.

- BELIEVE that a selling interview is never to be considered a contest between you and the prospect.

- BELIEVE that the power of your sales presentation will always lie in its simplicity.

- BELIEVE that the product purchase must be "helped along" and is most often made because you guided the prospect's behavior in an effective manner.

- BELIEVE that prospects buy financial products and services not so much because they understand the product thoroughly, but because they feel and believe that you, the agent, understand them, their problems and the things that they want to accomplish.

- BELIEVE that almost all of the development is, in fact, self-development—that personal growth is the product of practice, observation and self-correction.

- BELIEVE that staying physically fit is a prerequisite for maintaining a high level of energy.

- BELIEVE that top producers are ordinary people with an extraordinary determination to make every occasion a great occasion.

- BELIEVE that there is great power in holding a high ideal of your worth as a professional agent. Your image of yourself determines how far you will go in earning money, gaining clients and achieving influence.

Once you know what you believe and that your beliefs are sound, you can begin to work on your *attitude*.

The greatest discovery of my generation is that people can alter their lives by altering their attitudes of mind. What the mind attends to, it considers. What the mind attends to continually, it believes. And what the mind believes, it eventually gets done.
—William James

Your attitudes about your job, your relationships and your circumstances in life tend to become self-fulfilling prophesies. Assuming your beliefs are sound, it will be your attitudes that influence your outlook on life. Industry great Norman Lavine told me this when I was brand new in the business: "Young man, be very careful of what you want out of life, because you're sure to get it!" It will be your attitudes that form winning philosophies and give you a healthy outlook on life. Some characteristics of a good attitude include the following:

- *Optimism*—A sense of promise about the future that considers problems more as opportunities than obstacles.

- *Enthusiasm*—A passion for life and its rewards. Encouragement of individuality with a sense of team spirit.

- *Initiative*—The continuous pursuit of knowledge as well as the things that are good, true and beautiful in life and nature.

- *Resilience*—The ability to bounce back from temporary defeat or setbacks and never take them personally.

- *Perserverance*—The ability to sustain a positive attitude in a sometimes predominantly negative environment.

Some qualities are either a direct outgrowth of practicing a good attitude, or are virtues that are simply not possible to master without it. They include the following:

- *Self-discipline*—The habit of routinely doing the sometimes difficult things that self-indulgent people cannot or will not do.

- *Character*—The determination to live up to our commitments long after the mood in which we made them has left us.

- *Integrity*—The instinctive practice of doing what's right whether others are aware of it or not.

- *Focus*—The ability to keep the blinders on no matter what. Blinders, after all, don't really blind us; they keep us from being distracted by obstacles so we can concentrate on our goals.

To succeed in life insurance selling and in life, we must first embrace winning philosophies. To that end, we have suggested a foundation for this lifelong task: (1) *understanding that it's not what happens to us that matters, it's how we choose to respond to what happens;* (2) awareness that all motivation is self-motivation, linked directly to our needs and our value system as it relates to the fulfillment of those needs; and (3) maintaining a good attitude, when applied to valid beliefs, that will become self-fulfilling prophecies.

SYSTEMS THAT WORK

In my view, success in life insurance selling is anchored in philosophies that win and systems that work. Just as we form our winning philosophies around sound belief systems, so should we form our sales practices around sound selling systems.

There are as many selling systems out there as there are philosophies. Our purpose here is to share with you what works best for more agents. In fact, the tandem selling systems we will examine now have gotten more and better results for life insurance agents than everything else available combined. They are Al Granum's One-Card System and Tom Wolff's Financial Need Analysis.

We will take a look at a brief overview of each of these systems, then leave you to pursue your interest in learning more about them. Both have been copyrighted and packaged and are marketed by large publishing firms, the details on which we will give you at the end of this chapter.

The One-Card System (OCS)

In 1968, the first edition of *Building a Life Insurance Clientele* was published. Written by O. Alfred Granum, CLU, it was the beginning of over a quarter century of ongoing leadership in the field of agent development by Granum and his associates. When Granum introduced the One-Card System to the life insurance industry, he launched a lifelong dual career. He built a showcase agency that validated his teachings with the highest productivity and agent retention imaginable, and then shared his teachings and experiences as a speaker, writer and teacher of life insurance agents worldwide.

The One-Card System (OCS) is designed to help an agent successfully develop a clientele and, therefore, build a successful practice. It evolved over more than 25 years of monitoring and analyzing records of prospecting activities among agents as they took qualified referrals and eventually turned them into satisfied clients.

Al Granum found that for every ten qualified referrals contacted by an agent, three fact-finding interviews resulted and one new client was acquired. This relationship of 10-3-1 holds true for agents whether they are relatively new or well established, and regardless of age, gender, size of the agency or nature of the market. (As an aside, what *has* changed is the number of times an agent must dial the phone to contact a qualified referral. In this day of answering machines at home and voice mail at the office, we must use new techniques for establishing contact.)

However, as we all know, some qualified referrals who grant interviews don't buy at that time. This doesn't mean they are not good prospects; it's just that—for whatever reason—the timing is bad. Typically, the time lag can be as long as four years. What OCS devotees have learned is that of 1,000 qualified referrals contacted, 60 buy in year one, 30 in year two and 10 in year three. Once an agent understands and then accepts these two ratios—10:3:1 and 1,000:60:30:10—he or she has the makings for building a clientele and a successful practice.

The One-Card System is the tool for managing these ratios and maximizing the available results they can deliver. It breaks the big task of building a large clientele into bite-size, digestible pieces for the agent to take on every day.

The first goal is to obtain 1,000 qualified suspects (referrals) during the agent's first year in the business. This boils down to just four per day, five days per week for 50 weeks.

These 1,000 qualified suspects should produce about 300 fact-finding interviews and eventually 100 new clients. Of course, 100 paid cases is the one surefire way to ensure success in our business. In my opinion, nothing can stop you if you pay for 100 cases per year.

Naturally, this is not the whole story. The key to building your clientele is systematic follow-up. Follow up on qualified suspects through a series of systematic callbacks and contacts, and follow up with existing clients for reviews and newer selling opportunities.

The agent starts with a suspect card when he or she gets a qualified referral. He or she records every contact with the suspect until the agent has a successful fact-finding interview. Each time the initial interview is refused, the agent asks the prospect if, as things have a way of changing, the prospect would mind being called back at a later date.

In most instances, each subsequent call builds a little more rapport and familiarity between the suspect and the agent. Eventually, resistance gives way to curiosity and an appointment is obtained. However, if after three callbacks with three requests for an appointment on each call, or if the agent cannot obtain permission to stay in touch, the suspect card is torn up and dead filed.

Once the agent has a successful fact-finding interview with the suspect, he or she replaces the suspect card in the system with a qualified prospect card. This card is retained in the system until the prospect buys. This may be imminent (as in the next interview) or it may be awhile. When good qualified prospects don't buy, it is illogical to discard them. Instead, the OCS mandates that we return their card to our system for a regular series of contacts on, say, birthdays or at an agreed-to time when they promised to reconsider buying. When qualified suspects buy, their card is then exchanged for another one giving them client status.

Of course, clients—like prospects—need to be contacted not only on birthdays or important events, but also for their annual reviews. The OCS covers all of this in painstaking detail and provides the user with all of the documentation, filing systems and procedures to ensure there will be a list of suspects, prospects and clients to contact every day. It is the best tool our industry has ever produced to keep the agent focused on his or her priorities.

There are many reports, tools and aids included in the One-Card System package. A key tool is the OCS monthly report. It monitors agent activity by tracking key functions and then assigns activity/

Figure 7.1 Activity Tracking Chart

	TELEPHONING			FROM LUNCHES				FROM ALL ACTIVITY							WRITTEN		PAID	
DAYS MO-WKD	DLD	RCHD	APPTS MADE	NO.	SUSP	FTS-CO	CL'S	SUSP	FACTS	CO'S	CL'S	EFF PTS	APPTS KEPT	ACCUM. PAID MDRT	LVS-3'S	VOL-PREM	LVS-3'S	VOL-PREM

efficiency points to each. The agent can actually distill performance down to a simple numerical value that will reflect activities and put a weight on the value of those activities. The chart that appears in Figure 7.1 was developed for agents' use as a key part of training programs for new agents.

In summary, the OCS tells an agent whom to call (qualified suspects or OCS prospects), when to call (age change, birthday or callback) and why (first, to secure appointments with qualified suspects to gather facts; second, to secure appointments with OCS prospects having birthdays, to secure referred leads and to establish if needs have changed; third, to secure appointments with OCS prospects having age changes and to open cases).

There is much, much more to the One-Card System. For more information, contact The National Underwriter Company, 505 Gest Street, Cincinnati, OH 45203, 513-721-2140 (customer service, call 800-543-0874).

Financial Need Analysis (FNA)

By sheer coincidence, in 1968—the same year Alfred Granum introduced the One-Card System to the life insurance industry—another student of selling destined to become an industry legend introduced a sales system that would become the most successful point-of-sales training system in industry history. His name was Thomas J. Wolff, and his sales system was called Capital Need Analysis, the forerunner of Financial Need Analysis (FNA), the life insurance industry's most enduring and practical sales track.

Tom Wolff's sales system has endured over time and flourishes today for several important reasons. First, it was developed in the field through years of trial and error by a tenaciously studious life insurance agent who, although intellectually brilliant, by his own admission is someone who struggled terribly to make it in the business. While other agent-teachers have dazzled their audiences with tales of sales wizardry and artful cherry-picking among the rich and famous, Tom Wolff told a much different tale. His was the story of a young agent who ran into as much bad luck as the next guy and who was willing to acknowledge his human frailties. Tom became an industry giant by identifying a basic transferrable process for success in life insurance selling and creating a sales system that would work for almost anyone. Instead of trying to achieve his place in industry lore by showing everyone how good he was, he taught his students how easy it can be. In the process, he became the most credible and believable role model for new agents our industry has produced.

FNA is, and always has been, a needs-driven sales system, meaning that its purpose is not to create a sale based upon the salient points of the product (the solution) but rather to analyze needs and determine how life insurance can meet those needs (the problem). This is a fundamental distinction between FNA and many of the point-of-sale software and illustration products out there today. FNA helps the agent sell the right amount of life insurance to the client for the right reasons. In today's environment, agents cannot afford the legal exposure of makeshift or piecemeal sales practices or illustration software. We must have a complete, comprehensive selling system. We must do a needs-based analysis for our clients and generate recommendations we can defend and explain to critics if necessary. FNA focused on this important value many years before it became fashionable to do so.

The FNA sales system is focused on needs for another reason, too. In addition to needs being the best reason for a client to buy life insurance, it is also the best reason to sell life insurance. Sales based upon greed—meaning big returns on premium dollars paid—can be made by a lot of people other than life insurance agents. When we are making a greed sale, we are selling returns. As we have already pointed out, we are just selling configurations of numbers on a piece of paper. Selling numbers on paper can be done by stockbrokers, bankers and even accountants. This, in fact, is the basis on which many from these professions plan to enter our business. Selling a genuine need for life insurance is another matter. Needs selling is the thing that makes life insurance agents necessary; greed selling is the thing that could make them extinct!

Client analysis selling is only part of the story. FNA is much more than the uncovering of needs; it is a complete needs-based selling system. FNA uses a single method for obtaining the appointment, opening the interview and gathering factual data for all types of prospects. At the end of the fact-finding process, a joint decision is made between the prospect and the agent as to which financial cornerstone is the top priority. Once this decision is made, the data gathered provides a separate needs analysis for life, disability, accumulation and retirement planning. The FNA sales system breaks the sales process down into carefully engineered, bite-size pieces that agents can master one step at a time.

Preapproach This step is to get an appointment under favorable conditions for a face-to-face meeting. FNA offers proven methods to accomplish this objective and utilizes an extremely effective method to obtain referred leads.

Approach FNA utilizes the compelling power of visuals through point-of-sale software to help the agent make a favorable impression and gain positive interest from the prospect.

Problem The opening presentation shows the general financial problems most people have so that prospects begin to recognize the need. Then the problem is personalized to arouse interest in a possible solution.

Presenting FNA pictorially creates desire through vivid computer-generated graphics that create a desire to solve the problem by showing advantages of planning.

Close Both logic and responsible emotion are employed to motivate a prospect to action.

A great benefit of FNA is that it works effectively only when used as it is designed to be used. Because the system builds on itself in terms of both content and data, it is most effective when used from start to finish; shortcuts undermine the effectiveness of the process. What's more, if an agent follows the FNA system from start to finish, no one can ever realistically accuse him or her of less than professional point-of-sale practices. Today, this is no minor consideration!

Each step of the FNA sales process has been honed and polished over the years into the most eloquent prose in the world of selling. Each phrase, graphic concept and probing question has been field-tested by thousands of successful agents and managers. This is no canned sales talk; it is a selling system that has been refined over time through constant feedback given by Tom Wolff's legendary following of leading life insurance agents.

FNA goes into great detail in analyzing needs and creating recommendations that are based upon airtight logic and responsibly arrived at conclusions. As we have already emphasized, it is important that today's life insurance agent not only use objective and sound analysis to arrive at the proposed course of action, but that he or she also be able to provide a well-documented "paper trail" as to what transpired in the interview and what logic was employed to arrive at proposed solutions. With FNA, the agent is comforted by the goal of fair treatment of all involved, supported by a 25-year track record of sound sales practices.

The FNA system is characterized by the recognition of accurate needs by professional analysis. Through careful fact-finding, information is gathered about the prospect's desire to provide income to family members in the event of premature death or disability. The same is done for retirement planning. The goals are those of the prospect, not the agent.

Then an analysis is performed based upon the prospect's views about timetables, interest rates and inflation assumptions. FNA is truly an interactive sales process that lets prospects participate in creating their own solutions to their needs based upon what they consider important.

Business and Estate Analysis and Review

Once the agent has mastered the basic FNA system, he or she can advance to Business and Estate Analysis and Review (BEAR). This sales system was developed in the late 1980s by Tom Wolff to help agents to grow into the next step smoothly. The BEAR system gives the agent a way to make an almost seamless transition from the "kitchen table" market into business insurance and estate planning. Business owners and individuals with large estates have many unique problems and opportunities that can be addressed by the insurance professional.

The BEAR system provides the agent an approach to the business owner that is designed to get an initial interview based upon a 15-minute "Business and Financial Checkup" (BFC). On this initial interview, the agent is able to quickly qualify the suspect with regard to 12 business- and estate-planning needs.

1. Transition of business ownership

2. Optimizing personal benefits

3. Key-people maximizing benefits

4. Buy/sell planning

5. Key-person insurance

6. Section 303 redemption

7. Deferred compensation

8. Split-dollar

9. Disability

10. Executive bonus

11. Estate planning

12. Liquidity needs

One of the most important benefits of the BEAR system is that after the need has been uncovered, agents with limited experience can bring an expert or their manager to a second meeting for a complete business or estate fact-finding interview. Like FNA, the BEAR system provides a fully scripted data-gathering interview, complete with third-party influences and point-of-sale software that graphically supports the problems and opportunities of sound planning.

In most cases, newer or intermediate-level agents willing to learn the FNA and BEAR systems can save literally years of trial-and-error learning in the "school of hard knocks." It is important that agents understand the difference between a "canned" sales talk and a structured sales process. FNA and BEAR provide the agent with the framework for doing it right. Every base will be covered, every sale that could have been made will be made. There will never be reason to second-guess yourself as to whether you gave it your best. There is no better sales procedure. In that respect, our profession is no different from that of a doctor: There are certain universally accepted steps that must be taken to ensure a successful and properly done procedure. For my money, OCS, FNA and BEAR are foundation systems of a successful practice for the year 2000 and beyond. They only seem to get better as time and success story after success story validate them as the industry standard for professional selling.

For more information on FNA and BEAR, contact: Vernon Publishing, P.O. Box 2200, Vernon, CT 06066, 203-643-7799.

8

The Agent as a Businessperson

"We are not paid for how hard we work, we are paid for the results we get."

—Jack Kinder, Jr.

The biggest failures among life insurance agents are not those who don't do enough business to succeed financially. It is those who sell so much that they lose sight of *how to succeed financially.*

I used to have a framed statement on my credenza titled "Schulte's Law." It stated, "The annual standard of living for most life insurance agents is determined by taking their best month and multiplying it by 12!" In fact, my best advice on this subject is that agents should set their annual standard of living by multiplying their *worst* month by 12! Actually, the business of managing profitability goes far beyond the management of income. Income is what is left after the process of selling and servicing is complete. It's what the agent pays himself or herself after everyone else has been taken care of, both present and future. You see, as a proprietor, you must take care of not only the person you are today, but also the retired person you will someday be.

When we sell our product, we often show the frightening statistics on the financial condition of our aging population. Then we might ask the prospect, "Would you agree that the best person to take care of the person you someday will be is the person you are today?" In the next chapter, we will deal with this subject in greater detail.

As we examine the subject of profitability and later move on to the topics of service, creating equity in your practice and selling your practice, let's step outside of the traditional viewpoint of a life insurance agent. Instead of looking at you as a sole proprietor, let's look at you as a Fortune 500 company.

We have all read about the great entrepreneurs who started out as sole proprietors and then lost control of their companies when they broke into the Fortune 500. Thomas Edison, Henry Ford and Steven Jobs all struggled terribly with this transition. Well, suppose they had managed their companies as if they were giants right from the start. Impossible, you say? Look at what Fred Smith has done with Federal Express, what Bill Gates has done with Microsoft or what Sam Walton did with Wal-Mart. It is possible for certain entrepreneurs to make the transition from sole proprietorship to Fortune 500 company.

I'm not suggesting that your insurance practice can become the next Wal-Mart, although some industry legends might think I'm underestimating them. The point is that if you manage it right from the start, it will never grow to the point where it gets away from you.

So, as we look at the subject of profitability, let's look at our practice as a microcosm of a Fortune 500 corporation. Initially, divisions of your company might be only drawers in your file cabinet. Eventually, each drawer may become the full-time job for a staff member. Beyond that, I'll leave it to your imagination—but you get the idea.

MANAGING PROFITS

Let's call the practice of operating your business like a big corporation the "Rule of 500."

First, understand that a profitable practice is not related to production alone. *Commissions are not profits, they are revenues!*

There are only two ways to increase profits in a life insurance practice: Increase revenues or decrease expenses. I hope you will be effective at both.

Sources of Revenue

Commissions I define first-year commissions as the purest expression of your company's gratitude to you for putting business on the books. Companies pay what they need to pay to get the job done and not one dollar more if they can help it. This is as it should be if the companies wish to prosper and grow. It is your responsibility to understand every aspect of the compensation schedules in your contract. Remember the Rule of 500—learn to look at your commission revenues the same way Procter & Gamble or Wal-Mart examines the profitability of their businesses.

By line of business. Even though you will have an area of specialization, you are likely to sell a lot of different products to your clients over the years. Like large corporations, you'll want to develop product lines that complement one another. If, for example, you work with doctors, you'll want to put a lot of emphasis on disability income, because this is a huge seller in that market. Most physicians have invested a fortune in their education and at least a dozen years of their time. They understand death and are willing to insure their lives, but they genuinely fear disability and consider it a must to insure their capacity to earn a living. Therefore, disability is a must in your product line if you work with doctors.

It is also important to have different lines of product, because times change. Using our doctor example, changes in such things as trends in malpractice litigation, national health care and qualified retirement plans for the self-employed will all affect their choices in the insurance products they buy.

Finally, if your chosen market is subject to cycles, downward pressure on compensation, or declines in demand due to economic or legislative changes, you may wish to hedge your bets by offering an expanded product line. If, for example, you work with contractors and others in the construction business, you may need products such as security bonds, workmen's compensation or inexpensive term insurance to cover large construction loans.

By type of plan. Different policies pay different commissions. You should be familiar with how these differences affect your profits. The products you sell can differ significantly in the amount of commission they generate and the way that compensation is paid out.

While I hope you will always make recommendations based upon what is best for the client, you still must be aware of the profit margins on various products. This is simply good business.

For example, universal life products tend to pay a larger first-year commission and a smaller renewal, while whole life contracts tend to pay a slightly lower first-year commission with a stronger renewal. Interest-sensitive whole life tends to pay high commissions for both first year and renewal.

Are these discrepancies based on higher or lower competitive values to the consumer? Not necessarily. Actually, they usually have to do with the flexibility of the contract. As a general rule, the more freedom the policyholder requires in earlier years with regard to the scheduling of premium payments and access to cash values in the form of loans or surrenders, the lower the commission. Conversely, if the policyholder has the ability and intent to pay required minimum annual premiums with limited access to cash in early years, the ultimate values can be just as attractive as those of the more flexible contracts with lower commissions. There are a lot of other reasons an agent might select one plan over another for a client, but it is naive to think that commissions are not a part of the equation. The issue is whether the role of commissions in the choice is practical and professional or selfish and greedy. If you understand the profit margins in your business and require a fair and reasonable profit for the amount of work and overhead you must allocate to a given sale, you are no different from any other professional. After all, every doctor, lawyer and accountant you know probably arrives at a fair hourly billing rate by taking into account their fixed and variable expenses as well as the value of their time, not the least of which is the years of preparation that make the quality of their advice worth paying for. You have every right to do the same.

Cheaper insurance products than those you sell are, no doubt, available to your clients elsewhere. So is cheaper advice, but they will get what they pay for. If they call it to your attention, explain why you are worth what you charge and remind them that it's a free country. If they want to comparison shop, they can do so. On the other hand, you should have a compensation strategy in place that is consistent and can be comfortably defended should it be challenged.

By size of sale. Generally, big sales pay big commissions. They also tend to be more complicated, take longer and involve more competition. Be sure when looking at the profitability of a sale that you properly allocate your overhead. For example, as we discussed in the market focus section, certain markets require a great deal of specialized resources. The purchase of computers, software and support staff are all more important in the big-case market. Case preparation tends to be very labor-intensive if properly done. Thus, on the larger cases, although the absolute dollar amount of commissions is usually much greater, the net amount after expense allocations as a percentage of premium is usually somewhat less.

In addition to expenses, commissions are also affected by downward pressures on the percentages payable. This comes from two sources. First, companies must reduce commission percentages on certain products targeted at older insureds, such as second-to-die, in order to compete. With these products, it is simply not possible for companies to have enough time to recover commission loads from future premiums and still offer a competitive product. Life insurance works best as a long-term purchase. When people with short life expectancies buy it, something has to give.

The second downward pressure on commission schedules comes from the outside advisers and consultants who are sometimes involved in big cases. For example, in the corporate-owned life insurance market (COLI), accounting firms or compensation specialists commonly target an acceptable load into the product they want and ask various insurance companies to design a customized product that meets their specifications. Other times, clients will pressure the agent into giving a "legal" rebate or waiving commissions if they think the compensation is excessive or a product with lower loads is available to them elsewhere. These practices are becoming more and more acceptable in the competitive world in which we live.

All of these conditions are part of the realities of the big-case market. They certainly haven't been debilitating to the agents operating in these markets, who seem to be doing as well as ever, but they should be a consideration in the business planning of every successful agent.

By acquisition costs (costs per piece of business). Do some simple modeling to find out how you want to amortize your expenses over your book of business. This will be a real eye-opener. You will be able to test the effect on profit of an increase in case rate or in average premium. It can be a great motivator for improved performance.

As we have pointed out, certain types of business will use more of your time, overhead and resources. Know your cost of doing business. Then, using your average-size premium, take a look at what an increase in case rate will do to your acquisition costs and the resulting increase it will have on profits.

Every life insurance company knows what its acquisition costs are and how those costs are affected by an increase in paid cases or in average premium per case. You should know the same thing about your book of business. It will be a great source of motivation when planning your year to see how dramatic the impact of a 20 percent increase in premium per case and a 20 percent increase in case rate will be on your bottom line.

Renewals It has been my experience that most agents significantly undervalue the role of renewals in the building of a successful life insurance practice. This is partially due to the newer products in recent years, some of which pay lower renewals. Specifically, universal life and variable life generally pay a lower renewal than traditional whole life does. Still, your renewals are important to building a valuable practice. Remember, as the appeal of life insurance as a wealth accumulation vehicle continues to grow, the average premium will grow and, with it, the renewal commissions. In effect, the trend in renewals is a smaller percentage of a larger number.

It is incumbent upon the agent to know exactly how renewals work on every type of product sold. The term *renewals* is generally used to include the additional category of service fees, although service fees are actually a separate part of your contract.

Renewals are a portion of the commission that is deferred past the first year and is contingent upon the company receiving renewal premiums in later years. Because there is an inverse relationship between lapsation and profitability to the company in early policy years, it is worthwhile for the company to pay the agent additional reduced commission in early years (usually two to ten) on renewal premiums. The company hopes these payments will motivate the agent to stay close to the policyholder and ensure the payment of premiums until it becomes a habit and until the company has turned a profit on that particular piece of business.

Beyond the tenth year or so, companies usually pay a service fee to the agent or agency for handling any problems or questions that may arise, such as a change of address, change of beneficiary or policy loan request. Although usually modest, service fees can build up to a considerable amount over time on a large book of business. Agents should learn to budget their resources in the policyholder service department of their practice in such a way as to make service a profit center.

Vesting. An important consideration in any discussion of renewals is vesting. Most life insurance companies have a vesting schedule with regard to that portion of the agent's renewals that will continue to be paid to the agent should he or she leave the company at a given point.

As a general rule, vesting schedules are a direct function of the company's investment in the agent. One can probably look at vesting the way we look at surrender values in a life insurance contract. As we discussed in some detail in Chapter 3, life insurance companies incur acquisition costs when they put a piece of business on the books. If the policyholder surrenders the policy before the company has recovered its expenses, there is usually a surrender charge or a reduced policy value that is less than the insured paid in.

The acquisition costs for an agent are similar. If a company recruits, trains and develops an agent, it may take several years of solid production before the relationship generates a profit. If the agent leaves and applies those newly acquired skills elsewhere or leaves the business entirely, the company will likely hold all or a portion of the agent's renewals to recover its investment. On the other hand, if an agent stays with a company until the relationship has become a profitable one, then the company usually is willing to vest him or her in renewals, meaning commission will continue to be paid even though the agent has left the company.

I point this out because I have often seen agents become excited when a competitor offers them a "fully vested contract." There's nothing wrong with this, but the agent should understand that the only reason the competing company can do this is because it is not likely to invest any money in the agent's development. The nature of such a relationship is, therefore, going to be much different without the involvement, the dedication of money and resources, and the personal touch of sales management. Agents should be prepared for this should they decide to make such a move.

Persistency and quality business bonuses. The term *quality business* generally refers to the mortality experience and the persistency of a block of business. Any product actuary will tell you that the impact of persistency on the profitability of a given block of business can be dramatic. If the home office underwriters do their job and the agent is thorough and honest in the role of field underwriter, clients should die pretty much as expected. When an agent delivers policyholders to a company who keep their insurance and live as long as expected at the time of issue, the benefit to the carrier is substantial. Most companies want to recognize this with persistency and quality business bonuses. If you have such bonuses in your contract, congratulations! If you do not, you still will be rewarded because of the higher renewals paid to you because more of your policyholders renew each year.

If you want to develop a real sense of urgency about the importance of good persistency, do some modeling comparing how your contract will pay you overtime on a couple of good years of production if you have 95 percent persistency as opposed to 75 percent. It will motivate you to emphasize the service side of your practice in a hurry!

Volume bonuses and special services. Most companies and agencies want all of their agents' business, or at least the right of first refusal. For reasons we will discuss in the next chapter, I believe this is also usually in the agent's best interest. Of course, you must be your clients' representative, and you must feel the company you recommend is in their best interest. All other factors being equal, you can usually do the best job for your clients if you put them with a company that you know and are known by, whose people and products you are comfortable with and with whom you have some influence.

Because companies want as much of your business as they can get, they frequently offer incentives to bigger producers in the form of cash bonuses or special services. These perks are something today's agent will want to pay special attention to. They can make a compensation package that is run-of-the-mill for the mediocre agent into a pair of golden handcuffs for the exceptional producer.

Volume bonuses are usually paid at certain break points, such as $50,000, $100,000 or $250,000 of first-year premium annually. They are usually tied to persistency and also require a minimum number of paid cases annually. Volume bonuses are clear-cut, usually easy to understand and embrace a basic tenet of sales management: Because 80 percent of the business is produced by 20 percent of the people, give the rewards to the 20 percent who are making a difference.

A more subtle, but perhaps even more important form of volume bonus comes when companies or agencies provide special services for their top producers. All agents should be given an equal opportunity to succeed, but for my money, the exceptional performer should expect—and deserves—exceptional treatment. Special services usually come in the form of such things as secretarial services, office space, telephone and fax, postage, and allowances for CLU and ChFC courses and attendance at industry meetings. Of course, we should also mention the most popular perk of all for successful agents—paid attendance at industry sales conventions. These meetings typically cost the company several thousand dollars per attendee and should never be taken for granted. They are a wonderful benefit that is unique to our industry.

Other perks for the top performers can include co-op advertising allowances, club and association dues, visits to the home office and whatever else can be reasonably provided to reward superior performance.

A word of caution: When a successful agent squeezes the profit margins on his or her manager or company, the relationship is strained, and much more can be lost than gained. Before you go back to ask for more than is reasonable, think how you would feel if all of your clients knew your exact commission on everything you sold them and demanded what they perceived to be 100 cents on every dollar of service in return! You deserve to profit from your clients if you do a good job for them, and you will. If your agency and company do a good job for you, they, too, deserve to profit from the relationship.

Supplemental revenues. Many agents are able to charge fees for the planning work they do for clients even if it does not necessarily result in the purchase of insurance. There is also a growing number of fee-based products appearing on the market, most notably in the COLI and deferred compensation area.

Other agents have been able to generate considerable revenues from the fact that they have become well-known in their marketplace. Most significant, joint work can become a great source of supplemental income. We put this in a separate category from regular commissions, because joint work usually means the client relationship belongs to the person who calls you in, or in some cases, instead of splitting the case, the agent receives a finder's fee.

For many established, successful agents, speaking at industry meetings and functions for a fee can generate supplemental income as well as stimulate joint work activity. Many would be surprised at the amount of income the industry's leading agents garner by packaging themselves and telling their stories to the rest of the industry.

Finally, each agent can choose among several ways to supplement income by selling noninsurance financial planning products, such as mutual funds, limited partnerships and other investment-oriented products. Depending upon your licensing, qualifications and comfort level, you may want to consider one of these areas as a way to supplement your life insurance income.

Your second paycheck. In any discussion of revenue, we should always consider the value of any fringe benefits provided by the carrier you represent. It's difficult to back into a present dollar value to add to this year's revenue stream for things like health insurance, pension plans, deferred compensation, life insurance and other employee benefits. I will say that agents almost always seem to undervalue these benefits, especially when a competitor is dangling a high commission schedule in front of them. This can be a serious mistake. I can't tell you what dollar amount your fringe benefit package should be assigned in determining a value to add to your revenue calculations, but the human resources department of your company can give you a good idea.

All of these things then, make up the gross revenues from your life insurance practice: commissions, renewals, bonuses, fees, special services and fringe benefits. Therefore, to determine the profits each year, we must do a profit-and-loss statement (P&L) like any Fortune 500 company. Let's briefly look at how we might approach this task.

First of all, a life insurance practice, like any other business, has fixed costs and variable costs. The fixed are those that tend to stay the same whether you sell anything or not, such as automobile, rent and basic secretarial help, or tend to increase moderately with production, such as telephone and additional clerical support. Variable expenses are those that are the direct result of making a sale, such as medical examinations for applicants, policy wallets and the lunch you bought the client when you delivered the policy.

Some areas are gray, but you should try to break all of your expenses down into accounts or categories and assign a series of numbers to them so you can track results and compare them to sales. There are many simple software packages available to help you with this task. Figure 8.1 shows the type of output you will be able to generate either monthly or at least quarterly.

As your practice grows, you will no doubt want to become more sophisticated in your analysis of expenses as they relate to revenues. You will also want to track expenses to various lines and types of business, as we have discussed. In our simple example here, we can learn a great deal as we transfer the information over to simple graphics, available through most software vendors, that show us how sensitive our profits are to increases and decreases in sales. The same graphics can show the effect of persistency on profits.

In Figure 8.2, we see that our basic profit margins at our current level of production in the third quarter are 39 percent (divide the Operating Income of $22,050 by the Net Revenues of $56,200). In other words, for every dollar of revenue generated by our practice, we take home 39 cents.

YOUR KEY OFFICE PERSON

It is hard to measure the impact of superior service on the profitability of your practice. We do know that it is substantial. Obviously, better persistency is one immediate result of good service. Yet I tend to think there are several benefits that, when added up, are even greater.

Figure 8.1 Sample Quarterly P&L

John Sellmore, CLU, ChFC
3rd Quarter, 1995

INCOME

Account #	Description	Q1	Q2	Q3
2111	Life Sales	25,000	20,000	35,000
2222	Disability Sales	2,500	3,500	5,000
2333	Mutual Funds	1,500	6,000	3,500
2444	Renewals	4,500	5,500	5,700
2555	Bonuses	2,500	1,500	2,500
2666	Fringe Benefits	2,500	2,500	2,500
2777	Fees	0	1,000	1,500
2888	Other	500	500	500
Net Revenues (A)		39,000	40,500	56,200

VARIABLE EXPENSES

Account #	Description	Q1	Q2	Q3
3100	Meals	2,200	1,700	2,300
3200	Automobile	1,500	1,500	1,500
3300	Entertainment (other than meals)	500	600	800
3400	Birthday and Holiday Gifts	1,200	200	250
3500	Split Commissions	5,000	0	15,000
3600	Policy Wallets	250	200	300
3700	Client Newsletter	300	300	300
Total Variable Expenses (B)		10,950	4,500	20,450
Gross Profit (C) = (A – B)		28,050	36,000	35,750

FIXED EXPENSES

Account #	Description	Q1	Q2	Q3
4100	Key Office Person (agent's share)	5,500	5,500	5,500
4200	Telephone and Fax	1,400	1,800	1,800
4300	Rent (agent's share)	2,600	2,600	2,600
4400	Postage	400	500	600
4500	Copier	100	150	250

Figure 8.1 (Continued)

Account #	Description	Q1	Q2	Q3
4600	Printing and Office Supplies	300	600	800
4700	Educational Fees and Dues	250	250	350
4800	Depreciation	800	800	800
4900	Miscellaneous	1,000	1,000	1,000
	Total 4000 Series Expenses (D)	12,350	13,200	13,700
	Operating Income (E) = (C − D)	15,700	22,800	22,050

Today, among all Americans, there is a growing expectation of better service. With all of the pressure they get on their limited savings dollars, people know they have choices. The fact is that you must service your clients or you will lose them. The opportunity is that if you do an outstanding job of servicing your clients, they will not only stay with you, they will take care of you!

To manage service properly, we must apply our rule of 500 and look at service as a profit center within our enterprise. We can do this because, if we manage it right, service will pay big dividends through good persistency and more and bigger sales.

We've already discussed the benefits of good persistency. Service can generate more sales because your clients will buy an average of seven insurance policies over the course of their lifetimes, and if you stay in touch, there's no reason they shouldn't make every purchase from you. They'll buy bigger policies, because as they mature and succeed in life, their needs will grow.

Finally, even if you never sold them another policy, satisfied clients are a golden resource; they generate the highest quality of referred leads you can obtain anywhere. Prospecting is your life blood and your number-one job. Referrals are the unchallenged top category of leading prospects. If all you accomplish with your clients in their annual review is to obtain four or five good referrals, your biggest problem as an agent is solved.

Figure 8.2 Sample Quarterly P&L in Graph Format

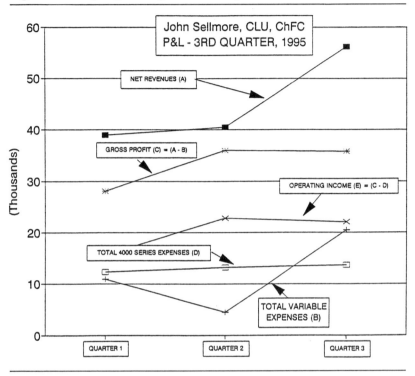

Let's look at a few keys to building your service profit center. Your executive assistant, or key office person (KOP), is the person who will eventually become the chief operating officer of your practice. Of course, the actual person occupying this post may change several times as your practice grows. Initially, it may be your spouse or a part-time high school student. Ultimately, it may be a part owner in your practice, with a CLU and ChFC behind his or her name, who manages a staff and does virtually everything you do except prospect, get appointments, fact-find and close.

Once you settle on who your KOP will be, it will be important to show this person a career path that may ultimately lead to sharing in the profits and learning the business from ground zero to a level that rivals that of most successful agents. However, the KOP's one-sentence job description will never change: "Do what it takes to keep the agent focused on those key functions of the job that are essential to success."

Outstanding producers I have worked with all have that key person, that "watchdog" who keeps them on track. Your KOP will become your confidant, critic, supporter and protector. Start simply with a part-time job you fill at the minimum wage. As your practice grows, the KOP position will grow, and when it's big enough, you will find the person who can fill it and grow with you. For now, let's start by identifying those functions your KOP will be responsible for.

Processing Prospects

We never delegate the key function of prospecting, but when we return to the office with the golden harvest of a day's worth of referred leads, certain actions should be taken.

The One-Card System, or whatever system you use, should be constantly monitored and updated by your KOP. Referrals, callbacks, reviews and all other "automatics" with regard to prospect and client contact should be assembled and put in front of you daily by your KOP.

Other activities involving new prospects you may want your KOP to handle include confirming appointments, sending a follow-up letter after the initial interview and even traveling to the prospect's home or attorney's office to pick up policies, wills, trusts and other documents.

Once a name is given to your KOP, it should enter a system that causes it to pop up on a regular basis as a suspect (callback), prospect (case in process), applicant (case in underwriting), client (policy-holder) or reject (not worth pursuing). Your KOP should navigate you through each step of the process.

Case Assembly

This may well be your KOP's most valuable and challenging task. It's second chronologically, but it's probably the last step you'll turn over to your KOP.

All clients' needs are different and each proposal you make should be customized to their needs, but the process for case analysis and for building your proposal should be consistent and transferable. Just as a highly successful lawyer walks into court backed by the research and preparation of the law clerks back at the firm, or a top surgeon walks into the operating room to perform a procedure on a patient someone else already has cut open and will suture up, you will eventually want your KOP to pull the case together for your presentation.

Of course, even when your KOP is as skilled as you in the analysis of needs and the preparation of recommendations, you will always want to review every detail of the proposal ahead of time to assure that everything is perfect. Inspect everything that is going to be put before a prospect, no matter who does it. And, because no one should ever edit his or her own work, on those occasions when you have built a case, be sure to have your KOP inspect your work!

Processing New Applicants

The new-business function is often not given adequate attention by agents. Many feel that their job is mostly over when the prospect agrees to buy. True, the lion's share of the selling may be done by this point, provided the applicant can easily qualify at the applied-for rate and the underwriting process goes quickly and smoothly. Even then, smart agents will go through the key points of the presentation all over again upon delivery of the policy.

The point at which your KOP will step in on the new-business process will vary. Some agents want to do everything up to the point of submitting the application, then have their KOPs push it through underwriting and turn the issued policy over to them for delivery. Others want to get a verbal OK or handshake from the prospect, then have their KOPs follow them in to complete the application and handle every other step until the policy is ready for delivery.

In either case, it is essential that your KOP be a licensed agent. No activity in your organization should be handled by anyone other than a licensed agent.

Processing New Clients

The point at which an applicant becomes a client is technically when the case has been settled and the commission has been paid. For purposes of breaking down your KOP functions, I suggest that this imaginary line is crossed when the policy is approved and comes out of the policy issue department.

In this phase of the new-business process, your KOP will typically schedule the policy delivery, go over any requirements or amendments with you, and be sure the policy is settled and commissions are forthcoming.

The client's file will now move from the pending file to the permanent file with other policyholders. Systems will be put in place for birthdays, annual reviews and holidays as well as inclusion in the agent's quarterly newsletter.

Other KOP Functions in the New-Business Process

You will want your KOP to facilitate each step in the new-business process by following up each significant event with a phone call, letter or other communication. A standard but personalized letter or telephone script should be developed and used by your KOP on each key occasion in the sales process. Figures 8.3 through 8.5 are examples of standard letters for the preapproach contact, appointment confirmation and following the closing interview.

SECRETS OF SERVICE

Continuing with our approach of running your practice like a microcosm of a Fortune 500 company, you will want to have a first-rate policyholders' service department. In my experience, there are actu-

Figure 8.3 Preapproach Letter

(Send to each referral before you call for an appointment.)

Dear Mr. Watkins:

For the last three years, John Sellmore has helped me analyze my business and estate problems with a financial planning service. I have asked him to contact you because I am impressed with his concepts and believe that you might be interested in them.

Obviously, I am not familiar with your personal and business finances. However, most people are aware of high income and estate taxes and are seeking individually designed solutions to these problems.

Whether or not you have any need of John's professional advice, I am sure you will find the visit stimulating and rewarding.

Sincerely,

(signed by Center of Influence)

---

ally two phases to the policyholder service issue: the basics of good professional service and the secret of going the extra mile. First, let's look at the basics that must be in place before we can learn about going the extra mile.

Policyholder Inquiries

Every policyholder inquiry should be either answered the day it is made or responded to with a commitment as to when an answer can be expected. The fax machine is an economical way to get answers from your home office that can, in turn, be faxed to the client.

Figure 8.4 Appointment Confirmation Letter

(Send after you have secured an initial appointment.)

Dear Bill:

It was a pleasure making your acquaintance over the phone.

Enclosed is some information about me and the work I have done for people like John Jones and others.

I look forward to meeting you on Tuesday, April 17, at 4 PM in your office.

Best wishes,

Note: This letter should be followed up by a confirmation phone call from your KOP an hour or so before the appointment to inform the prospect that you are on your way and expect to arrive on time.

The commitment to a prompt, accurate, cheerful response to every client inquiry or need should be fundamental in all that you do.

If your clients feel you have an interest in them and care about their success, they won't leave you for a lower rate or better deal. Your KOP or staff should see to it that each client hears from you at least quarterly. This communication can be newsletters, new product ideas or just a simple phone call.

Many agents have holiday open houses or even host events such as golf tournaments for key clients. Eventually, you will want to do something special for your important clients.

Figure 8.5 Post–Closing Interview Letters

(These letters are designed to suit all three of the possible circumstances that may follow a closing interview.)

<u>Congratulations</u>

Dear Jerry:

Today does not seem too soon to congratulate you on the tax-advantaged retirement plan you've started. It certainly is a big step in establishing a sound financial program that will benefit you in the years ahead.

I wanted to take this opportunity to thank you again for your business and wish you every success.

Best wishes,

<u>Think It Over</u>

Dear Eric:

I sincerely appreciate your time and willingness to share your financial goals and concerns with me last Monday.

I am confident that once you and Nancy have taken an objective look at the program the three of us designed, you will want to go ahead with it.

I will call you next Monday to arrange an appointment, if need be, to answer any further questions you may have.

Meanwhile, I have enclosed some information on [retirement planning, mortgage protection, estate tax rates, etc.] that will help you with your decision.

Best wishes,

Figure 8.5 (Continued)

<u>Put It Off</u>

Dear Judy:

Thanks for showing your confidence in me yesterday by discussing your financial plans in detail. I can understand your reluctance to immediately agree to my proposal for setting up [a retirement plan, health insurance, etc.].

As we agreed, I'll be in touch in six months to set up an appointment for us to review your situation.

I'd like you to know that when we do get together again, it will not be for an idle visit. The reason will be something that has a direct, important bearing on your financial security.

Best wishes,

<u>Policy Delivery</u>
(Confirmation)

Dear Bob:

As Jo Ann explained to you over the phone today, your policy has been issued exactly as we applied for it.

Congratulations!

I will review all of the details when I deliver it at your office on Tuesday, May 21, at 2:30 PM.

Have a great day!

Figure 8.5 Post–Closing Interview Letters (Continued)

<u>Postdelivery</u>

(Thanks for buying and thanks for the referrals.)

Dear Tom:

Once again, thank you!

Not just for the confidence you've shown by selecting me as your insurance adviser, but by referring me to John, George and Elaine.

I'll let you know how we get on together and I promise I will do my best to be helpful to them and earn their trust.

Best wishes,

The Management of Referrals

It's no secret that successful practices are built around referrals from satisfied clients. Given the importance of referrals, a system must be put into place to maximize the benefit of this precious resource.

We have already discussed this topic, but it bears revisiting. When the agent brings in a referral, it should trigger the following activities by the KOP:

- A thank-you letter to the client promising to report the results

- A preapproach letter to the referral, including your image brochure

- After the sale, a thank-you gift and letter to the client, including a request for more referrals

- A letter to the new client reminding him or her of how you met and asking that he or she do the same for someone else (to be sent before the policy delivery)

YOUR COMMISSION ACCOUNTING DEPARTMENT

Commissions are the primary source of revenue in your practice. We have discussed how we measure and optimize commissions; now let's briefly look at how we manage commissions.

Managing Persistency

The best way to good persistency is selecting the right prospect and selling him or her the right product for the right reasons. Beyond that, we must recognize that the most important thing you can do is jump—and jump hard—on every late or missed premium. The key to persistency management is quick reaction time. This is your KOP's opportunity to shine!

One Top of the Table agent I work with tells me his first rule in persistency management is not to wait until the company tells him there's a problem. By then, it's often too late. Instead, he says that the KOP's procedure should be triggered by your commission renewal statement. He wrote a simple PC program that allows his KOP to cross-check company statements the day they arrive and identify every missed premium.

Let your KOP make the first call to ask if there's a problem. If there is, then you step in. As a friend of mine likes to say, "If you overreact to the smoke in your business, you'll never have a fire."

If your clients know they will be hearing from you within days of a missed premium, they may choose to miss some other payment. If it's because of replacement, you will nip it early on and be able to save the case. You will probably still have a lapse on occasion, but when you do, you can let it go and move on, because you will know that if the case could have been saved, it would have been saved.

Managing New Commissions

The payment of a new case should trigger a series of checks and balances with your KOP. The first is a careful check to ensure an accurate commission payment. Home office personnel are only human; they make mistakes, and when they do, it's usually at settlement of the case and it's not always in your favor. At settlement, a separate record should be set up to track the renewal commissions on the case as they come due. This may sound superfluous, but I've seen many examples of how well this practice pays off for those agents who take the time to check and double-check every commission statement.

Managing Profits

We've always been told that we must pour profits back into our business if we are to build a successful practice. This is an incorrect statement. Most of us are spoiled when we come into the business, because the company that hires us finances our initial years with subsidies and continues to pick up various expenses ranging from office space and telephone costs to health insurance and retirement plans. Then, as we get our practices off the ground, we find we are expected to pay for an ever-increasing portion of our overhead.

Sometimes we complain about it. When we do, it is a classic case of seeing the glass as half-empty rather than as half-full. If we are lucky enough to be with a company that not only provides training but also helps finance us into the business, we are truly fortunate. However, we must understand that some of our reserves should be used to pick up our expenses before we even determine our profits. In other words, we're not investing our profits back into our business when we use commission revenue to pay for things like automobile expenses and entertainment. These are costs of doing business. After we have calculated our profits, we then decide what to do with them. Most will be taken out of our practice in the form of compensation. However, some may be used for the purchase of a new wardrobe or our education through LUTC or CLU. These are examples of investing in our business—doing those things that build a foundation for growth—as opposed to merely paying for those things that are the cost of doing business today.

Thus we have those expenses that are automatic—in effect, the cost of goods sold. Then we have those items that are optional—an investment of present profits for future growth—new plant and equipment.

The easiest time to discipline ourselves to set aside these funds is at the time our commissions are paid. One good approach is to have your accountant act as your payroll deduction administrator. After your accountant pays your bills, he or she can set aside an agreed-to additional percentage of profits to be earmarked for reinvestment into the business.

GOING THE EXTRA MILE

As it pertains to clients, "going the extra mile" means simply doing more than is expected (and more than your competition is willing to do) with regard to the way you run your business.

Over the years, I have studied leading life insurance people all over the world. Although they are all quite different, there are certain qualities, values and practices that they seem to possess in common. Going the extra mile in servicing their clients is the most universal quality I have identified. Following are just a few of the actual practices I have observed among leading agents. Obviously, you will not want to adopt all of them at earlier points in your practice and, in fact, you shouldn't. What you may want to do is pick up an idea or concept from some or all of them to try out in your practice.

Top 250 Club

While visiting Top of the Table agent Greg Acosta a while back, I noticed a set of about a dozen very thick, leather-bound ring binders along the back of his credenza. Each had a name embossed in gold on the spine. At first, I thought they must be some type of compendium of estate-planning materials or part of an advanced underwriting library. I was mistaken. Greg told me that those binders contained a summary copy of the files of the members of his Top 250 Club. He explained that this group consisted of individual and business clients who were paying $250,000 or more per year on annual premium life insurance purchased through him! Members of Greg's Top 250 Club get the following special treatment:

- An instant fax response to all inquiries

- All documents, requirements or service forms delivered by courier

- Special holiday gifts—a $50 box of chocolates on holidays, a $75 floral arrangement on birthdays and anniversaries

- Comprehensive financial planning service, regularly updated

- Transportation by limo to and from medical exams

The records for each client that are kept in the ring binders on Greg's credenza include copies of every policy owned, a full and current benefit summary sheet on each policy, copies of every letter sent from the agent or carrier and an up-to-date, complete financial plan. The binders are displayed in a prominent place under Greg's watchful eye but also where all staff members have immediate access.

The most interesting thing about this extraordinary example of going the extra mile is that Greg has turned it into a public-relations and motivational tool. He tells all substantial clients about his Top 250 Club and lets them know the benefits of membership as they approach $250,000 in annual premium. Incredibly, Greg tells me that most clients look forward to the day they qualify and regularly indicate a commitment to eventually getting there!

Most of us would not have a very big membership in our Top 250 Club if we had one, but the concept will work just as successfully with more modest membership requirements. A Top 25 Club ($25,000 in annual premiums) or a Top 10 Club ($10,000 in annual premiums) might be a more realistic starting point for most of us.

Make Every Occasion a Great Occasion

Many agents don't think about it, but *our sales presentations are a preview for our clients as to the level of service they can expect from us.*

We have long advocated the philosophy of "making every occasion a great occasion." There is no more important occasion in your career than when you present a case. If your preparation is less than perfect when you are asking clients to buy, you are telegraphing what they can expect when they encounter a problem after you have spent your commission.

Here are some customs followed by leading agents that you will want to consider.

Have a dress rehearsal for every presentation with your staff, your KOP, your spouse or your manager. Sit them down and walk through the presentation with them. Ask, "If you were the prospect, what reasons might you come up with not to buy?" Don't hope objections won't come up, because they will. If you are prepared, then you will retain control of the interview and, therefore, of the outcome.

These reviews are good for your staff and will ensure that you arrive at the presentation prepared and ready to earn the client's business.

Try to anticipate questions the prospect may have and prepare your answers in advance. The prospect's questions are an indication of interest. Your preparedness to answer questions is an indication of your worthiness of his or her business.

Bring a tool kit to every selling interview that contains all of the facts, information and third-party influences needed to answer every conceivable question or objection. The Financial Need Analysis Sales Maker™, discussed in Chapter 7, is a good example of this tool. If you don't have such a point-of-sale aid, you are really not adequately prepared for objections and your closing ratio will suffer. This is not just good salesmanship, it is also an impressive demonstration of your desire to serve the client. Clients ask questions to test your conviction and gain your reassurance as well as to satisfy their need to understand.

When the prospect gives the OK, make it easy to close. Have the paperwork ready, and be sure your staff or KOP is on the alert for a call to set up medicals and follow up with any questions or problems that came up in the interview.

Make the underwriting process a smooth transition from prospect to client. These examples of practices used by our Top of the Table friends may not be possible for every agent today, but some or all eventually will be. Meanwhile, you can perform these functions yourself until the fruit they bear enables you to delegate them to staff.

- Have your KOP go to the client's office to complete all documents.

- If the exam has to be done by an internist (as in bigger cases), send a car and driver to transport the client to and from the appointment.

- Have your KOP go by the client's personal physician's office to pick up APSs.

- Deliver the policy with a full delivery kit, including a leather binder.

- Give a meaningful gift to a client who refers you to a prospect who buys.

Stay in Touch (But Don't Pester)

- Flowers on birthdays

- Christmas and holiday baskets

- Quarterly newsletters

- Updates on the progress of your agency

- Congratulations on important events in clients' lives

The Magic of a Personalized Letter

Today we get junk mail, junk faxes and junk telephone calls from computerized voices.

Form the practice of sending your clients a personalized letter (no labels or signature stamps) on important occasions. This often overlooked and very appreciated practice is the ultimate example of going the extra mile and is also the most economical of the practices we've discussed. Figure 8.6 shows some examples of letters you may wish to send your clients on various appropriate occasions.

Figure 8.6 Annual Policy Review

Dear Jerry:

Congratulations on nearing the first [second, etc.] anniversary of your life insurance policy. It is a pleasure to send you the enclosed Annual Policy Report.

This Annual Policy Report includes your dividends and shows the scheduled changes or options effective on the approaching policy anniversary, which will be March 12. All figures—protection, premiums and values—are also shown as of the anniversary on March 12.

I will contact you prior to the policy anniversary to discuss the current options and to answer any questions you may have. If you need to contact me before then, just phone.

Sincerely,

Universal Life Policy Annual Review

Dear Jerry:

By now, you should have received your annual report from the home office on your universal life policy.

To illustrate the remarkable flexibility of your universal life policy, I have requested a computer illustration showing how a $25 monthly increase in premiums would improve the values.

I will contact you next week to explain the illustration and discuss the requirements for making changes in premiums.

Sincerely,

Figure 8.6 Annual Policy Review (Continued)

Birthday

Dear Wendy:

Have a Happy Birthday on Tuesday!

I wanted to get into the act by wishing you lots of good health, good spirits and good friends for the coming year. Many more in the future.

Sincerely,

Compliment to Wife

Dear Mrs. Primary Beneficiary:

John has just paid you the greatest compliment that any husband can possibly pay to his wife. A man can buy flowers, fine jewelry, cars and many other things in an attempt to demonstrate his love for a woman. However, such an effort is only a shallow indication compared with what your husband has just done.

In my business, we know that the person who buys life insurance is a person who loves someone. It is truly an unselfish act of love, because the buyer is obligating himself into the future for the sole benefit of the beneficiary. For this reason, you should really feel complimented. As the years pass, I hope I shall have an opportunity again to add further to your security.

Sincerely,

Figure 8.6 (Continued)

Engagement

Dear John:

I just heard the happy news that you and Mary are engaged to be married in July. Best wishes for achieving your hopes and dreams and all the good things in life.

Sincerely,

Holiday Greetings

Dear Client:

The holiday season and the end of another year are upon us. As we celebrate, count our blessings and enjoy good times with family and friends, it seems appropriate for me to express my thanks to you for your continued trust and confidence.

I hope that this year has been a good one for you and the people you love, and that the holidays will bring happiness to every member of your family.

Sincerely,

Service Review

Dear Policyholder:

Your annual review checklist is enclosed. I sincerely urge you to take a few minutes to complete the information form and be sure your personal and business financial affairs are in order.

Please return your annual review checklist, and don't forget to indicate if you wish me to phone you.

I appreciate the continuing opportunity to be of service; please feel free to call at any time you might need me.

Sincerely,

9

Selling Your Practice

"The secret to my success has been simple; when everyone wants to sell, buy; when everyone wants to buy, sell."

—J. Paul Getty

In the life insurance industry, the economic life of our prospects can be separated into two distinct phases: wealth accumulation and wealth conservation. We sell two distinct groups of products to accommodate prospects, depending upon whether they are in the accumulation or the conservation stage of their lives.

As agents, we face the same two issues in the life cycle of our insurance practice. Earlier chapters of this book were devoted to building and managing a successful sales career. Now we come to the fun part—payday! Now that you've built it, what are you going to do with it?

The business of selling your practice is not just the concern of the established or mature agent. On the contrary, it should be an issue of concern even for new agents. If you build your practice from the start with an eye on what you want it to look like on the day you sell it, chances are what you build will be of greater value when that day comes.

The reality is that you must have a careful plan in place many years before "payday!" or payday may never arrive. That is why it is important to think about it now.

Another important issue we must understand when we consider the subject of selling our practice is that we are not always talking about age 65 or retirement. In fact, the opportunity exists for the younger agent to build two or three practices over a career that he or she sells or transfers.

I am familiar with many cases where agents have built practices over a ten-year period or even less, then sold them and started a different practice in a new area. Living in southern California, we get a lot of visitors who come out for a special event, such as the Rose Bowl, and decide they want to settle in the area. I have two friends, one from Shreveport, Louisiana, and another from San Antonio, Texas, both of whom sold substantial practices and moved to southern California. Certain types of practices lend themselves especially well to acquisition. For example, pension and profit-sharing practices are probably the best examples of a specialized clientele that often can be acquired by a large pension administration firm.

As barriers against banks, accounting firms and law firms entering the insurance business fall over time, all of these, in my view, will make outstanding candidates for acquiring agents' practices. I know the idea of banks, accountants and lawyers being in our business has met with a great deal of resistance in the past, but that could change when they realize it may be more practical to buy a clientele than to build one. We'll touch on this subject in greater detail in the final chapter. The goal should be to follow certain procedures and practices that enable you to build something of transferable economic value.

Here's a good question to start with: What would you define as the ultimate economic expression of the value of your life's work? There can only be one answer: *How much someone is willing to pay for it.* With this in mind, let's look at the key issues leading up to the successful capitalization (sale) of a life insurance practice and what you should be doing today to ensure that your insurance practice doesn't stop when you do.

PRINCIPLES OF PERPETUITY
IN A SMALL BUSINESS

Sole proprietorships and closely held corporations are a wonderful form of business for those with the entrepreneurial spirit. They all, however, have one problem in common: Their greatest strength can eventually become their downfall. Small businesses are usually built around one key personality, a founder whose vision and hard work are the very soul of the enterprise. When that person dies, retires or becomes disabled, the business can evaporate.

Of course, as life insurance agents, we make our living solving this very problem through a series of solutions offered by our products and services. But what about our own business? How do we create lasting value that can be capitalized when we die or want to quit or retire?

I believe the value that matters most in a practice is not the actual book of business but rather the clientele. If the client base is properly constructed, everything else will take care of itself. This is an important departure from some contemporary views on the selling of a practice. Many programs we hear about refer to selling your book of business or your premium stream. We will look more closely at this approach in a moment, but for the most part, when we talk about selling your practice, we mean selling your clientele. When we talk about a book of business or premium in force, we are talking about numbers and cash flow. This can be important, but for my money, the thing you have to sell that's really worth something is the relationships with your clients. The strength of those relationships and the value to a would-be acquirer will be greatly affected by the intangible qualities you build into your practice—primarily the goodwill that will make the practice continue to grow after you are gone.

So first let's look at the seven key things we can do to be sure we build an insurance practice that is more likely to have an ongoing value. I call these the seven rules of perpetuity in a small business.

Rule 1: Manage with an Eye on the Long Term Rather Than on Fads or Hot Markets A practice with a mixed clientele, built around outdated products like RLR, Section 416 or Section 79, is not likely to have much value. This is primarily because the clients bought for the wrong reason. Sadly, there has been a long-standing practice in certain quarters in our industry of developing sales concepts that seemingly enable the insured to get the life insurance portion of the scheme for nothing. We know this is not possible, and eventually all such approaches go sour. Who, for example, would want to buy a practice consisting of a large number of fully loaned-up policies that were sold back in the late 1970s and early 1980s on a minimum deposit basis (policy loans used to pay premiums on a zero net outlay basis for the insured)? Sales that attract customers because of a gimmick or loophole do not build a true clientele. Whether sales built around "windows of opportunity" are considered opportunities or outright abuses is of little consequence. The fact is, if the customer bought because of a perceived tax or legal condition that eventually closes or loses its appeal, you don't really have much of a client. Just remember, those who bought for a better deal will leave for the same reason as soon as your deal is no longer the best or slickest.

Sales concepts and package sales are a vital component in a client/agent relationship, but they should not be the basis of the relationship.

There are several strategies you can use to develop long-term value for your practice. For example, when you pick your area of specialization, pick one that will be around for a long time. That means avoiding tax gimmicks or loophole products. Instead, look for legitimate, tax-advantaged products, such as pension plans or the use of irrevocable life insurance trusts in estate planning. These tax advantages have been blessed by the IRS and will not be challenged if properly executed.

Develop a relationship with your client's children. This will allow you to leverage your influence with clients in a way that will multiply their value. Think what this could someday mean to the value of your practice. Suppose you have 2,000 clients (households or businesses) and, on average, they have 2.5 children. If you have kept accurate, up-to-date records and data on your clients' children, regardless of whether or not you sold them insurance, think of the value. That's 5,000 highly qualified prospects, each in varying degrees of coming into their own as insurance prospects, and each of whom you have the best reference possible to use when calling on them.

Let's just say you took the time to acquire this information over a 20-year period, which certainly would take almost no extra effort at all. Now you are 50 years old and you bring a 25- or 30-year-old intern into your practice. What would such a person pay for those 5,000 files? What would your return on your investment be?

Use living trusts to be sure your client's assets are all in a known safe place. Assets under management have become the name of the game in the securities industry, and we should think along the same lines. By now, you know that wills and probate are antiquated, and virtually all estate-planning lawyers are using inter-vivos or living trusts as the depository for all client assets. Affiliate yourself with a first-class estate planning attorney who knows how to draft a quality living trust for a reasonable fee. Work with him or her on every client's behalf, not just on your estate-planning cases. The fact is, every client you have should have a living trust. If you have any doubt, just read the best-selling paperback *Loving Trust* by Robert A. Esperti and Renno L. Peterson (published by Penguin Group, 3rd ed., 1994).

An important side benefit to you is that you will know where all of your client's assets are and you will be part of the team that put the plan together. Once again, this greatly enhances the value of your clientele to a would-be acquirer.

Rule 2: Build the Practice Around Customer-Oriented Values Rather Than on the Strength of Your Own Personality Don't build your image around your ego. Center your image-building efforts around the agency you are part of and its clientele. Trade on the strengths of an organization that will be there for your clients long after you are gone. This is why banks enjoy such loyalty. They are institutions. You must think of ways to institutionalize your practice—for example, by sending clients a quarterly newsletter and familiarizing them with the agency and its management. You will also want to promote your company's good name and image whenever the opportunity arises.

Promote what you sell and the services you offer in your community. Be known for what you do and how you serve clients. These are the things your clients will value and for which a successor will be willing to pay.

Make certain your clients are aware of everything you sell; mutual funds, disability insurance, annuities and senior care products are all things that they should hear about from you rather than the competition.

Sell your high level of customer service to every client. Service, and the reputation that accompanies it, will be a big portion of what you will sell someday. Be sure you save and catalog every letter you get from clients that is complimentary about your service (save any complaint letters, too, for liability purposes, but there is no need to put them in a scrapbook for your successor!). Incidentally, when a client pays you a compliment, it doesn't hurt to say, "Would you mind putting that in a note and dropping it in the mail to me? It would mean a great deal to me, and I would like to share it with my key office person [spouse, manager, etc.]." This is the goodwill portion of your practice that is part of the value added to your balance sheet.

Rule 3: Work Toward a Successful Program of Multiplying Yourself Through Others Build a staff that can run the organization without you. As we discussed, this may be a part-time high school student or your spouse in the beginning. Later it will be your key office person (KOP) and other staff. It will be a big help if your KOP stays on with the practice after you are gone, at least for a while.

Develop at least one intern who will eventually own part of the business. As previously mentioned, the best approach to this I know of is the mentoring program developed by Richard McCloskey. Over a number of years, Dick has perfected a program in his agency whereby newer agents are promoted to intern under a mentor, or established senior agent.

Consider eventually merging with another successful practice that complements yours. One plus one can equal three with the right team! There have been many great partnerships in our industry. Typically, the best fit is between an opener and a technician: one person who is outstanding at prospecting, uncovering needs and building relationships, and another whose strengths lie in casework, case presentation and follow-up.

A word of caution: Partnerships are the most fragile form of business entity. They almost always wind up splitting. However, they can work successfully for many years before growing stale, and the result can be very rewarding for both parties. Also, partnerships can provide a natural market if one partner wishes to buy out the other.

Do joint work with younger agents who may someday be potential buyers of your practice. Every time you are invited by a less experienced agent to accompany him or her on a call, you are being paid the ultimate compliment. You are also being given a chance to showcase your skills in a way that may interest that agent in working with you on a more permanent basis. It is a great way to ease into a relationship on a trial basis and then take it in any number of directions—mentoring, junior partner, partner or acquirer. Again, the virtues of joint work cannot be overemphasized. Creating a market for your practice is just one more reason to make it a part of your modus operandi.

Rule 4: Put Systems in Place That Work Whether You Are There or Not For prospecting, the importance of a solid One-Card System is at the center of almost any valuable practice. In my opinion, a well-managed One-Card System is the primary asset you will be selling when you sell your clientele. With this in mind, you may wish to go back and reread Chapter 7.

Service to clients should be automatic, automated, prompt and responsive. When you decide to sell your clientele, it will be extremely important that you be able to demonstrate a system with a history, reputation and capacity for giving first-rate service.

Client review and update systems are critical. Documented evidence of an ongoing client relationship with every client can be tracked by well-placed systems such as the client management system from CMS. (CMS is a Pismo Beach, California, company that specializes in client prospect management systems.) This is an automated tool that will support your OCS (One-Card System) as well as generate other types of prospecting activities. Remember that access to information is what your successor is really paying for.

Rule 5: Have a Corporate Mission and Purpose Bigger Than You Are Don't name your practice after yourself. Name it to describe what you do. Better yet, just use the name of your company if it employs you or your agency. When people are giving you their money, they want to deal with an institution. True, you must win their trust and gain their confidence, but a big part of that today has to do with the company that stands behind you.

Make your mission known to all with whom you do business. This is one area where you can promote yourself by promoting your values as an agent with such slogans as "Solutions for Life" or "Your Choice for Life." Your practice should be a reflection of your beliefs and the value of the work you do.

Promote the practice, not the practitioner. In promotional materials, be sure to emphasize what you do for the client, and when you refer to yourself, do so in a way that communicates what your credentials mean to them. A small picture and brief résumé in the back of your image brochure will do. Too much self-promotion quickly wears thin with everyone except, perhaps, your mother.

Rule 6: Develop Revenue Sources That Complement One Another Sell disability income and related morbidity products. From a liability standpoint, today's agent must understand that the client may expect to at least be informed of those products you sell that protect him or her against losses other than death. In addition, disability income and related products will expand your renewal base and strengthen your performance.

Offer investment products to fund client retirement plans. Most agents today are security licensed, and as such, you owe it to your clients to learn about those equity-based products that you feel qualified to sell. Don't get in over your head, because the securities arena is a big place with thousands of products. Instead, learn all you can about a few good mutual fund families that cover the investment spectrum. These products are excellent accumulation vehicles and will complement your traditional insurance products well.

If your practice focuses on a single market, such as pension plans, mix the clientele so that when one industry—for example, construction—encounters adversity, you can focus on another industry that tends to do better during difficult times—for example discount retailers.

Rule 7: Keep Accurate Records Maintain every production, persistency and bonus record in a single Gross Revenues ledger that shows what you have been paid for your efforts. The years will pass more quickly than you think. You will want to maintain your production records for many reasons, but showing a steady pattern of growth will eventually be very important. You will also want to create some graphs, charts and the like at the end of each year showing cumulative performance in key areas.

Do an annual report just as a public company does for its shareholders, including a balance sheet and profit-and-loss statement. We suggested this earlier, but it bears repeating: Run your practice by the rule of 500. It will pay big dividends. If you were the CEO of a Fortune 500 company, you would be expected to provide your board with a business plan, annual statement, profit-and-loss report, and a detailed explanation of every important event in the company. Don't you owe at least the same level of accountability to yourself? Then, when it's time to sell your practice, think of the impression such records will make on the purchaser.

Keep a scrapbook containing your achievements, endorsement letters from clients and recognition from company officials and industry figures. This is something you will want to keep for yourself after you leave. However, it will be a wonderful third-party influence piece to show anyone interested in buying your practice.

Record your goals and objectives for each year and track performance against objectives. Past performance is the best indicator of potential. Anyone buying your practice will want your past performance to be the benchmark of theirs as your successor. After all, when you were building the practice, you weren't able to hit the ground running with an established clientele the way your successor will. Part of the justification for the price you ask should be the fact that, given the head start he or she will have, your successor should be able to do somewhat better than you did.

The best advice I can give you is to repeat that the value of your practice will depend upon the perspective from which you build it. Make your choices about your practice not from your perspective today, but rather from the perspective of the person who will someday buy it from you. Think of yourself walking arm-in-arm through your practice 10 or 15 years from today with the person who will be your successor. As you make decisions today, make them with your successor's best interest in mind. This will work in your best interest, too.

The nice thing about using this perspective in building your practice is that it also is in your clients' best interest. If you review this chapter, you will see that every piece of advice portends well for the policyholder. What it really translates to is this: *If you want a practice to be worth its weight in gold, just build it by practicing the Golden Rule.*

CHOICES FOR BUILDING EQUITY IN A LIFE INSURANCE PRACTICE

All of the seven principles of perpetuity we just discussed can be applied to any type of conventional distribution system. I have indicated no preference toward one or the other, because I have none. It is my conviction that, with hundreds of companies competing for the business of the successful agent, on balance, no one company has a substantial advantage over the rest. If they tell you they do, you probably should look elsewhere—or better yet, stay where you are.

As we have discussed from the start, the important difference is in the agent and his or her performance. There are, however, differences in the packages and choices that various companies offer. Some may work more effectively for you or better fit your style of operating, but none is meaningfully better than another in and of itself. What most of them do have are strengths in certain areas that can work to your advantage. So avoid thinking in terms of one company being better than another on an absolute basis. Realize that the strengths of one company may be more important to your needs than the strengths of another. With these thoughts in mind, let's look objectively at the choices of distribution systems available today and examine their strengths and weaknesses.

In each type of distribution system discussed here, you can build equity in your practice. The means may differ, but the ultimate outcome will vary only with the agent's performance. In other words, the issue is not which is the best deal, but rather from which platform you are most likely to give your best performance.

During my 12 years as a senior marketing officer throughout the 1980s and early 1990s, I had the unique experience of being in charge of all of the primary types of distribution systems practiced in our industry: Career Agency, PPGA, Brokerage, Producer Group and Agent-Owned Reinsurance Companies. There are few areas in which I claim absolute expertise, but I am not aware of any senior marketing officer who has managed all five methods of distribution popular today. So, I guess I may be the closest thing to an overall expert the industry has at this moment. During those historical years in our industry's history, I spent a great deal of time studying the strengths and weaknesses of each type of distribution system, and I concluded that the biggest differences from an agent's perspective are subjective rather than objective. The differences in compensation have more to do with agent needs and how the distribution choice meets those needs than anything else. If it works for you, it's the best distribution system. If it doesn't work for you, it doesn't matter how attractive the payout is. Note also that our purpose here is to evaluate the forms of distribution *only from the point of maximizing performance and building equity* in a practice for purposes of someday selling it.

Independent PPGA

If you are an independent personal producing general agent (PPGA), you have chosen to have a relationship with your carrier similar to that of a retailer to a manufacturer. The person or entity between you and the carrier is the wholesaler. In exchange for less support, the company gives the agent a higher first-year commission percentage, out of which he or she is expected to provide most of the necessary support (which we described earlier).

The advantages and disadvantages you will want to consider in building equity as a PPGA include the following:

Advantages	*Disadvantages*
Your perceived independent status can be helpful in establishing your credibility with clients.	Most PPGA companies are not household names. If you represent several companies, you must be sure of your potential liability.
Being on your own gives you complete autonomy.	Many people perform better on a team than they do solo.

First-year compensation is usually higher.	Renewals are often lower.
You can set up your own deferred compensation program.	It takes a lot of discipline and autonomy, because there is no support framework.
You can incorporate and take in partners, sell stock and sell your book of business.	It can be cumbersome to administer your practice because companies offer limited support.

Producer Group Member

Producer groups are a phenomenon of the 1980s that have gained popularity among some of the industry's leading agents. Typically, a producer group is a federation of agents across the country who pool their production power to win Master General Agent (MGA) contracts with leading carriers. The number of producer groups that have enjoyed meaningful success in the 15 years or so they have been in existence can be counted on one hand. It isn't that they are a less valid form of distribution, it's just that they don't fit the style of most mainstream agents.

Advantages	*Disadvantages*
The agents run their own distribution system.	Agents typically are not well suited to manage large sales organizations, and buyers know this.
The agent has a choice among several qualified carriers with whom he or she can place business.	The agent's identity is seldom well-known to the carriers. He or she is a cog in the larger machine.
Because of their high profile, producer groups may have a significant perceived value to would-be suitors.	The independent nature of producer group members makes the group volatile and subject to easy dissolution.

Producer groups are able to exert significant influence on their carriers with regard to product compensation issues. Some carriers feel hostage to producer groups and pull out of relationships.

Agent-Owned Reinsurance Companies

Agent-Owned Reinsurance Companies (AORCs) started on the West Coast about 1980 and gained wide acceptance throughout the decade. The versions varied, but the basic idea is for the company to share its profits on the agent's book of business in exchange for a financial investment and a production commitment.

The next phase of this concept was the development of AORCs by producer groups rather than carriers. In these arrangements, the AORC takes business from several companies in the group.

Sometimes career agency companies offer a share of the profits on the agent's book of business that is tantamount to an AORC.

Advantages	*Disadvantages*
Because he or she shares in the profits, the agent is on the side of the insurance company.	Some consumers perceive AORCs to be a conflict of interest that removes the agent's objectivity.
The agent stands to gain substantially if the company earns a profit.	There is usually an up-front cost in cash or reduced commissions.
The agent takes a more active interest in the quality of the business, its mortality and persistency.	Even though the agent does everything right, the company can still lose money or get into financial trouble.
The agent has a piece of the action based upon level of performance.	Poor results of the business of some agents can have an adverse effect on everyone.

It ties the agent to the company for a long period.

The internal rate of return potentially available to the agent on his or her investment is attractive when the buy-out occurs.

The company's culture and practices can change over time, leaving agents stranded.
Most AORC buyouts are not guaranteed and the list of potential buyers is short.

They are very complicated and few agent participants really understand the deal.

Career Agencies

Career agencies, the most enduring form of distribution, have evolved into a potent factor that agents must take into consideration when deciding how to succeed into the year 2000 and beyond.

Typically, career agencies house their agents (who are usually employees), pay their expenses and provide fringe benefits. The characteristics of this distribution system are fairly consistent across the industry.

Advantages	*Disadvantages*

The carriers are often household names that add goodwill to the agent's practice.
The companies usually have a very broad product line.

The fringe benefits, renewals and overhead expense payments make for a very attractive package and lets the agent focus on his or her job.
The training, sales support and agent development programs help build the practice at little or no cost to the agent.

The agent must usually identify solely with that carrier until he or she is established.
Agents are usually expected to give their company first right of refusal on their business.
The net compensation is sometimes perceived to be less than what is available elsewhere.

Once established, some agents feel they are subsidizing the newer agents coming up through the system.

The deferred compensation packages, bonuses and recognition programs often negate the need for any type of AORC or extra compensation. By doing all of his or her business with one carrier, the agent's due care burden and potential liability are greatly reduced.

If the company encounters difficulties, fringe benefits could be diminished or jeopardized.

Thus, each system has its advantages and disadvantages. All are very suitable for successful selling in the year 2000 and create equity you can eventually sell or pass on to new owners. What constitutes equity, however, may differ among distribution systems. Generally, there is a clear distinction between three types of equity that can be sold as part of a practice.

Book of Business Equity   The first type of equity is the actual book of business produced by the agent. This consists of the flow of premiums and the future profit those premiums create based upon persistency, mortality, expenses and the investment performance of the company. This aspect of equity is usually perceived to be owned by the insurance company. The exception to this is the AORC, in which agents actually share in the ownership of their block of business. Of course, with the thin profit margins most companies are experiencing today, rest assured that nothing a company gives you is free. In such instances, agents usually trade things like benefits, retirement plans, support, training and managerial guidance for their ownership. Usually, agents also take some sort of cut on their commissions, perhaps as much as 10 percent. This, however, is perfectly understandable in light of surplus strain (see Chapter 3). When a life insurance company puts up surplus to put business on the books, it must get a return (profit) on its investment. It stands to reason, then, that if the company gives a portion of the profits to the agent, the agent should put up part or all of the surplus representing those profits. Many agents don't understand this and, as a result, back away from AORCs. Others do understand it but conclude that it's more profitable to just go out and sell another policy and reap the profits today instead of waiting ten or more years for an AORC payout.

Another drawback of the AORC approach is that it seems to detract from the value of the clientele approach we will discuss later. Due to the somewhat convoluted nature of an AORC, the agent looking at buying your clientele may back away because of uncertainty as to who owns what and what eventually will become of the block of business. Clearly, if an agent buys the clientele, he or she will want to know where the policies reside and what the expectations are of the former owner. (AORCs, when sold, always have a protracted payout to the seller with conditions that must be met regarding service and persistency. The company is usually a pure manufacturer.)

Vested Renewal Equity The second type of equity consists of vested renewal commissions. This item is usually perceived as being owned by the agent.

When selling your practice, you can handle renewals in different ways. You can sell them, too, or assign them to the purchaser for some lump sum payment. The problem here is that if you get an accurate valuation of a lump sum based upon present values and allowing for lapses and terminations, you might not be pleased with the number. Actuaries are not nearly so optimistic as agents are.

A second approach is to split the renewal stream or to let the purchaser use it to help fund the payments. This would typically increase the purchase price, because you are turning more of an asset over to the new owner.

A final approach is to keep the renewals but leave the service fees to the purchaser, because he or she will be servicing the clients.

Whichever approach is used, you will add to the purchase price the value of renewals passed on to the new owner using a formula that allows for persistency and a discount factor that allows for the present value of future renewals.

Goodwill Equity The third type of equity in your practice consists of goodwill, which is based on the value of your relationship with your clients. This is the most intangible equity but, in my view, the most valuable. Under most circumstances, the best package I believe an agent can put together for selling a practice is a combination of assigned renewals and the clientele.

The renewals are tangible, measurable and can easily be valued with the help of a valuation actuary. Getting a valuation from an agreed-upon third party (actuary) is a relatively simple and inexpensive matter.

You should be aware that some companies have restrictions on the assignment of renewals even if they are vested. Other companies may want some say in who is appointed to service their policyholders. However, both of these issues can be negated if the acquirer is an agent in the same agency or employee of the same company as you are. Therefore, typically you will want to pick a fellow agent, affiliated with your company, to ensure that the company blesses the transaction. No company is going to obstruct an effort between two of its agents to pass the baton of a successful practitioner to an understudy.

TWO PERSPECTIVES ON CLIENTELE VALUATION

The value of renewals is what it is, but how do you value a clientele? Well, let's look at the two extremes.

Most valuation actuaries will value the goodwill portion of your practice at very little. They deal only with the realities of premium streams and cash flow. For example, when one life insurance company acquires another, the actuaries almost always value the sales force at zero! I have been involved in at least a dozen acquisitions, and I have never been able to persuade the actuaries to put any meaningful value on the sales force. They nearly always look at it as frosting on the cake if the agent stays on board and services his or her clientele. They consider it a "push" between the nonpayment of nonvested renewals if an agent leaves as opposed to the payment of renewals if the agent stays. This is the world actuaries live in—numbers—not people.

You and I live at the other end of the spectrum. For us this is a people business, and relationships are our most valuable asset. Also, keep in mind that when we sell a clientele, we are selling access to distribution and access to prospects—a harvest of future sales. These things are of great value to the agent with the skill and know-how to reap the harvest, but of little value to those without the skills or inclination to do anything with it.

From the perspective where you and I sit, the value of a well-managed, quality clientele is substantial. One fact that even the actuaries can't argue with is that for many years now, the biggest profits, on new business in our industry have been made on distribution, not manufacturing. That's not to say companies aren't making profits, but I can guarantee you that if they could have your profit on a given sale (assuming you are applying the techniques offered here) as opposed to theirs, they'd take yours in a heartbeat. After all, I don't know of a company worth its salt where the top ten agents don't out-earn the top ten senior officers by a considerable margin.

The answer to valuing a clientele, then, probably lies somewhere between my opinion and that of the actuaries. Let's look at some of the things you will want to consider in arriving at a number.

- Client ages, professions and socioeconomic status. A clientele that is past its prime insurance-buying age (over 50) will be less valuable. The important exception, of course, will be those clients with a net worth that makes them candidates for estate planning (above $600,000). This is typically the biggest life insurance purchase a person is likely to buy.

- Records and files on client's children, including, of course, the insurance you sold them to start out their programs.

- Types of coverage in force. Policies with excess cash beyond that needed to carry them at the minimum guaranteed interest rates (as in many universal life contracts) can be a source of new premium dollars.

- Other products sold to them, such as mutual funds, limited partnerships or annuities that have liquidity and can be reallocated in the client's portfolio as needs change.

- Planning that has been executed and is in place, such as an updated estate plan and living trust that contains all of their current property.

- An up-to-date One-Card System with a detailed record of all contacts, reviews and correspondence.

- A client management system on a good database that will allow your successor to page through the client files based on such characteristics as age, income, premiums in force and ZIP code.

When you sell a clientele, you are selling relationships. This is purely a goodwill asset, but if properly managed, it can be the most valuable aspect of your practice. Think of what it would have meant to you if, after four or five years of paying your dues in the business, an agent of good reputation and credentials turned over to you an up-to-date One-Card System and client file of, say, 1,000 families and businesses. What would it be worth to you?

WHAT IS THE GOAL?

"To a ship without a destination, no wind is favorable." Just as a successful practice isn't built by accident, you will not capitalize your life's work in a way that pleases you without a plan for what you are going to do after the sale is consummated. (When we us the word *capitalize,* we mean sale, liquidation or transfer of your business so that the final disposition is favorable to you.)

Retirement

Full retirement is the most common reason to sell your practice. If this is your target, then you should have a long while to get ready for it. In cases of retirement, the value of your practice as an ongoing entity may be greatly enhanced if you have an understudy in position and ready to carry on. In fact, the intern is usually the best prospect to buy the practice.

Typically, any sale of a practice involves a payout period, but this is especially true if the seller is going to retire. The place to start is to look at the number of years you would like to have other retirement income supplemented and the number of years you are willing to wait to get your money.

Most payouts are between five and ten years. Less than five years will tend to discount the value too harshly due to unknowns about persistency and mortality, and more than ten years tends to drag things past the point of any ongoing value.

Partial or Early Retirement

Early retirement is often a goal of younger agents, but once they get there, many find they really don't want to slow down.

The best route to this approach is to bring in an ambitious partner 10 to 20 years your junior. Create a working arrangement that gives you the flexibility to slow down and turn your clients over to your partner or continue at your current level. There are as many ways to structure this type of relationship as there are agents willing to enter them. Just be sure that whatever you agree to is in writing. Remember what we pointed out earlier: Partnerships are the most fragile form of business.

Moving On to New challenges

Throughout this discussion, we have emphasized that selling a life insurance practice is not a subject just for agents wanting to retire. The fact is that many capitalization plans enacted today are completed between parties at the peak of their careers. One agent wants to sell his or her practice to go into a new area of specialization, move to a different state or replace himself or herself in an existing partnership. The buyer may be an agent or group of agents wishing to expand or diversify by acquisition. The reasons will vary based upon individual circumstances, but retirement is only one situation.

Actually, the prudent agent should probably build his or her practice around a series of five-year plans providing for the possibility of selling out at the end of any given five-year period. Thus, it's conceivable that an agent may sell his or her practice two or three times over a lifetime, and that is exactly what some agents have done with notable success.

When you sell a practice early in your career, it is likely you will have a smaller clientele and premium base than you would have with a sale later on. On the other hand, you are more likely to have clients just approaching their peak buying years. You should understand that the smaller the client base, the lower the per capita client price will be. In other words, all other things being equal, 1,500 policyholders are worth more than five times as much as 300 policyholders. This is because the larger group, if properly worked, will no doubt keep the buyer busy full-time and generate enough cash flow to pay for a full-time staff member. The smaller group, on the other hand, will only supplement the buyer's income and activity.

Thus, a sale of a small practice or a book of business acquired over five or so years should probably have a payout period of no more than five years. Otherwise, the numbers are typically not very attractive to the seller.

HOW DO YOU WANT TO BE PAID?

Most capitalization plans of successful practices involve a payout over a protracted period of time. As previously mentioned, lump sum buyouts can be calculated, but the discount factors applied by a valuation actuary are likely to make this approach unattractive.

In some cases, an agent has a book of business with a renewal stream attached to it that the company allows the agent to sell or assign. The choices in these instances can include the following iterations based upon persistency, mortality and the growth or shrinkage of the client base:

- A ten-year payout of a flat percentage of all renewals on the existing book of business

- A ten-year payout of a decreasing percentage of all renewals, including those generated from new sales

- A ten-year payout of a percentage of the renewals and a percentage of the emerging statutory profits on the business

- A lump sum and reduced renewals

- Reduced renewals and a balloon payment

- A multiple of in-force premiums, usually one to two years, then spread out over a number of years

- A payout of emerging statutory profits only (usually an AORC)

- A payout based on a future production commitment (usually a producer group)

- An exchange of all renewals for a fixed retirement income (usually a career agency)

Whichever plan of payment you choose, you will want to study all of the options, assumptions and logic that went into the formula. Most agents will want to seek the help of a qualified third party, such as a valuation actuary, before signing off on any plan for selling their book of business or their renewals.

In evaluating the purchase price you can get for your clientele, you are going to be much more subjective. The value consists primarily of the thing that a would-be acquirer considers the most precious resource in a life insurance practice: *prospects.*

The best measure of the worth of prospects is how much they eventually buy, so this is where most agents begin. They sell the clientele portion of their practice for a percentage of new sales generated. There is usually a time factor involved; sales made to your clients early on by the new practitioner tend to warrant more compensation to you than do sales made later on.

For example, a clientele might be worth 25 percent of the first-year commissions on each case sold in the first three years and 15 percent of each case sold in the next five years, with nothing on sales made after year eight. In some instances it may be appropriate to split each case 25 percent/75 percent, including renewals, while in others it may be more equitable for the seller to just take a cash payment of the first-year commission.

Looking just at a cash payout of 25 percent of first-year commissions in year one and 15 percent in years four to eight, you will see that the value of the clientele is going to be equal to about one year of first-year commissions. Add to this your renewals, free of any service work, and you're walking away with a significant value that might have been lost without careful planning.

Regardless of whether you have vested renewals you can sell, shares in an AORC or membership in a producer group, in each capitalization plan a would-be buyer should be required to consider the goodwill factor. If you have built a successful practice, it has value beyond the stream of premiums you leave behind. In fact, when one agent buys a clientele from another, the cost recovery for the purchase price should easily come from new sales generated by the existing momentum.

I know I am at odds with the actuaries on this issue, but I also know what I have seen working with agents who have built and sold a quality clientele.

You will also want the agreement to contain a covenant as to what the buyer can do with your practice once he or she has control. There are several important considerations here, not the least of which is your potential liability. For example, you wouldn't want to sell to someone whose objective was to roll your book of business or move policyholders in a direction you felt was not in their best interest. This could lead to problems for both you and the company. It is worth getting the help of a good insurance lawyer, perhaps from the staff of your company's home office, to work on the drafting of your agreement. You will especially want to work out a smooth transition plan during which each party has specific responsibilities to the other. It will be important to introduce your successor to your clientele in the most favorable light possible and in a way that makes it a positive event that your clients support.

WHAT TO DO TODAY TO MAXIMIZE TOMORROW'S RESULT

As with everything else in life, in selling your practice, preparation is the prelude to good performance. Many of the principles we have discussed throughout this book are all-important to building valuable equity in your business.

The more consistent and stable your life insurance career, the more attractive it becomes to a would-be acquirer. Change is inevitable, but in my opinion, the longer you build your business around one market, one carrier and one type of distribution system, the more stable and valuable people will perceive it to be.

Finally, include your plans for selling your practice in your long-term business plan. Earlier we discussed planning for purposes of production results. Once you have committed to your course of action, learn about the payouts available under your form of distribution and what your company's rules and practices are on the issue of selling your clientele. Do regular modeling and develop periodic projections of the value of your enterprise. This will be motivating and will help keep you on track for "payday."

In conclusion, we take you back to the quotation at the beginning of this book: "The business you are in is no business at all, except for the business you create." The same can be said for the practice you sell. It can be sold only if you create the value that makes someone want to pay you for it.

The value of a life insurance practice is a combination of goodwill and a solid client base that will continue to buy on into the future. The agent's task is to establish philosophies that win and systems that work in his or her practice. The purchase price you attract will be a direct result of the talent, quality and love with which you build your clientele. They are paying for your legacy—nothing less. Make sure it's a good value.

10

Trends Toward the Year 2000

"Any manager who thinks he or she is going to manage their business over the next ten years anything like they managed it over the last ten years, is going to be out of business."

—Roberto Goizueta
Chairman & CEO, The Coca Cola Corp.

The discussion of our industry's future has been a topic somewhere on the agenda of just about every major life insurance meeting in recent years. There are usually three major areas people want to hear about: the regulatory environment, new products and trends in distribution. Actually, it's not so much what will happen that concerns most of us as how what happens is going to affect us personally. So let's look at how changes through the turn of the century in these three areas will affect the life insurance agent.

Let me preface this discussion of regulation, product and distribution by stating that I am neither a regulator nor an actuary, and I'm not even a marketing officer any more.

I am simply a guy who has spent over 25 years working with and trying to understand all three. This will be a discussion of the future as I see it affecting the person on the firing line—the agent. I have grown very weary of hearing the diplomats of the podium massage painful change into unrealistic sermons of the way things used to be, or ought to be. I respect the men and women who sell life insurance for a living too much to end this book by gilding the lily with another "the more things change, the more they stay the same" dose of pablum. The fact is, things are going to change—and the more they do, the less things will stay the same.

REGULATION

As we all know, the insurance industry is among the most regulated businesses in America once a policy is on the books. This will intensify even more, but at long last, we will also see potent regulation at the point of sale.

As far as what happens to the regulation of business on the books, three trends will continue: one good, one unfortunate and one uncertain.

The good trend will be the continuing emphasis by the National Association of Insurance Commissioners (NAIC) on the protection of policyholders. Additional reserving requirements such as risk-based capital—imposed on companies to ensure policyholder safety—will continue. What this means to agents and policyholders is that the likelihood of an insurance company failure will continue to diminish.

The regulators will see to it in every way they can that companies honor their contractual guarantees to policyholders and, to a degree, even the de facto guarantees made in policy illustrations.

As far as I am concerned, this is a necessary form of regulatory intervention. It would have been better had the industry disciplined itself in the past so that its reach (illustrations) did not exceed its grasp (performance). When this happened at most companies, the result was just disappointment, but at a few companies the result was devastation. The NAIC realizes that the industry can ill afford more six-year vanished premiums that result in a 12-year premium-paying period before premiums vanish, not to mention those instances when the company vanished rather than the premiums! So, like it or not, the regulatory requirements for reserving assets for future obligations will continue to be stringent. The consequence will be a lower yield to companies on invested surplus because of the increased down payment on their book of business (see Chapter 3). Nonetheless, this is an intervention that industry practices invited, and it should be at least accepted if not welcomed by responsible companies.

The unfortunate trend in regulation has to do with point-of-sale practices. Due to the fact that this aspect of our business has remained comparatively underregulated, many problems have emerged in recent years. The biggest problem is that unbridled sales practices in certain segments of the industry have caused concern for the way in which we sell our product. Some of that concern is well-founded.

The positive side of this intervention is that agents will be required by companies and regulators to return to needs selling. We are going to have to substantiate the logic behind every sale in terms of why it was in the prospect's best interest to buy—in other words, did he or she need it? The problem comes with the political baggage that inevitably accompanies reform. American Council of Life Insurance president Richard Schweiker has pointed out four groups of professionals that he thinks will keep the issue of point-of-sale practices before us for a long while: investigative reporters, ambitious attorneys general, plaintiff attorneys and insurance commissioners. I tend to agree with him.

Investigative Reporters

There is a real desire among reporters in the financial services arena to uncover and publicize perceived injustices to the consumer. The idea of a large, faceless insurance company misleading a trusting, unsophisticated consumer will sell a lot of newspapers. If the story is valid, it should be reported. If, however, it's a case of a few bad apples, then to imply that it is a company or industry conspiracy is, in my view, irresponsible.

Earlier, we defined the term *psychomedia risk* as a real risk insurance companies must consider. The power of the media to impugn the character of a public figure or a large corporation is well documented—perhaps better so than the facts behind their aspersions. The unfortunate result can be a crisis in confidence and the abandonment of rational behavior. For the foreseeable future, this is a concern the life insurance industry must live with.

Ambitious Attorneys General

The state prosecutors appointed by the administration in power in Washington at any given point in time have a long agenda and face formidable challenges for relatively modest pay. Their best hope in terms of their careers is to exploit a highly publicized issue in a way that wins popular support. The bashing of big business has long been a proven vote-getter. If controversial issues concerning insurance companies can be pursued, they may become a cause célèbre for the upwardly mobile attorney general in a given jurisdiction. If we deserve it, so be it. Either way, it is a reality we must live with.

Class-Action Litigation

For many years, those occasional stock life insurance companies encountering public criticism have been subjected to shareholder suits based upon perceived misconduct. Now the current criticisms of point-of-sale practices by large mutuals have opened up the floodgates for class-action suits by policyholders against their insurance companies. In a country that has between 5 and 20 times the number of lawyers per capita as our peer economic powers (Great Britain, Germany and Japan), we have become far and away the most litigious society in the world. Some believe the preponderance of plaintiff lawyers in America may find insurance companies the perfect sustenance needed to sustain their disproportionate numbers. As they attach themselves to the issue of point-of-sale practices, we may as well hold onto our hats, because it's going to be a long and turbulent ride. Unfortunately, there will be no winners among the plaintiffs and the defendants. The only result will be lower profits to the companies and higher costs to policyholders.

I think it is appropriate to add that the industry's lack of resolve about self-policing point-of-sale practices has created the opportunity for litigation. Had we been better able to work together on the problem, the matter may have steered clear of most courtrooms. Every issue has two sides, and the industry has done its share to create the opportunity viewed as a meal ticket for our bloated population of plaintiff lawyers.

State Insurance Commissioners

The state insurance commissioners and their governing body, the NAIC, are struggling with a challenging agenda of their own. In addition to regulating things like the protection of policyholders, they must deal with point-of-sale practices and a multitude of other issues to which they have only limited resources to allocate. Theirs is a difficult job, and their performance, in general, has been very favorable when compared to other regulatory bodies. Part of the problem with the system is the way insurance commissioners view their jobs.

Insurance commissioners are either elected officials or political appointees and, like the investigative reporter, the attorney general or the litigator, they, too, need a cause to champion if they are to advance their careers. Of course, most are dedicated public servants, but with so many others investigating the insurance industry, the regulators must be prepared to either defend the companies or jump on the bandwagon. Like others in the public eye, they must deal with perceptions before attending to reality. Most do a commendable job; those who do not are eventually exposed.

The fact that there is also often balance and accuracy in the press was demonstrated not long ago by one state insurance commissioner with shamelessly transparent political ambitions. Attempting to use his office as a steppingstone to the governor's mansion, he routinely called press conferences to denigrate insurance companies as culprits and himself as the protector of the people. This worked for awhile, until the public and press became aware that this insurance commissioner was not so much a protector of the public interest as a promoter of his own interests. Eventually, one of America's leading and most respected financial journals did a cover story exposing him as a self-serving opportunist. What's more, other insurance commissioners applauded the exposé. His political ambitions were subsequently dealt a setback by a crushing defeat at the polls.

The point of this story is that the American system is fundamentally sound, and the truth will usually prevail about our industry. In the meantime, we most likely will have to endure some hardships.

An uncertain trend in regulation has to do with how our product will be viewed in the future and, therefore, how it will be regulated. The first issue concerns who will be regulating us.

One movement afoot in Washington is for a single federal body that would oversee the financial integrity aspects of the insurance industry in all 50 states. The argument is for one set of uniform rules and regulations similar to those governing the securities industry. It's a compelling argument, but the transition would be a nightmare that could take years.

The NAIC, meanwhile, argues that it is doing a pretty good job, so "if it ain't broke, don't fix it." This, too, is a compelling argument. For those of us in the industry, the concern is whether we would rather deal with 50 monkeys or with one gorilla! Each has its advantages and disadvantages from an agent's point of view. The danger, as I see it, is that the bureaucrats will divvy up the regulatory pie in a way that creates an additional layer of regulation with no reduction in taxpayer expense.

Another uncertain trend in regulation concerns sales practices. A number of authoritative sources have challenged the way we illustrate our product and the point-of-sale practices of some agents. The American College (CLU, ChFC) has long promoted uniform illustration procedures, called the I.Q. index, which many companies have subscribed to using. The ACLI is introducing the concept of a SRO (self-regulating organization). Either way, the industry needs to do much more in this regard or it will be done for us.

Some feel that if we are going to sell life insurance as a security, then perhaps it should be overseen as such by the Securities and Exchange Commission (SEC) and the National Association of Securities Dealers (NASD). After all, if it walks like a duck and quacks like a duck... This, of course, may all soon become moot as the industry movement toward variable life takes hold. If we all sell variable life, we will, in effect, be assimilated into the jurisdiction of the SEC and the NASD.

One thing I think the life insurance industry should do right away is to replicate the Consumer Central Data Bank provided by the NASD for prospective customers. By calling the 800 number or writing, the inquirer can get a printout containing information regarding any infractions or violations by or pending suits against a broker.

In general, the insurance industry has performed admirably for the public it serves. In some areas, we have invited regulation by not being more proactive in policing ourselves. The one thing we can count on about regulation between now and the year 2000 is that it is not going to diminish.

My advice to the agent is to practice the suggestions made throughout this book: At every sale, leave behind the equivalent of a prospectus in the form of printed material from the company. Use only those sales materials and presentations that have been cleared by the compliance department of your company. Do a "memo to file" regarding every significant conversation you have with a client or prospect. If you make a sale that involves taking advantage of current tax law, get a disclaimer signed by the client making it clear that he or she understands that tax laws may change. In summary, over-prepare for every sale and overcommunicate every transaction. Promise to exercise due care, but do your best to practice due diligence!

THE NEW PRODUCTS

For a number of reasons, the big event in the product arena is that by the year 2000, most agents will be selling variable life. Variable life will eventually, in my view, be the preferred product for most companies to offer.

The first reason is that under current practice, variable life can be illustrated more competitively than can a traditional product. This is especially true in times of lower interest rates, such as those experienced in the first half of the 1990s. Even in environments of higher interest rates, the variable products can justify a more attractive growth picture over the long term. This is because a responsible illustration of a traditional product will not extrapolate long periods of high interest rates over a 20- or 30-year period. Instead, the traditional policy illustration will tend to create an average interest rate or dividend schedule that, when compared to the growth of the equities market, will generally produce a lower total return.

The possible lower return of traditional products, when compared to variable life, is for a very good reason. With a fixed life insurance product, the policyholder is risking only the return *on* the money. With variable life, the risk is on both the return *on* and the return *of* the money (cash values and death benefits can fluctuate with performance of the equity funds into which the policy assets are invested). However, most variable life marketers are addressing the safety of principal issue by offering a fixed-asset strategy as an option contained within the variable policy. In other words, the insured can determine where cash values will be invested from a mixture of growth funds, income funds, government securities, bond funds, etc. The client can periodically switch from one option to another within the policy based upon where he or she perceives the opportunity for the best return to be. Thus, the concern about risk of lost principal is mitigated to a degree by many variable life products.

The second reason we will continue to see a major push toward variable products has to do with the companies that sell it. We have discussed in some detail the ever-increasing surplus strain created by reserving requirements to be sure that policy guarantees are met. With variable life, the cash value guarantees are much lower, and as a result, so are the reserving requirements. To a large degree, variable life passes on the risk of protecting the principal within the policy to the consumer.

Actually, the consumer delegates the risk to the portfolio managers who are selected to manage the cash value in the policy. This, in turn, takes even more pressure off the insurance company with regard to its financial ratings. The asset in the policy is, in effect, walled off from the company when it is invested in a mutual fund. Should the insurance company encounter financial problems and experience a run at the bank, these separate account assets would remain inaccessible and illiquid to anyone other than the policy-holder. What's more, the problems of the insurance company are less disturbing if the policyholder's cash values are safely walled off in a separate account invested in a mutual fund or bond fund that has nothing to do with the insurance company.

Another big benefit of variable life to companies is that, due to restrictions on dual licensing by the NASD, it is difficult for an agent to represent multiple carriers for variable life. It is more likely due to liability issues and the complexity of the product that most agents will license for variable life with only one broker-dealer. Logically, that will be the one through which their primary company sells its variable life product. Brokering variable life or representing multiple carriers is often perceived as too risky and cumbersome for most agents to undertake. This bodes well for the larger career agency companies that want a dedicated sales force.

Variable life offers benefits to everyone that are real and fair. It is, in my opinion, a win/win product that is here to stay.

Other product changes on the horizon will tend to draw their appeal from variable life. In the family insurance market, we will see a resurgence of the agent as financial planner due to the variety of investment-oriented products available through variable life. This, too, is a win/win situation. Agents will have more to talk to mainstream America about, and families and individuals will have more opportunity to plan for their financial security.

The annuity market has, in terms of volume being sold, already gone variable. The variable annuity, first introduced by Aetna Life in the 1960s, has passed the test of time and been proven beyond any doubt to be one of the best values ever delivered by the life insurance industry. The stockbrokers have done an outstanding job of marketing variable annuities; now it's the insurance agents' turn to take this product to its next plateau.

I don't have a great deal more to say about the life insurance products for the year 2000, because the real product revolution is over. It occurred in the 1980s, when the product of life insurance was unbundled, examined and reassembled into an attractive, consumer-oriented value that, by any measure, should be an important part of the average American's financial plan. Now, in the late 1990s, we are effectively under way with a conversion from the fixed to the variable product (which retains fixed product features) while preserving most of the consumer-oriented benefits introduced a decade earlier. The real revolution on the horizon is the distribution revolution.

DISTRIBUTION CHANGES

The biggest change in product development is that it will shift from being distribution-driven to becoming market-driven. This, in turn, will drive the changes we can expect to see in distribution. Historically, the agent distribution system led the industry to markets and products. For example, when the IRA was created, agents needed a product to penetrate that market. Therefore, companies developed a series of insured IRAs, IRA alternatives and, eventually, the Private Pension Plan, which caused more than a few problems in that the distribution system had lost sight of the original customer expectations in this market. This led to a great deal of criticism regarding some industry sales practices. The real problem was that the distribution system was trying to adapt the market to its criteria for success, rather than succeeding by adapting to the market and its needs.

Today and into the future, we will see a continued trend toward companies examining a market objectively and then seeking out the appropriate distribution system or strategy to meet the needs of that market. In other words, the tail will no longer wag the dog. LIMRA guru Walter H. Zultowski, PhD, calls this development "distribution pluralism." He says companies will no longer be bound by their primary distribution system to the product they sell and the markets they serve. Instead, companies will decide what markets they want to serve and what products they want to sell in those markets. They will then seek out distribution systems that can serve those markets effectively and profitably and to the satisfaction of the consumer.

What this means to agents is that companies are, in effect, going to be doing target marketing for the very reason they have encouraged their agents to do the same for at least a decade—economics. Just as agents should pick an area of specialization, then select the products that can effectively and profitably be sold in those markets, so will a company develop products and delivery systems that meet the needs of its target markets. Traditional agents may or may not fit into the plans.

In the future, companies are more likely to look for access to existing distribution to penetrate new markets. The reasons for this are fairly obvious given the scarcity of working capital and the high cost of building distribution internally. These efforts are already under way in banks and stockbrokerage firms and are soon to come to accountants, management consulting firms and any other credible venue for accessing a given target market.

Banks Despite considerable efforts by industry organizations to resist banks entering our business, the proverbial genie is out of the bottle. The issue is really no longer whether or not the alternative distribution systems, such as banks and credit unions, will sell our product; the only question is how their role will evolve over time. While publicly fighting bank involvement in selling life insurance, many companies have privately—or even publicly—been preparing to launch full-scale efforts to get their piece of the pie the minute it's out of the legislative oven. This feast won't take long to be served up to insurance companies and banks eager to increase their share of the consumer's savings/investment dollar.

Stockbrokers As for the stockbrokerage industry, perceived by many as the other threat to traditional distribution, there are no meaningful entry barriers to the marketing of life insurance. It's simply a matter of putting together the right set of motivating circumstances. Like the banking industry, stockbrokers had little success selling life insurance to the traditional mainstream market early on. They then found the annuity market a while before the banks did. Older, high net worth clients were perfect prospects who were not being called upon by traditional agents, especially regarding an annuity purchase. Today, stockbrokers are selling a tremendous amount of second-to-die life insurance for purposes of estate planning. However, it is extremely important to note that the lion's share of this selling is being done on a joint-case basis with qualified estate-planning life insurance agents. When the banks move from annuities to life insurance, I believe they, too, will find they must work with qualified agents.

What does all of this mean to the individual life insurance agent wanting to prosper to the year 2000 and beyond? From where I sit, it looks pretty good. Although these changes may not portend well for some companies, I fail to see any cause for concern from an agent's point of view. In fact, I would have to say that I believe these developments are a blessing in disguise.

The Ambergris Factor

Before drawing any conclusions about the effects of alternate distribution, let's look at the issues of distribution expense and profitability. If you are going to grow and prosper beyond the turn of the century, an understanding of the history of agent development is valuable. The problems of agent productivity and retention have plagued our industry from the start. The average paid case rate among agents is less than 50 per year, and the retention of new recruits into their fifth year continues to hover between 10 and 15 percent. The industry has browbeaten itself over these statistics forever, but little has been done to improve the situation. I have an entirely different view of the productivity retention issue. I call it the "ambergris factor."

In the American whaling industry, which got under way during the 18th century, whalers slaughtered the giant sperm whale for sperm oil, which was used as fuel for lamps. Another type of oil, called spermaceti, extracted from the head, became the chief ingredient in candles. While boiling up the blubber and parts of the sperm whale, whalers occasionally noticed a very pleasing fragrance. It turned out this was a third oil-like substance located in the intestines of the whales. Called ambergris, it became the basis for very expensive perfume. The problem was that whalers found ambergris in very few of the whales they killed; nevertheless, the substance brought them a good income because the perfume manufacturers paid extremely high prices for it, so the whalers killed a lot of sperm whales looking for those chosen few who had the right intestinal stuff.

The life insurance industry is a lot like those whalers. We can get along okay without the perfume. But finding that occasional person with the right intestinal stuff sure makes things smell a lot better, not to mention the profitability such a catch brings to the enterprise. With a true success ratio of less than 1:10, it is hard to believe that the typical career agency company is solely dependent upon the occasional survivor—or, even more rarely, the genuinely successful agent, for its survival. Rather, I believe that the occasional successful agent is the ambergris, the perfume, that provides extra profitability. The rest of the blubber in the sales force is still profitable without him or her. I know this is a very harsh view, but we live in a very competitive world, and it's time the industry looked at itself in the brilliant light of our global economy.

Please bear in mind that this analogy is how you might look at the issue as an *agent*. For those who run companies, it's quite a different matter. They must share in all of the problems as a team, but agents must use their talents to overcome these problems personally while the industry struggles with them.

If you're part of the ambergris in our industry, forget all of the trendsetters and futurists writing so prolifically about our fate, because none of the changes that occur will keep you from succeeding. You are beyond being adversely affected by external conditions. Your values and beliefs are too sound to be corrupted by intruders.

The fact is that the biggest challenge facing the alternative distribution systems—namely, banks and stockbrokerage firms—is profitable distribution! Despite their huge client bases, so far most of them have been unable to put business on the books any less expensively than you do. This has been confirmed by one study after another. So what's the threat? Are they going to beat you to a prospect? Hardly. After all, according to LIMRA, in the decade from 1984 to 1994, the number of life insurance agents per American household shrank from one for every 200 households to one for every 400. During the same period, the number of policies sold per year in the United States declined from a high of 17 million to about 10 million. Clearly, the life insurance industry is not getting the job done in the traditional individual market. That is a problem the industry must and will address through alternative distribution. Meanwhile, it is not a problem the individual agent can do much about, other than to enjoy the shrinking competition.

From the perspective of life insurance agents who have paid their dues and established themselves in the business, the horizon looks very bright. The industry's efforts at alternative distribution will have to become wildly successful before they recover the loss of market share that will be experienced in the individual agent market between 1985, when noticeable declines began, and the turn of the century!

Regardless of the reasons behind these industry difficulties, the fact is that no one who sells life insurance for a living in the year 2000 or beyond, is likely to be tripping over competition.

Concerning agent attitudes about banks and stockbrokers selling our product, we should wish them all the success in the world! The companies we represent who have embraced this distribution pluralism need these efforts to succeed and flourish into the future. Because these distribution methods are currently no more cost-effective than the agency system, and companies have a fortune invested in establishing their sales forces, it isn't likely they will scrap them anytime soon in favor of a short-term successful experience with an outside distribution source.

In fact, I would encourage agents to consider launching their own joint ventures with bankers, stockbrokers, accountants or others interested in sharing their client base in exchange for your expertise. A word of caution: Be certain you check with your company's compliance officer before forming any partnerships.

AN INDUSTRY IN TRANSITION

Many feel that ours is a mature industry; some feel it is an industry in decline. I tend to think of the life insurance industry, from the agent's point of view, as an industry in transition. In economic terminology, we are making the transition from imperfect competition to perfect competition. Imperfect competition exists when, due to a controlled supply, such as the DeBeers diamond empire, and increasing demand, such as more and more affluence, a company can enjoy very substantial profit margins. With this, of course, eventually comes complacency, bureaucracy, inefficiency and resistance to change. Historically, the life insurance industry has consisted of hundreds of companies who were ostensibly competitors but, in reality, enjoyed the same control over their product and its profitability as DeBeers over its diamonds or the old AT&T over telephone systems. That control, however, was not over supply but over knowledge. We sold a product that everyone needed and almost no one understood. Thus, it didn't matter how many competitors there were as long as the lack of apple-to-apple comparisons conserved exceptional profit margins.

Perfect competition exists when multiple providers compete toe to toe, center stage on a level playing field. This is where our industry is today. The consumer is now sophisticated and has the help of the press, regulators and plaintiff lawyers to point out the chinks in our armor. We had it our way for a long while. Now we must perform or perish. For the agent who is ready, this is only good news.

PREPARING FOR THE FUTURE

Now we must perfect our product and educate our agents to meet the challenge. These issues are at the heart of the transition, but with them will necessarily come improvements in expense management, investment performance, distribution efficiency and customer service. Eventually, these changes will be good for everyone, including the individual agent. The journey will probably have a few bumps in the road along the way. One of these will be the expense of bringing new agents into the business. The average career agency admits to a cost of about $250,000 for every agent it delivers into a fifth year in the business. It's important to note that this statistic applies to the cost of one *survivor*. What the cost is for an agent most would regard as successful is unknown and, to my knowledge, unsought. This is the ambergris factor. It works if you are some of the ambergris, but the industry can no longer afford this expense—especially now that the amounts available for financing new agents have been reduced on a per capita basis. The result has made it harder than ever to attract good people.

Law firms, accounting firms, medical practices and even casualty agencies all finance their own new people. The life insurance agency system must bite the bullet and do the same. It can be accomplished through the adoption of intern and apprentice programs such as those discussed in this book. It isn't the entire distribution system that's inefficient, it's the portion controlled by the companies. Let the companies turn the manpower development function over to those they hold accountable for it—their field managers. The companies can then focus their energies on doing what they do well: asset management and the management of risk.

Life insurance companies should earmark the funds available for the three key functions of recruiting, training and agent development and turn them over to their field management instead of spending money on financing new agents. Recruiting and training dollars should be given to the manager for use within the agency as well as the support of LUTC, AMTC, CLU and ChFC and other industry-recognized freestanding programs such as those provided by KBA (Kinder Bros. & Assoc.).

With this logical transition, life insurance companies could focus on being manufacturers of product, which is what they do well, and give up on being distribution specialists, which is something they usually don't do well. This doesn't mean giving up control, which is, unfortunately, the underlying concern that keeps most companies from taking this logical step. As long as companies offer quality products, operate at an acceptable profit and maintain a good public image, their agents are not likely to leave. If companies have a sales force they want to save, they must let go and earn the agents' willingness to stay, for if they try to hang on, they will surely lose much more. Let them make their wonderful product of life insurance, for which there is no substitute, and let others deal with the arcane business of agent development.

What all of this means to the agent looking to the year 2000 is opportunity, challenge and vocational fulfillment. If the business as we know it has become antiquated, so be it. There's a subtle but important difference between antiquity and obsolescence.

I once purchased a home in my native Detroit that was constructed by a Depression-era master craftsman. It had an oak spiral staircase, jeweled leaded-glass windows and a walnut-paneled study, and was surrounded by 50-year-old pine and maple trees. It was, in every way, a treasure. Visitors, without exception, lamented that the re-creation of such a masterpiece of architecture and craftsmanship "would be impossible today."

They were right. I savored every walk down the marble hallway beneath the crown moldings and into the canopied garden. It was a house that would not be practical to build today, which caused me to cherish it all the more. Yet it was anything but obsolete. Its beauty and functionality exceeded that of the finest new housing available. It was one of a kind—something of great value, into which those before me invested resources unavailable today. I was the beneficiary of their labors, and I drank deeply from the well that my benefactors had so lovingly dug.

With patience and care, all of us can preserve and improve this remarkable industry, and in turn it will shelter and provide for us and our clients into the future.

Appendix A

The National Network of Estate Planning Attorneys

Esperti Peterson Institute
for
Estate Planning

INCORPORATED

INNOVATION & LEADERSHIP

Strategic Overview

Leadership in the research and development of innovative estate planning techniques, and sharing this knowledge with professionals so they can assist families, preserve wealth and perpetuate philanthropy

The Institute is the leading national organization dedicated to superiority through education and the interrelationship of a diversity of estate planning skills.

Robert A. Esperti and Renno L. Peterson, Co-Founders and Co-Chairmen of The Institute, are leading estate and tax planning attorneys. Together, their expertise exceeds forty years. They are nationally known authors and educators who have authored thirteen books on estate and business planning and related subjects. These include the highly-acclaimed *Handbook of Estate Planning* and *Protect Your Estate* published by McGraw-Hill, and *Loving Trust* and *The Living Trust Revolution* published by Viking-Penguin. In 1989, they created the first of a series of information and educational services which have evolved into the present-day Institute.

Edward M. Lee, President, is a national leader in the information and education industries. He was one of the founders of Xerox Learning Systems, a pioneer education company. As a founder, President and CEO of The Information Technology Group, he built a major multi-national information company serving worldwide engineering, legal, architectural, governmental and academic markets.

Esperti Peterson Institute for Estate Planning

Incorporated

410 17th Street, Suite 1260   Denver, Colorado 80202   Phone: (303) 466-6100
Fax: (303) 446-6060

**National Network
of
Estate Planning Attorneys**

INCORPORATED

THE NEW PRACTICE PARADIGM

Attorneys helping attorneys to
serve clients better and build
prosperous and satisfying
professional careers

The Network is comprised of hundreds of estate planning attorneys who are committed to providing superior legal advice, counsel and documentation to their clients. The national electronic telecommunications network is supplemented by several *Advanced Estate Planning Techniques Seminars* each year which foster idea-sharing and continuing education.

Members take special pride in determining client needs and desires and tailoring recommendations which empower their clients to achieve their objectives.

MARKET SEGMENTS

Firms
Sole practitioners
Boutique firms
Specialized firms
Full-service firms

Attorneys
Estate planning specialists
Tax specialists
General practitioners
Litigation counsel
Commercial transaction counsel
General business practitioners

PRODUCTS / SERVICES

Multi-volume drafting compendium
Document creation software:

Individual & Joint Revocable trusts-
(Common law and community property states)-
All living trust ancillary documents-
Irrevocable life insurance trusts-
Charitable remainder trusts-
Grantor retained trusts-
Generation-skipping trusts-

Scripted/slide supported client seminar programs
Technical support
Update service
Technical texts
Marketing texts
"How to" audio/video tapes
Interprofessional electronic-bulletin board
Practice marketing aids
Advanced technical seminars
Advanced marketing seminars

National Association of Estate Planning Advisors

INCORPORATED

INTERDISCIPLINARY COOPERATION

Empowering professionals to plan together with attorneys to achieve superior planning results and client satisfaction

The Association is an independent organization of professionals in the financial services industries. These specialists exchange information on estate planning needs and client requirements. Members benefit from innovative publications, seminars and educational materials.

MARKET SEGMENTS	PRODUCTS / SERVICES
Firms	Advisor action plan
Life insurance companies	Audio sales series
Full-service financial	Audio technical series
institutions	Electronic mail bulletin board
Broker dealers	Technical update service
Corporate fiduciaries	Marketing aids and brochures
Banks	Advanced technical seminars
Credit unions	Advanced marketing seminars
Accounting	Prospecting seminars
	Video sales series
Advisors	Video marketing series
Tax professionals	Script/slide-supported client
Accountants	seminar programs
Life insurance professionals	
Financial planners	
Stockbrokers	

Appendix B

VitalSigns Carrier Analysis

Life Insurer Financial Profile

Company	New York Life	Top 25 US Companies
Ratings:		
A.M. Best Company (Best's Rating)	A + + (1)	
Standard & Poor's (Claims Paying/Solvency)	AAA (1)	
Moody's (Financial Strength)	Aaa (1)	
Duff & Phelps (Claims Paying Ability)	AAA (1)	
Comdex (Percentile in Peer Group)	100	80
Assets & Liabilities		
Total Admitted Assets	53,570,943	40,887,109
Separate Accounts	2,898,101	8,604,687
Total Liabilities	46,394,743	29,787,127
Total Statutory Surplus	4,278,099	2,495,295
As % of General Account Assets	8.4%	7.7%
Invested Asset Distribution & Yield		
Total Invested Assets	48,737,314	31,231,452
Bonds (%)	67.3%	62.1%
Stocks (%)	4.7%	4.1%
Mortgages (%)	10.6%	19.7%
Real Estate (%)	2.0%	4.2%
Policy Loans (%)	10.3%	5.3%
Other (%)	5.0%	4.6%
Yield on Mean Invested Assets		
1993 (Industry Avg. 7.87%)	8.04%	8.14%
5-Year Average (Industry Avg. 8.86%)	8.62%	8.85%
Non-Performing Assets as % of Statutory Surplus		
Bonds In or Near Default	0.6%	3.1%
Problem Mortgages	1.8%	10.0%
Real Estate Acquired by Foreclosure	7.7%	13.6%
Total Non-Performing Assets	10.2%	26.7%
As a % of Invested Assets	0.9%	2.1%
Bond Quality		
Total Value of Bonds	34,029,904	20,095,473
Class 1: Highest Quality	74.6%	68.5%
Class 2: Higher Quality	20.5%	25.0%
Class 3: Medium Quality	3.2%	3.4%
Class 4: Low Quality	1.5%	1.9%
Class 5: Lower Quality	0.2%	0.7%
Class 6: In or Near Default	0.1%	0.4%
Weighted Bond Class	1.3	1.4
Income & Earnings		
Total Income	13,051,427	8,669,870
Net Premiums Written	8,874,455	5,812,161
Earnings Before Divs. and Taxes	1,743,879	856,861
Net Operating Earnings	313,420	228,840

V05/94 Data for Year End 1993 provided by the National Assoc. of
Insurance Commissioners (000's omitted in all dollar amounts.)

Life Insurer Financial Analysis

Page 1	New York Life	Top 25 US Companies

Ratings

A.M. Best Company (Best's Rating)	A + + (1)	
Standard & Poor's (Claims Paying/Solvency)	AAA (1)	
Moody's (Financial Strength)	Aaa (1)	
Duff & Phelps (Claims Paying Ability)	AAA (1)	
Comdex (Percentile in Peer Group)	100	80

Asset Analysis

Total Admitted Assets	53,570,943	40,887,109
Separate Accounts	2,898,101	8,604,687
Total Liabilities	46,394,743	29,787,127
Total Statutory Surplus	4,278,099	2,495,295
As % of General Account Assets	8.4%	7.7%
Invested Assets	48,737,314	31,231,452
Bonds	67.3%	62.1%
Stocks	4.7%	4.1%
Mortgages	10.6%	19.7%
Real Estate	2.0%	4.2%
Policy Loans	10.3%	5.3%
Other	5.0%	4.6%
	100.0%	100.0%
Yield on Mean Invested Assets		
1993 (Industry Avg. 7.87%)	8.04%	8.14%
1992 (Industry Avg. 8.58%)	8.47%	8.55%
1991 (Industry Avg. 9.09%)	8.74%	9.11%
1990 (Industry Avg. 9.31%)	8.96%	9.13%
1989 (Industry Avg. 9.47%)	8.91%	9.31%
5-Year Average (Industry Avg. 8.86%)	8.62%	8.85%
Asset Growth		
1993 Total Admitted Assets	53,570,943	40,887,109
1-Year Growth	14.2%	9.3%
3-Year Compound Growth	10.3%	8.9%
1993 Total Statutory Surplus	4,278,099	2,495,295
1-Year Growth	26.0%	15.0%
3-Year Compound Growth	15.6%	14.8%

V05/94 Data for Year End 1993 provided by the National Assoc. of
Insurance Commissioners (000's omitted in all dollar amounts.)

Life Insurer Financial Analysis

Page 2	New York Life	Top 25 US Companies
Asset Quality Analysis		
Non-Investment Grade Bonds (Class 3-6)		
N.I.G. Bonds/Total Bonds	4.9%	6.4%
N.I.G. Bonds/Statutory Surplus	39.2%	51.7%
Non-Performing Bonds (Class 6)		
N.P. Bonds/Total Bonds	0.1%	0.4%
N.P. Bonds/Statutory Surplus	0.6%	3.1%
Non-Performing Mortgages & Real Estate		
N.P. Mort & RE/Total Mort & RE	6.6%	7.9%
N.P. Mort & RE/Statutory Surplus	9.5%	23.6%
Non-Performing Assets/Statutory Surplus		
Bonds In or Near Default	0.6%	3.1%
Problem Mortgages	1.8%	10.0%
Real Estate Acquired by Foreclosure	7.7%	13.6%
Total Non-Performing Assets/Stat. Surplus	10.2%	26.7%
As a % of Invested Assets	0.9%	2.1%
Bond Portfolio Analysis		
Quality		
Class 1: Highest Quality	74.6%	68.5%
Class 2: Higher Quality	20.5%	25.0%
Class 3: Medium Quality	3.2%	3.4%
Class 4: Low Quality	1.5%	1.9%
Class 5: Lower Quality	0.2%	0.7%
Class 6: In or Near Default	0.1%	0.4%
Weighted Bond Class	1.3	1.4
Maturity		
1 Year or Less	5.6%	8.1%
1 to 5 Years	27.2%	25.5%
5 to 10 Years	28.8%	28.8%
10 to 20 Years	12.9%	17.0%
Over 20 Years	25.6%	20.6%
Weighted Bond Maturity (Years)	11.3	10.7

V05/94 Data for Year End 1993 provided by the National Assoc. of
Insurance Commissioners (000's omitted in all dollar amounts.)

Life Insurer Financial Analysis

Page 3	New York Life	Top 25 US Companies
Operating Income Analysis		
Total Income	13,051,427	8,669,870
Total General Expenses	1,079,537	631,721
General Expenses/Total Income	8.3%	7.3%
Earnings Before Policy Divs. & Taxes	1,743,879	856,861
Policy Dividends	1,093,810	508,970
Policy Dividends/Earnings	62.7%	59.4%
Pretax Earnings from Operations	650,069	347,891
Federal Income Taxes	336,649	119,051
Income Taxes/Pretax Earnings	51.8%	34.2%
Net Earnings from Operations	313,420	228,840
Net Realized Capital Gains	22,321	-55,704
Net Income	335,741	173,136
As % of Admitted Assets	0.6%	0.4%
Unrealized Capital Gains	234,401	35,148
Premium Growth		
1993 Total Premium Income	5,327,311	3,366,615
1-Year Growth	7.0%	5.0%
3-Year Compound Growth	2.1%	3.4%
1993 Ordinary Life Premium	3,919,706	1,430,236
1-Year Growth	4.5%	17.5%
3-Year Compound Growth	7.0%	11.0%
Profitability		
Return on Assets	0.7%	1.5%
Return on Equity	8.2%	9.8%
Net Investment Income	3,598,002	2,371,144
Required Interest	2,291,424	1,549,810
Interest Margin	57.0%	53.0%
Expected Mortality (Ordinary Life)	1,417,041	512,850
Actual Mortality (Ordinary Life)	403,685	168,112
Mortality Margin	71.5%	67.2%
Total Expenses/Total Income	8.3%	7.3%

V05/94 Data for Year End 1993 provided by the National Assoc. of Insurance Commissioners (000's omitted in all dollar amounts.)

Life Insurer Financial Analysis

Page 4	New York Life	Top 25 US Companies

Analysis of Face Amount of Insurance

	New York Life	Top 25 US Companies
Total Insurance In Force	367,985,871	228,166,013
Ordinary Life	73.3%	48.5%
Group Life	26.7%	50.9%
Other	0.0%	0.5%
Total Reinsurance Ceded	65,822,018	23,461,685
% of In Force Ceded		
Ordinary Life	24.2%	14.3%
Group Life	0.7%	6.3%
Other	0.0%	21.0%

Analysis by Line of Business

	New York Life	Top 25 US Companies
Net Premiums Written	8,874,455	5,812,161
Individual		
Life	44.2%	24.7%
Annuities	1.9%	18.7%
Health	1.4%	1.1%
Group		
Life	3.4%	6.9%
Annuities	41.4%	34.6%
Health	7.7%	13.8%
Credit Life & Health	0.0%	0.1%
Net Earnings from Operations	313,420	228,840
Individual		
Life	68.2%	31.3%
Annuities	4.6%	23.8%
Health	-0.3%	-3.3%
Group		
Life	4.0%	8.6%
Annuities	16.5%	24.3%
Health	6.7%	10.7%
Credit Life & Health	0.0%	0.2%
Misc. Lines	0.2%	4.3%

V05/94 Data for Year End 1992 provided by the National Assoc. of
Insurance Commissioners (000's omitted in all dollar amounts.)

Life Insurer Financial Profile
List of Company Ratings

Company :   New York Life
Domicile: NY
Established: 1845

A.M. Best Company Rating   A++ (1)

Superior overall performance when compared to the norms of
the life/health insurance industry. Strongest ability to
meet policyholder and other contractual obligations.

Standard & Poor's Claims Paying Ability Rating   AAA (1)

Insurers rated AAA offer superior financial security on
both an absolute and relative basis. They possess the
highest safety and have an overwhelming capacity to meet
policyholder obligations.

Moody's Financial Strength Rating   Aaa (1)

Insurance companies rated Aaa offer exceptional financial
security. While the financial strength of these companies
is likely to change, such changes as can be visualized are
most unlikely to impair their fundamentally strong position.

Duff & Phelps Claims Paying Ability Rating   AAA (1)

Highest claims paying ability. Risk factors are
negligible.

Comdex - Vital Signs Composite Index   100

The Comdex gives the average percentile ranking of this
company in relation to all other companies that have been
rated by the rating services. The Comdex is the percentage
of companies that are rated lower than this company.

The ratings on this report are current as of May 1, 1994.
These ratings have been selected by your life insurance
advisor from among the ratings assigned to this insurer.

New York Life

Asset Distribution

Investment Yield

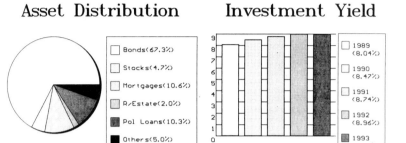

Bonds(67.3%)

Stocks(4.7%)

Mortgages(10.6%)

R/Estate(2.0%)

Pol Loans(10.3%)

Others(5.0%)

1989 (8.04%)

1990 (8.42%)

1991 (8.74%)

1992 (8.96%)

1993 (8.91%)

Non-Performing Assets

Bond Quality

Statutory Surplus

Non-Perform. Assets

Industry Average

Highest (74.6%)

Higher (20.5%)

Medium (3.2%)

Lou (1.5%)

Louer (0.2%)

In or Near Default (0.1%)

Appendix C

Data Taker

The Funnel Is Hard To Fill
Because It Has Two Siphons

Equipment
Inventories
Real Estate

Receivables
Cash
Investments

Good Will

Key People

Value of Business

Roadblocks
While Alive
Taxes
Inflation
Competition
Mistakes
Business Cycle
Fringe Benefits

Cash Needs
At Death
Lost Value of Key Person
Loss of Good Will
Professional Fees
Income to Heirs
Buyout of Deceased
Debts and Estate Taxes

Income and Capital
for Ourselves and
Our Families

PASSING THE BATON

On retirement / death, business is to be: (PB 1)

☐ **Sold** (PB 5)	☐ **Kept** (PB 4)
To Whom? _____	Who will run it? _____
_____	_____

Agreement? ☐ Yes ☐ No (BSP 9, 11)	Agreement? ☐ Yes ☐ No (BSP 9)
If yes, ☐ Stock Redemption ☐ Cross Purchase	
(BSP4) (BSP5)	
☐ Entity Purchase (Partnership)	
(BSP4)	How will owners/heirs be paid?
For How Much?	☐ Salary ☐ Salary Continuation
☐ Price to be determined at time of sale	☐ Dividends ☐ Not to be paid
☐ Price set in agreement	
☐ Price which IRS sets (303-4)	What value will IRS place on business? _____
☐ Have not considered (BSP 11)	(BSP 11, 303-4)
☐ Other	How will Estate Taxes and Expenses be paid?
$ _____	☐ Cash (LN 13-15) ☐ Borrow (LN 13)
(Total Value of Your Equity)	☐ Sell Assets (LN 13) ☐ Insurance (LN 16, 17)
How Paid? (BSP7)	☐ Section "303" (303-1,2) ☐ Deferred Payments
☐ Cash (BSP 17) ☐ Borrow (BSP 12-15)	(LN 10, 11)
☐ Installments to Sellers ☐ Insurance (BSP 16,17)	Are heirs to inherit ownership equally?
(BSP 12-15) ☐ Don't Know	☐ Yes ☐ No (Give details below)
Insured Amount	
_____ $ _____	_____
_____ $ _____	
_____ $ _____	Optional – Continue datataking in the "Estate
_____ $ _____	Planning" section of the Datataker.

Name _____   Date _____

Company _____   Phone _____

Address _____

Present Ownership

Owner	% Owned	Earnings	Age/Health	Smoke (Y/N)
_____	_____	_____	_____	_____
_____	_____	_____	_____	_____
_____	_____	_____	_____	_____
_____	_____	_____	_____	_____

☐ Sub S Corporation	Top Tax Bracket (Including State and Federal) _____ %
☐ C Corporation	Gross Sales $ _____
☐ Professional Corporation	Earnings $ _____
☐ Sole Proprietor (BSP 20-22)	Book Value $ _____
☐ Partnership	Name of Attorney : _____
☐ Professional Partnership	Name of Accountant : _____

B2

NOTES

_____

_____

_____

_____

_____

_____

_____

_____

_____

_____

_____

_____

_____

_____

_____

_____

_____

VALUING A BUSINESS (303-4)
(Revenue Ruling 59-60)

	Compound Interest Factors

1. Book Value $ _____
2. Industry Return*   _____ %
3. "Expected" Earnings (1 times 2) $ _____
4. Actual Earnings** $ _____
5. Earnings Above "Expected"
   (4 minus 3) $ _____
6 Capitalization Rate***   _____ %
7. Good Will (5 divided by 6) $ _____
8. Plus Book Value (1) $ _____
9. Value of Business $ _____

Compound Interest Factors

Years	4%	6%	8%	10%
1	1.040	1.060	1.080	1.100
2	1.081	1.123	1.166	1.210
3	1.124	1.191	1.259	1.331
4	1.169	1.262	1.360	1.464
5	1.216	1.338	1.469	1.610
6	1.265	1.418	1.586	1.771
7	1.315	1.503	1.713	1.948
8	1.368	1.593	1.850	2.143
9	1.423	1.689	1.999	2.357
10	1.480	1.790	2.158	2.593
11	1.539	1.898	2.331	2.853
12	1.601	2.012	2.518	3.138
13	1.665	2.132	2.719	3.452
14	1.731	2.260	2.937	3.797
15	1.800	2.396	3.172	4.177
16	1.872	2.540	3.425	4.594
17	1.947	2.692	3.700	5.054
18	2.025	2.854	3.996	5.559
19	2.106	3.025	4.315	6.115
20	2.191	3.207	4.660	6.727
21	2.278	3.399	5.033	7.400
22	2.369	3.603	5.436	8.140
23	2.464	3.819	5.871	8.954
24	2.563	4.048	6.341	9.849
25	2.665	4.291	6.848	10.834

PROJECTED GROWTH

In _____ Years at _____ % Growth

$ _____ x _____ = $ _____
   Current Value   Compound Interest   Projected Value
   of Business   Factor   of Business

 * Use 8% for Low Risk – Stable Business, 10% for High Risk – Hazardous Business
 ** Before Tax Earnings, Average of 5 Years, Add Amount Paid to Owners Which Exceeds
    Amount Paid to an Employee Performing Same Work.
 *** Use 15% for Low Risk – Stable Business, 20% for High Risk – Hazardous Business.

B3

KEY PEOPLE — MAXIMIZING BENEFITS (KPMB 1)

Besides yourself, which of your employees are critical to the operation of your business?

Employee	Earnings	Age/Health	Smoke (Y/N)

Name _____   Date _____

Company _____   Phone _____

Address _____

Present Ownership

Owner	% Owned	Earnings	Age/Health	Smoke (Y/N)

☐ Sub S Corporation
☐ C Corporation
☐ Professional Corporation
☐ Sole Proprietor (BSP 20-22)
☐ Partnership
☐ Professional Partnership

Top Tax Bracket (Including State and Federal) _____ %
Gross Sales $ _____
Earnings $ _____
Book Value $ _____
Name of Attorney: _____
Name of Accountant: _____

B4

OPTIMIZING PERSONAL BENEFITS (OPB 1)

Name _____ Date _____

Retirement Age _____ Health _____

Family Status _____ Date of Birth _____

Annual Salary $ _____ Smoke (Yes/No) _____

Company Name _____ Phone _____

Address _____

Complete when interest is shown in a particular question on Salesmaker page OPB1

Question 1:   • How much additional income is desired? $ _____
            Complete "Key People – Maximizing Benefits" section (page B4)

Question 2:   • How much additional income is desired? $ _____
            Complete "Key People – Maximizing Benefits" section (page B4)

Question 3:   • Record details on existing retirement plans, i.e.: Qualified Plans, Deferred Compensation, etc. in Notes section (page B3) and complete "Key People – Maximizing Benefits" section (page B4)

Question 4:   • Record existing Individual Coverage (use "Insurance Information" section, page E2)

            • Record existing Group Coverage (use "Insurance Information" section, page E2)

Question 5:   • Complete Present Ownership section in "Passing the Baton" section (page B2)

            • Estate Value: $ _____

            • Dollar Value of Your Business Interest: $ _____

Question 6:

Amount of Note	Bank	Duration	Who Signed
1.			
2.			
3.			

Question 7:   • Record details on personal life insurance (use "Insurance Information" section, page E2)

Question 8:   • Complete "Estate Planning" section (pages E2-E7)

         B5

The Funnel Is Hard To Fill
Because It Has Two Siphons

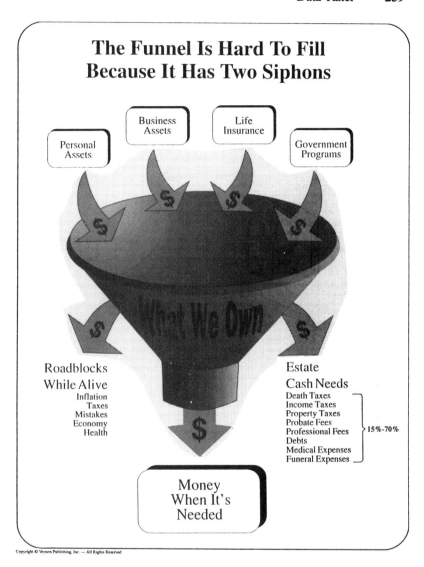

Personal
Assets

Business
Assets

Life
Insurance

Government
Programs

What We Own

Roadblocks
While Alive
Inflation
Taxes
Mistakes
Economy
Health

Estate
Cash Needs
Death Taxes
Income Taxes
Property Taxes
Probate Fees
Professional Fees   } 15%-70%
Debts
Medical Expenses
Funeral Expenses

Money
When It's
Needed

ESTATE PLANNING (EP 10, 11)

Family Information

Date _____

	Name	Birth Date	Birth Place/Citizenship	Health/Smoke
You				
Spouse				
₁ Children				

Residence Address _____ Tel. # _____

Own Home ☐   Renting ☐   Monthly Rental $ _____ Mortgage Balance $ _____ Int. Rate _____%

Father Living _____ Age _____ Health _____

Mother Living _____ Age _____ Health _____

Parents' Financial Status _____

Spouse's Father Living _____ Age _____ Health _____

Spouse's Mother Living _____ Age _____ Health _____

₂ Spouse's Parents' Financial Status _____

₃ Attorney _____ Accountant _____

Your Will Date _____ Provisions of Will _____

Spouse's Will Date _____ Provisions of Will _____

₄ Trusts _____ Trustees _____

Occupational Information

₊₅ Employer _____ Occ. _____ Tel. # _____

Business Address _____

₊₅ Spouse's Employer _____ Occ. _____ Tel. # _____

Business Address _____

Social Security # Yours _____ Your Spouse _____

Insurance Information

	Life Insured	Company	Policy No.	Date	Amount	Type	Premium	Beneficiary	Owner	Cash Value	Dividend Status
6											

	Disability Insured	Company	Policy No.	Date	Monthly Benefit	Type	Annual Premium	Waiting Period	Benefit Duration
7									

Medical Insurance _____

₈ Pension Plan _____

₉ Expiration Dates: Car _____ Homeowners _____

Financial Information

Bank Connection _____ Marginal Tax Bracket _____%

Your Annual Income $ _____ Spouse's Annual Income $ _____

Date of Next Salary Review _____ Date of Next Salary Review _____

₁₀ Anticipated Increase _____ Anticipated Increase $ _____

*If Business Owner: Review fringe benefits
Numbers in the left-hand margin reference the "feeling/finding" questions on page E3.

E2

GOALS

1. a. Are you planning any (more) children?
   b. How do you feel about insurance on a spouse and children?
2. a. Do you think you might ever have to support your parents/in-laws?
   b. Do you expect an inheritance? How large?
   c. Do you have brothers or sisters? Married? Where do they live?
3. Are you pleased with your attorney/accountant?
4. Do you believe your spouse could properly manage and conserve your assets?

5. How do you feel about your career?
6. a. What do you want your life insurance to do for you?
   b. How do you feel about permanent insurance and term insurance?
7. How long could you live on your reserves if you were disabled tomorrow?
8. How do you feel about saving for retirement?
9. If I could show you a better buy for your auto and homeowners insurance, would you be interested?
10. What are your most important personal and financial goals?

E3

BALANCE SHEET

Date _____
Name _____   Review Date _____

Assets[1]		Liabilities	
Net Equity in Home			
Market Value: _____ Mortgage: _____ $ _____		Current Bills	$ _____
Other Real Estate (Net of Mortgages) _____		Notes	_____
Personal Property _____		Other Debts	_____
Death Benefits under Retirement Plans _____		Cost of Exercising	
Listed Securities _____		Stock Options	_____
Stock Options (market value of stock) _____			
Life Insurance _____			
Business Interest (303-4) _____			
Checking, Savings, Money Funds, etc. _____			
Other _____			
Total $ _____ (A)		Total $ _____ (B)	

Satisfied with Amount Saved? Yes ☐ No ☐   Regular Monthly Savings Plan? Yes ☐ No ☐

Amount Being Saved Monthly $_____ Additional Monthly Amount That Can Be Saved $_____
[1]Include only half the value of any jointly owned property. Place an asterisk next to any item which is non-income producing or is producing income but is not to be sold.

CAPITAL ANALYSIS

Total Assets		$ _____ (A)
Liabilities	$ _____ (B)	
Taxes and Other Final Expenses (LN 1, 2)	_____	
Emergency Fund (Guideline: 50% of Annual Income)	_____	
Payment of Mortgage/Rent Payment Fund	_____	
Cost of Education ($45,000 per child is usually the minimum that should be provided)	_____	
* Non-Income Producing Property and Income Producing Property which is not to be sold	_____	
Total Deductions		_____ (C)
Capital Available for Income (Subtract C from A)		$ _____ (D)
Income Producing Assets not owned by you (Including non-owned personal life insurance on your life)		_____ (E)
Total Capital Available for Income[2] (Add D and E)		$ _____ (F)
Projected Earnings to retirement ($_____ X _____ years)		$ _____

Note: Complete shaded areas on this page and pages E6 and E7 during first interview, also complete applicable sections on page E5.
[2]If this number is negative, it should be listed as a positive number and shown on Line "F" on page E6, Line "A" should show no Capital available for income.

E4

BALANCE SHEET
(Detail)

Details On Other Real Estate:

					YOU	SPOUSE
a. Joint Ownership	Yes ☐	No ☐	List Amounts of Money			
b. To Be Retained?	Yes ☐	No ☐	Checking		$_____	$_____
c. Income Producing?	Yes ☐	No ☐	Savings		_____	_____
d. Other Details			Certificate of Deposit		_____	_____
			Money Fund		_____	_____
			Other		_____	_____
			Total		$_____	$_____

Details On Business Interests — Complete the "Passing the Baton" section, page B2.

Details on Other Assets _____

Details on Liabilities _____

CAPITAL ANALYSIS
(Detail)

Taxes and Other Expenses:

Federal Estate Tax (LN 1)	$_____	
State Death Tax	_____	
Administrative Expenses (LN 2)	_____	
Other Final Expenses (LN 2)	_____	
Total	$_____	

Home to be Retained? Yes ☐   No ☐   Mortgage to be Paid? Yes ☐   No ☐

Rent Payment Fund (10 years suggested) Monthly Rent $_____ X_____ months = $_____

Details on Non-Income Producing Properties (Items in the estate that will not produce income for heirs)

1. Net Equity in Home (Unless Sold)	$_____
2. Any Non-Income Producing Real Estate	_____
3. Personal Property	_____
4. Any Non-Income Producing Business Interests (PB 1)	_____
5. Any Other Asset Which Will Not Produce Income, i.e. Antiques, Stamps, Coins	_____
6. Income Producing Assets that are not to be sold*	_____
Total Non-Income Producing Assets	$_____

Details on assets not owned by you: _____

*Income from these assets to be shown on page E6, line(c)

INCOME ANALYSIS

Income Objective

Based on a Government study by the Bureau of Labor Statistics[1], the following are typical income objectives in order to permit a family to "remain in their own world" after the death of a wage earner. Assumption is the mortgage on residence is paid, or a rent fund has been established, and educational expenses are provided for separately.

Annual Gross Income			Percentage of Gross Income Required
Up to		$44,000	70%
$44,001	to	$49,000	66%
$49,001	to	$54,000	63%
$54,001	to	$60,000	60%
Over		$60,000	57%
Two Income Families[2] (At all income levels)			70%

Present Income (All income of both spouses) $_____

Income Objective (_____% of above) $_____

Income Presently Provided:

Total Capital
  Available for Income $_____ @_____ % $_____ (A)

Social Security[3] and other Government Benefits $_____ (B)

Other Income (if any) $_____ (C)

Total Income Provided Now $_____

Income Shortage[4] $_____ (D)

New Capital Required ($_____ ÷ _____ %) $_____ (E)
                        Income Shortage   Assumed Interest
                                              Rate

Capital Shortage (Line F on page E4) - if any $_____ (F)

Total New Capital Required (Line E plus Line F) $_____ (G)

[1] Source: Bureau of Labor Statistics Consumer Expenditures Survey; updated with Bureau of Labor Statistics Consumer Price Index through 5/91.
[2] The study found two-income households outspend their one-earner counterparts. Therefore, if both spouses are presently working, 70% of their Total Gross Income should be provided regardless of the Income Level.
[3] Only available until youngest child reaches age 16 unless beneficiary is over age 60. (See Total Income Analysis for calculation of a spouse's subsequent income needs.)
[4] If there is an income surplus, proceed as follows:

  Show the surplus on Line (D) with a minus sign.
  Using the discount compound interest table on page E7, multiply (D) by the appropriate factor. (To determine factor, calculate the number of years until youngest child is 16 and use same interest assumption as in the Income Analysis.)
  Enter the result, with a minus sign on Line (E) above.

TOTAL INCOME ANALYSIS

New Capital Required During Child Rearing Period $_____ (G)

Income Objective After Child Rearing Period (_____%) $_____
(See Below)

Social Security only available until youngest child reaches
    age 16, thus income will be reduced _____
    years from now to Total of A + C + D' $_____

Income Shortage After Child Rearing Period $_____ (H)

New Capital Required ($_____ ÷ _____%)   _____ (I)
             _{Income Shortage (H)}   _{Assumed Interest Rate}

Amount of Capital Required today to Equal $_____ (I)
    in _____ years $_____ (J)
    (Multiply (I) by Discount Factor[2])

Total New Capital Required (G + J) $_____

[1] If D is a negative number use total of A & C only

Percentage of Gross Income Required			Years Until Youngest Child Reaches 16	[2]Discount Factors			Discount Compound Interest Factors ($1 Per Annum in Advance Compounded)		
				4%	5%	6%	4%	5%	6%
Annual Gross Income		Children Gone	1	.962	.952	.943	.962	.952	.943
Up to	$44,000	60%	2	.925	.907	.890	1.886	1.859	1.833
			3	.889	.864	.840	2.775	2.723	2.673
$44,001 to	$49,000	55%	4	.855	.823	.792	3.630	3.546	3.465
$49,001 to	$54,000	51%	5	.822	.784	.747	4.452	4.329	4.212
			6	.790	.746	.705	5.242	5.076	4.917
$54,001 to	$60,000	48%	7	.760	.711	.665	6.002	5.786	5.582
Over	$60,000	45%	8	.731	.677	.627	6.733	6.463	6.210
			9	.703	.645	.592	7.435	7.108	6.802
			10	.676	.614	.558	8.111	7.722	7.360
			11	.650	.585	.527	8.760	8.306	7.887
Two Income Families[3]		60%	12	.625	.557	.497	9.385	8.863	8.384
(At all income levels)			13	.601	.530	.469	9.986	9.394	8.853
			14	.577	.505	.442	10.563	9.899	9.295
			15	.555	.481	.417	11.118	10.380	9.712
			16	.534	.458	.394	11.652	10.838	10.106

[3]A Bureau of Labor Statistics study found two-income households outspend their one-earner counterparts. Therefore, when children are gone, if both spouses are presently working, 60% of their Total Gross Income should be provided regardless of the income Level.

"The Box" by Guy Baker and Jeff Oberholtzer

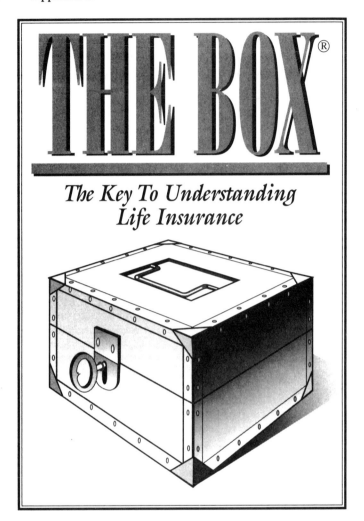

By Guy E. Baker & Jeff Oberholtzer

Most people are confused by life insurance. Buyers are often mystified by its complexity, structure and pricing. In fact, most people don't feel very comfortable with the entire subject of life insurance. But it's too important to the financial fabric of the family and business to be ignored. That's why we're writing this booklet to help readers understand the basics. We call it "The Key to Understanding Life Insurance."

Many financial writers and commentators have made their living trying to explain the fundamental principles of how insurance actually works. The jargon and vocabulary often stop people cold. What most buyers want to know is quite simple. Their questions are the same whether they're purchasing term insurance, whole life, universal life or some form of variable life. "What is the best policy for me?" "How much insurance should I buy?"

When these questions go unanswered, a mystique or confusion clouds the real value of the insurance product. It often causes buyers to make an unproductive purchase, or no purchase at all. In this booklet we hope to clear up some basic confusions, and provide a simple vocabulary to let you communicate your questions.

> *But it's too important to the financial fabric of the family and business to be ignored.*

What is life insurance?

Before we explain the key to understanding life insurance, let's define insurance and a few fundamental terms.

Insurance is a legal contract referred to as a policy. It guarantees to pay a certain sum of money (death proceeds) to a specified person or entity (the beneficiary) when the insured dies. The policy remains in effect as long as the cost for it (the premium) has been paid according to the contractual provisions.

You can own the policy personally, or have someone else own it instead. The owner has the legal right to name the beneficiary, and may change the beneficiary at any time. The owner is responsible for the tax consequences of the premium and the death benefits.

Most people don't think of it this way, but life insurance is risk sharing between a group of people with a common goal to provide money for their beneficiaries when they die. It is most often purchased because someone loves someone or something. It can be used to:

- pay a debt
- finance a tax
- purchase an interest in a business
- buy a piece of property
- or provide a guaranteed income and financial security for your loved ones.

Life insurance can also be used by a corporation to recover the cost of an obligation (or a promise) made by the employer to an employee. For instance, an advance for insurance payments or promised retirement benefits. Life insurance is often the ONLY way the owner of the policy can provide money to meet these needs. And, in most cases, it is the least expensive alternative solution to these problems.

> *...life insurance is based on the fundamental mathematical principle of probability.*

As you will see, life insurance is based on the fundamental mathematical principle of probability. People die according to a predictable pattern. This pattern, called a mortality table, is based on accumulated historical data. Insurance companies don't know who will die when, just how many. This predictable pattern, and the amount of coverage, is then mathematically converted into a lump sum amount. This lump sum amount the company needs in order to make the contractual payment at death.

The lump sum is usually financed with annual payments based on a specified rate of interest. By providing coverage to hundreds of thousands of people, insurance companies can offer coverage to each insured for a small amount of money each year. By each insured paying their proportionate share, a large lump sum is available to their family or business when they die. Life insurance is NOT a gamble. It's a proven mathematical principle based on probability. And it's available to anyone who can qualify.

With this background, let's look at why insurance works.

The KEY to Understanding Life Insurance

Life Insurance is based on the statistical odds of one person dying among a group of insureds. As we explained above, mortality tables are used to predict the chances of a person's death in any given year.

Table 1 Age 45 Mortality Table			
Age	Chance of death	Number living	Number of deaths
45	0.11%	1,000	1
46	0.12%	999	1
47	0.13%	997	1
48	0.14%	996	1
49	0.15%	995	1
50	0.16%	993	2
51	0.17%	991	2
52	0.19%	990	2
53	0.21%	987	2
54	0.23%	985	2
55	0.25%	983	3
56	0.28%	980	3
57	0.32%	977	3
58	0.35%	973	3
59	0.39%	970	4
60	0.44%	965	4
61	0.49%	961	5
62	0.54%	955	5
63	0.60%	950	6
64	0.66%	943	6
65	0.73%	937	7
66	0.82%	929	8
67	0.94%	920	9
68	1.03%	911	9
69	1.14%	900	10
70	1.68%	885	15
71	2.25%	865	20
72	2.88%	840	25
73	3.59%	810	30
74	4.26%	776	35
75	5.01%	737	39
76	5.89%	693	43
77	6.93%	645	48
78	7.81%	595	50
79	10.22%	534	61
80	11.10%	475	59
81	12.36%	416	59
82	13.41%	360	56
83	14.55%	308	52
84	15.78%	259	49
85	17.09%	215	44
86	18.51%	175	40
87	20.03%	140	35
88	21.66%	110	30
89	23.40%	84	26
90	25.26%	63	21
91	27.24%	46	17
92	29.34%	32	13
93	31.57%	22	10
94	33.92%	15	7
95	36.40%	9	5
96	39.00%	6	4
97	41.72%	3	2
98	44.55%	2	1
99	49.00%	1	1
100	56.00%	0	1

So let's suppose we have a group of 1,000 men all 45 years old. Insurance company mortality tables assume all to be in good health today, but project that none will be alive by age 100. The mortality table shown in Table 1, predicts the chances of a person's death in any given year between ages 45 and 100.

Insurance is simply a group sharing the risk to fund the dollars at death for its designated participants. The first to die are paid for by the last to die. First, let's assume no interest earnings on the money. If all participants die according to their statistical probability, there will be enough funds to pay each participant their share of the account. Those who die first will benefit most based on the ratio of their contribution to the proceeds. Those who die last will still receive proceeds, but they will have paid more to receive them.

When we factor in interest earnings, the last to die will still have to pay more into the fund than the first. But the compound interest earnings will offset the need for them to place the full value of their expected benefits into the pot.

Staying with our group of 1,000 healthy 45 year old males, let's follow what is likely to occur if they want $1,000,000 of insurance.

5

Determining the cost of insurance (the premium)

The cost of their insurance is determined by the relative probability of death at various ages. If the people in this group die as predicted by the mortality table, one of them will die in the first year. The cost to the group of this death is $1,000,000. When we spread this cost over the group of 1,000 people ($1,00,000/1,000 people) this results in a cost of $1,000 per person.

However, at age 50, 2 of the original 1,000 will die each year. This equates to a cost of 2 deaths times $1,000,000 of insurance divided by approximately 1,000 people or $2,000 per person. At age 60, the cost is $3,000 per person, and at age 70 the cost is $12,000 per person, and so on.

When you graph the outcome of this analysis, the curve looks like Chart 1. Notice the flat part of the curve in the beginning. Obviously, the coverage is very inexpensive to own during the early years. The real increases in the cost of the coverages come in the later years.

So how does an insurance company develop the information about a group of people to build a mortality table? Each insurance company has created its own data bank of experience based on their own book of insurance in force. In addition, the industry has calculated nationwide statistical measurements of mortality probabilities.

Each company's table is based on death claims over an extended period of time. The national statistics are developed without the benefit of any physical determinations. But the company tables all assume quality underwriting and good health. This means that company underwriters have received full disclosure of any medical history so they can make an accurate assessment of the insured's health. If, from the outset, a company can eliminate people who are in poor health from their table of experience, it stands to reason that their table will be more reflective of the actual statistical probability of death for their insureds.

Now ask yourself. Which would you rather buy? Insurance based on statistics developed from the population at large? Or insur-

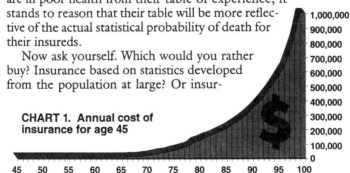

CHART 1. Annual cost of insurance for age 45

ance based on a select group of people who are all in excellent health, with a socio-economic life-style that suggests they will maintain their health over time?

To determine pricing, insurance companies select the mortality table most appropriate to the risk they are willing to insure. If medical information is not readily available, the company uses the mortality table that best reflects that higher risk.

Without dwelling on the relative merits of these tables, it is important to understand that each measures the cost of dying for different groups of people. The following graph compares the difference between 5 commonly used methods for deferring premiums.

Premiums for $1,000,000 of life insurance from various sources

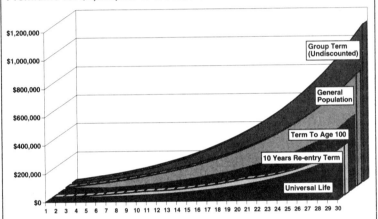

The Best Time to Buy Life Insurance

When is the best time to measure the cost of insurance? Age 50? Age 60? or Age 90? Any specific age would be arbitrary. We think life expectancy is the most meaningful calculation. But most people don't understand the true meaning of life expectancy.

When the newspapers announce that the life expectancy of a male in the U.S. is 71.2 years, it sends shivers down most spines. Fortunately, life expectancy is not the age a person is expected to die. Instead, Life Expectancy (LE) is the predicted age at which half of the people in the measured group will be dead. It is the average age of death for the group. But LE is different for each given age group at a point in time.

So, when the papers say that LE is 71.2 for males and 75.4 for females, they mean for people being born at the time of the statistic. The LE for a 45 year old from our sample table is 73.49. That means that 50% of all 45 year olds in the group will be dead by age 73.49. But it also means 50% of the group will still be alive. In other words, you have a 50% chance of living longer than LE. An 80 year old male has a LE of 85.49. Even a 95 year old has a LE. Table 2 shows life expectancies for various ages of males and females in the general population.

Counting the Cost of Insurance

Many people don't count the cost of insurance over an extended period of time. They only focus on today! But, what happens when you add up the cost of insurance (the mortality costs) from today, until life expectancy?

Chart 2 shows the results of this study. Assume you're part of our example group of 45 year old males. The sum of the mortality costs to LE is 74.7% of the face amount for a 45 year old male. That means, if you wanted to own $1,000,000 of insurance starting today, and you paid the annual mortality costs every year until life expectancy, you would need to pay $747,000.

We have measured this cost for over 20 major companies, and the cumulative rates all come out within dollars of each other. Actuaries (mathematicians trained to calculate the cost of insurance) work from the same base of statistics. Every insurance carrier must mathematically be near the same target, or they have violated the fundamental theory of risk sharing.

But next let's look at what happens if you are "unfortunate" enough to live one standard deviation beyond the mean. The standard deviation is the next statistical breaking point from the mean

TABLE 2. Life Expectancy

Current Age	Age at Life Expectancy	Current Age	Age at Life Expectancy
45	80.58	73	82.20
46	80.59	74	82.51
47	80.60	75	82.86
48	80.61	76	83.26
49	80.62	77	83.72
50	80.63	78	84.21
51	80.65	79	84.84
52	80.67	80	85.49
53	80.60	81	86.17
54	80.70	82	86.87
55	80.72	83	87.60
56	80.75	84	88.34
57	80.77	85	89.09
58	80.80	86	89.86
59	80.83	87	90.66
60	80.87	88	91.47
61	80.91	89	92.28
62	80.95	90	93.09
63	81.00	91	93.93
64	81.05	92	94.79
65	81.11	93	95.67
66	81.18	94	96.56
67	81.25	95	97.44
68	81.33	96	98.30
69	81.42	97	99.17
70	81.55	98	100.00
71	81.72	99	100.90
72	81.93	100	

(usually 6-8 years later). Let's add up all of the mortality costs for $1,000,000 of insurance at one standard deviation. It equals 119% of the face amount. That's right, you would have to pay $1,196,000 for $1,000,000 of coverage.

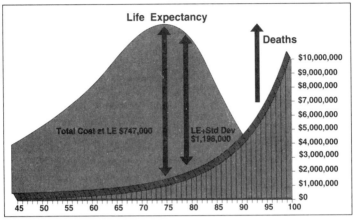

CHART 2. Cost at life expectancy

But it gets worse. What if you should live two standard deviations (approximately 14 years) beyond the mean, the ratio of mortality costs to benefits increases to 240%. That means you will have paid $2,400,000 for $1,000,000 of insurance. It's expensive to live a long time and retain your insurance.

The Natural Consequences of Aging

Okay, here's a test. What would you do if you were 82 years old and your insurance premium notice came in the mail telling you to pay $100,000 this year for your $1,000,000 policy? Answer: Not pay it and throw the notice away.

Most would let the policy lapse and laugh at the absurdity of the premium notice. All except who? The person who was in bad health or had reason to believe they might die in the next few months.

Most of us have had enough experience with people dying to know it is only the fortunate who die quickly. There are those who linger for many months, sometimes years. They still get mail, and their mail may actually consist of insurance premiums which become due on a specified date. Would you laugh and throw those away as well? Of course not.

This decision to retain a "bad" risk policy creates adverse selection against the insurance company. The ability to decide whether to keep the insurance, based solely on the probability of claim, ruins the mathematical principle. Insurance must have statistical randomness to protect the integrity of the product.

> *Insurance must have statistical randomness to protect the integrity of the product.*

It has been said that the actuaries calculate insurance premiums so the policy will lapse the day before the insured dies. But statistically, very few (less than 1%) pure insurance policies (term) ever pay a claim. People can't afford to pay the term insurance premiums at the time they are most likely to die. As the price rises, if the only insureds who retain their policies are those who know their chances of claim are certain, the insurance carrier faces financial crisis.

Insurance history reveals an interesting footnote. In the early 1800's, only people who were "near dying" retained insurance. And since there were no healthy insureds left to pay premiums, what happened? If you guessed bankruptcy you are correct. Notice that every old line insurance company started in business after 1820. That's because all of the older companies went out of business due to this adverse-selection problem.

So the carriers solved the problem from their perspective. They incorporated into the cost of term insurance the effects of the healthy people dropping their insurance.

Where did that leave the policy holder faced with rapidly growing premiums in old age?

The carriers hired actuaries to figure out the problem. They sat with their abacuses and determined there was only one solution.

Introducing THE BOX

The actuaries came up with only the solution which could make life-long insurance attainable, a whole life policy. Insurance carriers had to help insureds "pre-fund" their insurance premiums so they could afford to retain their coverage throughout their lives. If they only offered insurance premium plans on a "pay-as- you-go" basis, no one would ever be able to keep their insurance past life expectancy.

And that's where The Box comes in. The Box is your individual account with your insurance carrier. It will hold all of the premium payments you make. From The Box, you must pay the annual cost of insurance (mortality costs) and the policy expenses.

Unfortunately, the cost of funding The Box without interest is too expensive. So the actuaries had to add an interest element to The Box.

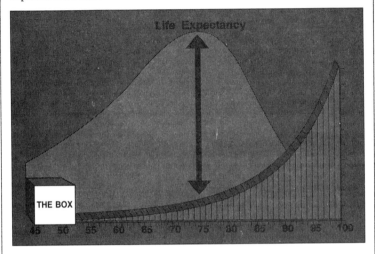

The insurance company invests the premiums they receive, (net of expenses) then allocates some portion of those earnings to The Box. The amount allocated varies according to the insurance contract.

In 1913, Congress passed the 16th amendment authorizing the collection of income taxes. The insurance industry successfully sought regulatory relief to allow the money in The Box to grow without tax. So, government actually participates in the cost of insurance as a contribution to the welfare of society.

How The Price Is Determined

First let's recap what we learned earlier. Probability is the key to insurance. People die according to a predictable pattern called a mortality table. This predictable pattern, and the amount of coverage, is mathematically converted into a lump sum target that the company needs in order to make the contractual payment at death. The lump sum is usually financed with annual payments based on a specified rate of interest.

And we found that the mortality costs at life expectancy for our 45 year old male wanting $1,000,000 of insurance would equal $747,000.

11

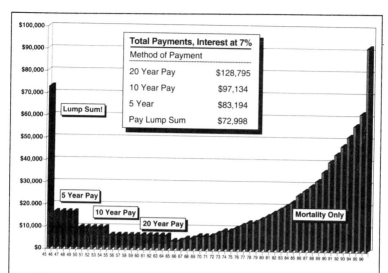

Total Payments, Interest at 7%	
Method of Payment	
20 Year Pay	$128,795
10 Year Pay	$97,134
5 Year	$83,194
Pay Lump Sum	$72,998

Now by putting $72,998 into The Box today, the interest earnings would pay all the costs associated with the policy until death. But not everyone can deposit $72,998 as a lump sum. So the company allows you to finance the cost over a defined period of time. You can define the period.

The Factors That Impact The Price

The amount of each deposit (premium) has only four determining factors:

1. The predictable pattern of death (mortality costs).
2. The cost of doing business (expenses).
3. The amount of interest earned each year (sometimes called dividends).
4. The number of people who actually keep their insurance policies (called persistency).

Your individual account (The Box) holds your annual payments or your lump sum deposit so long as you retain the insurance contract. As long as all the original assumptions are achieved, the value of The Box will grow to meet the projected lump sum targets according to the illustration provided by the insurance company.

Each year, The Box must pay the annual cost of insurance (mortality costs) and the policy expenses. The Box also receives the interest credited each year by the insurance company. The Box provides a way to pre-fund the cost of insurance so that compound interest can actually pay the insurance costs at the older ages. What happens if someone wants to cancel their insurance early? The Box must be assessed a surrender charge if the insurance company hasn't recovered all of it's start-up expenses. It usually takes ten to fifteen years for a company to recover their costs.

What Happens When The Assumptions Are Incorrect?

The insurance company projections are based on assumptions. So the illustrated results will vary based on the four factors listed above. The Box will either get larger or smaller, depending upon what happens to these factors.

So what if interest rates fall, expenses rise, or people die faster than expected? The Box will need more money than originally illustrated. The Box will have to become larger to hold the additional money needed to meet your obligations. To increase the size of The Box, you will either have to pay premiums for a longer period of time, or you will have to increase your annual payments to reach your targeted contractual results.

But the opposite is true if interest rates rise, expenses fall, or people live longer. The Box will not need as much money from you as originally illustrated. The Box can become smaller to reflect the improved performance. As a result, you might pay premiums for fewer years. Or you could reduce your annual payments.

In the final analysis, The Box must have enough money to equal the mathematical lump sum targeted by the insurance company for your age. Otherwise, the company will be unable to stay in business. If they have underfunded all of their contracts, they won't have enough assets to meet their obligations.

A Closer Look at the Four Pricing Factors

Let's examine the four pricing factors mentioned above to see how much impact future economic conditions can have on The Box. Illustrations of The Box can vary from company to company based on how they handle these four factors. And if a carrier uses assumptions which are too aggressive, The Box has no real chance of attaining the performance illustrated.

It is virtually impossible for most insurance buyers to know for certain how these factors will impact the specific product they purchase. But the surest way to protect yourself is by asking for a copy of the company IQ. This is the Illustration Questionnaire that all insurance companies have been asked to voluntarily provide. The questions have been clearly asked regarding pricing assumptions for these four factors. And the answers should be easy to understand. If they are not, or the carrier does not have an IQ, perhaps you should look elsewhere for your coverage.

Many insurance buyers believe that an illustration comparison between companies is a valid method for determining the best product to purchase. But purchasing a policy because one illustration looks better than another one is dangerous business. The "best" illustration may contain aggressive assumptions that make a direct comparison with another company impossible.

Let's look at some of the specific issues that impact the pricing structure of The Box.

1. Mortality costs. As medical technology improves, people have been living longer. What happens to The Box if the mortality experience for the insurance company is different than projected in your illustration?

> *But purchasing a policy because one illustration looks better than another is dangerous business.*

The company's mortality experience results from how long the people they select to insure actually live. If their underwriting assessment was inaccurate and the pool of insureds die too soon, the company's financial reserves will be impaired. This will impact your policy. It will cause the company to raise mortality costs, which will drain money from The Box faster than expected.

Unforeseen negative events can also cause problems for an insurance company. For instance, the AIDS epidemic could impact the overall mortality experience of the industry, or of a particular company. An outbreak of some unknown virus or other illness might adversely affect the statistics. Any of these occurrences could cause The Box to be underfunded and unable to generate enough compound interest to pay the increased mortality costs in future years.

On the other hand, breakthroughs in medical care could reduce the company's mortality costs. The Box will then grow faster because less costs are being deducted. But be careful! Some insurance companies are very aggressive and have already anticipated these improvements in mortality experience when designing their illustrations. Check to make sure the carrier's IQ clearly discloses these assumptions, and how much these savings will improve their product. If they haven't, you should stay away from their *Box*.

2. Expenses. Expenses associated with an insurance policy include administration, premium taxes, DAC taxes and sales commissions.

Another cost factor is risk capital. Companies have to price for the impact poor investment results might have on their products. A conservative company will project expenses in their illustrations using some inflation factor for expenses. A more aggressive company will often hold expenses steady, assuming there will be no increases for the maintenance of their contracts over the next twenty or thirty years. Again, the IQ will disclose how the carrier has priced their product to reflect these costs.

3. Interest credits. Interest credits are the third factor of pricing equation. Premiums (net of expenses) are invested by the companies in a variety of bonds, stocks and mortgages. The returns credited to The Box are based on this investment performance.

In recent years, some insurance companies credited interest in anticipation of earnings they had not yet achieved. The company illustrations showed The Box growing much faster than their current performance could support. Carriers justified this because the interest rates were rising and their investment portfolios were benefiting from the higher investment yields. But when interest rates decline, the illustrations which were originally based on higher rates will look substantially worse since they never achieved the original level of illustrated returns and now are dropping.

4. Persistency. Persistency refers to the number of policies which stay in force from their inception until death. We have already discussed how adverse selection can negatively impact the financial stability of a company. Persistency is directly tied to this problem.

An aspect of persistency is the acquisition costs for each policy. It requires several years (often 15 to 20) before an insurance company can recover their costs. If a policy terminates before the company has recovered all of their costs, it could adversely impact other policyholders and the profitability of the company.

The size of The Box can expand or contract with these four factors.

Persistency can also affect your policy through lapse supported pricing. Some companies assume an inordinate number of policies will actually terminate prior to the death of the insured. By assuming lower death benefits will be paid, they can project higher insurance benefits for a lower premium cost. But if these policies do not actually lapse, then the higher benefit payments will hurt the company's performance and impact The Box.

The size of The Box can expand or contract with these four factors. If mortality or expenses go up, or interest goes down, The Box must either get taller (more dollars in sooner), or longer (more years of the same premium payments).

So, The Box isn't just a static box. The long term nature of the insurance obligation makes The Box quite dynamic. Carrier illustrations are impacted by the investment performance of the insurance company. They are also affected by the ultimate results achieved in their underwriting (mortality costs), expense control, and business retention (persistency). A conservative company is more likely to attain their original assumptions than an aggressive company trying to use illustrations to attract new business.

It would be wise for the fiscally prudent insurance buyer to consider overfunding The Box to minimize the possible consequences of poor investment performance or the overstatement of pricing assumptions.

So ask yourself this question. If you are purchasing life insurance for your entire life...Do you want to pay the mortality costs on a pay-as-you-go basis each year with your money or would you rather have The Box pay them for you from the compound interest and tax benefits?

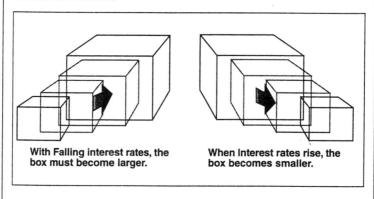

With Falling interest rates, the box must become larger.   When interest rates rise, the box becomes smaller.

How Much Can You Put in The Box?

Before we answer this question, let's review! The Box is very flexible. When you start your BOX, you can select how you want to fund it. You can put in one lump sum. You can fund it over 5 years...10 years...until age 65...or for life. In most cases, you can change your mind and raise or lower your contributions at any time. It is important to remember that the sooner you fill The Box, the less you will have to pay from your own pocket.

When you select your BOX, the funding is based on certain

interest credit, mortality cost and expense assumptions. If interest rates decline, or mortality costs rise, The Box will need more money. Likewise, if interest rates rise and/or mortality costs drop, The Box will need less money. The Box will be evaluated every year to determine whether it is on target or not.

Interest earned by The Box is tax deferred and potentially tax free if the policy is held until death. Tax is owed on withdrawals in excess of the amount you have deposited into The Box. This is a real economic advantage. So in 1984, Congress instituted IRC §7702. It defines life insurance and limits the amount of money you can put in The Box. If you exceed that limit, then all of the earnings in The Box are taxable. Your insurance carrier monitors this for you each year to make certain that your plan does not exceed the guidelines.

The amount of the contribution you can put into The Box, and still qualify as insurance, ranges between the minimum cost of insurance and the maximum allowed under IRC §7702.

The minimum amount needed to fund The Box is just enough to pay a level contribution to fund the mortality costs until Age 95. At this point, the policy is cancelled and you receive nothing back. However, you can fund for amounts greater than the minimum.

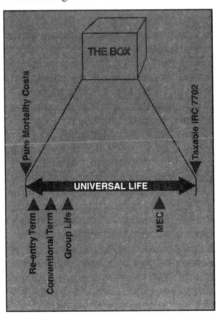

But whatever your targeted premium, it is an individual choice and based on your individual needs.

For instance, let's again assume that you are 45 years old. And let's say you want to have your insurance fully paid by the time you retire. Then you want to set the premium to fill The Box during the next 20 years. At that time, if the assumptions are accurate, the policy will stay fully funded for life.

Another option might be to fully pay the policy in 10 years. In this instance, the premium would be set to fill The Box in ten equal installments. At the end of ten years, if the assumptions are accurate, The Box will need no further payments. However, if the performance of The Box declines, it is possible you will have to deposit some additional premiums after the ten year period is reached. It is better to be conservative and over-fund The Box than to play it too close. We think you need a margin to protect against economic change.

There is one final consideration in determining the amount you can put into The Box.

In 1989, Congress placed another limitation on the advantages of life insurance. IRC §7702 already limited the amount of money you can place in The Box. But Congress was concerned that life insurance taxation still offered too many income tax benefits when compared to other investments especially annuities. Annuities are taxed as interest income paid to the income recipient. This is sometimes referred to as Last in, First out (LIFO). This means that interest is the last in, and taxed first when it comes out. Life insurance income on the other hand is taxed on the First in, First out method (FIFO). The interest is the last in and the premiums are the first out. First is a return of premium (non-taxable), and then the income earned (taxable).

So Congress enacted the MEC limitation (Modified Endowment Contract) to minimize these life insurance tax benefits. This is sometimes referred to as the 7 pay test. The MEC limitation causes distributions from life insurance to be taxed in the same way annuities are taxed, but only if the policy qualifies as a MEC. Otherwise the FIFO rules apply to life insurance withdrawals.

As you can see from the chart, a MEC reduces even further the amount of money you can place in The Box. However, the only disadvantage occurs if you want to remove the money during your lifetime. If you are willing to keep the money in The Box, the death benefit will grow untaxed for the benefit of your beneficiaries. This offers a significant advantage to the beneficiaries.

Retail Insurance Pricing

Carriers "markup" insurance premiums based on the amount of risk they feel they are going to assume in each specific situation. This risk is usually determined by asking the potential insured to provide evidence of health. However, some policies are issued with no evidence of health being required by the carrier. In this situation, the company usually adds a mortality surcharge to offset the possible risk they are accepting. These loads can increase the pure cost of insurance as much as 30%-50% or more.

The chart on page 7 illustrates different premiums based on the amount of risk carriers feel they are being asked to accept. Group term (sometimes referred to as New York Table Y) is the base rate for all group life insurance products. Depending upon competitive pressures and the size of the group, carriers will often discount these costs to obtain the business. Sometime discounts run as much as 50%-70%. Annual Renewable Term to age 100 (ART-100) prices the risk based on one physical provided only when the policy is first issued. After the beginning of the policy, the insurance company must continue to provide insurance coverage so long as the premiums are paid.

...carriers often discount these costs to obtain the business.

Re-Entry Term assumes the insured will submit to new evidence of insurability before the policy will be renewed. The frequency of requalification depends on the contract. It can be every 5 years, 10 years, 15 years or 20 years. If you can not requalify, you can still keep the policy, but at a significantly higher rate that increases each year.

It is apparent that carriers can price their products based on the amount of risk they must contractually assume and their ability to cancel the policy. If the company has a reasonable expectation of retaining the policy for a lifetime of the insured, it can price the mortality costs closer to their actual experience. The Box is the only way for the insurance company to provide this savings. In fact, most carriers offer mortality rates as low or lower than the "lowest" term rates if the policyholder purchases The Box.

Two Types of BOXES

There are two basic BOXES that insurance carriers offer:

1. a fixed premium policy called whole life, and
2. an indeterminant premium policy called universal life.

A fixed premium BOX means the contractual premium must be paid every year. It can not be higher or lower. If you are unable to pay the premium with new premium dollars, it can be paid from the cash values of The Box using policy loans or withdrawals. If there are insufficient values available, the policy will lapse.

An indeterminant premium policy allows you to increase or reduce the premiums each year based on your financial circumstances. If you do not pay the premiums, The Box just does not grow. You do not have to borrow from the policy to pay the premium. But you do need to make up any shortfalls if you want your Box to remain "on target." If there are insufficient values in The Box to pay the monthly charges, the policy will lapse.

Investing Money in The Box

Once you start to put money into The Box, there are again two different strategies used by insurance companies to credit interest earnings to The Box.

1. Declared credit rate. Most policy owners are content to accept the carrier's stated interest rate. This rate will change based on the overall performance of the underlying assets. Two types of underlying assets (investments) may be offered by carriers. A rate credited to a policy based on the overall assets of the carrier is called portfolio yield. A rate based on the return attributed to new money received by the company each year is called new money yield. Over time the two rates should blend together and achieve a similar rate of return. In these types of policies, the insurance carrier will provide a guarantee of the principle in The Box.

2. Market rate. The policyholder may wish to assume the investment risk by selecting a variable life product. This product offers a range of investment options which can be diversified according to the risk tolerance of the policyholder. These selections range from cash equivalents, (money market, guaranteed government securities) to fixed returns (bonds, high risk bonds) to equity (balance, index, international and growth). Funds may be shifted through telephone transfer as often as the policyholder desires.

Typically, each fund is managed by experienced, professional investment analysts specializing in each particular field. All funds grow tax free during the accumulation period. When the policyholder assumes the risk of investment by selecting a particular combination of funds, there is some risk of losing principle. This risk is offset however by the potential for gains over the more conservative carrier investments. If the plan fails to meet the basic growth assumptions of the funds, the values in The Box could be much lower than projected. In this case, the death benefit could decrease or the policyholder would be forced to put more premium into The Box to maintain the planned benefits

Conclusion

The application and selection of life insurance products for sophisticated tax and retirement solutions requires more than a computer illustration.

"Mortality only" products offer a temporarily inexpensive solution to the "high cost" of life insurance. However, not everyone wants their insurance coverage to disappear (or become too expensive) when they need it most...near life expectancy.

The Box offers a unique way to take advantage of compound interest in a tax advantageous way, plus pay significantly less for the mortality charges.

Either way, insurance provides a unique product which delivers large amounts of capital for a nominal cost. Over time the cost of coverage reflects your older age. But if coverage is still required, The Box provides the best economically acceptable long term solution to pay those costs.

Index